Competition Law in Hungary

Competition Law in Hungary

Csongor István Nagy

This book was originally published as a monograph in the International Encyclopaedia of Laws/Competition Law.

General Editors: Roger Blanpain, Frank Hendrickx
Volume Editors: Francesco Denozza, Alberto Toffoletto

Published by:
Kluwer Law International B.V.
PO Box 316
2400 AH Alphen aan den Rijn
The Netherlands
Website: www.wklawbusiness.com

Sold and distributed in North, Central and South America by:
Wolters Kluwer Legal & Regulatory U.S.
7201 McKinney Circle
Frederick, MD 21704
United States of America
Email: customer.service@wolterskluwer.com

Sold and distributed in all other countries by:
Turpin Distribution Services Ltd.
Stratton Business Park
Pegasus Drive, Bigglewade
Bedfordshire SG18 8TQ
United Kingdom
Email: kluwerlaw@turpin-distribution.com

DISCLAIMER: The material in this volume is in the nature of general comment only. It is not offered as advice on any particular matter and should not be taken as such. The editor and the contributing authors expressly disclaim all liability to any person with regard to anything done or omitted to be done, and with respect to the consequences of anything done or omitted to be done wholly or partly in reliance upon the whole or any part of the contents of this volume. No reader should act or refrain from acting on the basis of any matter contained in this volume without first obtaining professional advice regarding the particular facts and circumstances at issue. Any and all opinions expressed herein are those of the particular author and are not necessarily those of the editor or publisher of this volume.

Printed on acid-free paper

ISBN 978-90-411-6942-6

This title is available on www.kluwerlawonline.com

© 2016, Kluwer Law International BV, The Netherlands

All rights reserved. No part of this publication may be reproduced, stored in a retrieval system, or transmitted in any form or by any means, electronic, mechanical, photocopying, recording, or otherwise, without the prior written permission of the publisher.

Permission to use this content must be obtained from the copyright owner. Please apply to: Permissions Department, Wolters Kluwer Legal & Regulatory U.S., 76 Ninth Avenue, 7th Floor, New York, NY 10011-5201, USA. Website: www.wklawbusiness.com

Printed and Bound by CPI Group (UK) Ltd, Croydon, CR0 4YY.

The Author

Csongor István Nagy PhD, LLM, SJD, dr. juris is research chair at and the leader of the Federal Markets 'Momentum' ('Lendület') Research Group at the Hungarian Academy of Sciences (Center for Social Sciences), associate professor at and head of the Department of Private International Law at the University of Szeged, Faculty of Law. He is admitted to the Budapest Bar. Furthermore, he is visiting professor at the Central European University, the Riga Graduate School of Law and the Sapientia University of Transylvania. Nagy graduated at Eötvös Loránd University (ELTE), at the Faculty of Law in Budapest, in 2003, where he also earned a PhD in 2009. During his studies, he became a member of Eötvös Loránd University István Bibó College of Law and Political Sciences and of the Invisible College. He received master (LLM, 2004) and SJD degree (2010) at the Central European University (CEU) in Budapest. He pursued graduate and postgraduate studies in Rotterdam, Heidelberg and New York. He had visiting appointments in the Hague (Asser Institute), Munich (twice, Max Planck Institute), Hamburg (Max Planck Institute), Edinburgh (University of Edinburgh) and London (British Institute of International and Comparative Law) and was visiting faculty, among others, at the Central European University Business School, the Corvinus University of Budapest, the International Business School, Budapest and at the Masarykova University, Brno. In 2015–2016, he was Fulbright visiting professor at Indiana University, Bloomington. He was Eurojus legal adviser in the European Commission's Representation in Hungary. In 2014, he won the support of the 'Momentum II' programme of the Hungarian Academy of Sciences, which is awarded to 'internationally recognized leading scholars, who have a steadily outstanding and increasing performance'. In the frame of this, he founded the 'Federal Markets' Research Group in the HAS Center for Social Sciences. Nagy has published more than 140 pieces in English, French, German, Hungarian, Romanian and (in translation) in Croatian and Spanish. This monograph is based on research conducted with the generous support of the Hungarian Scientific Research Fund (OTKA PD-101612 research programme). The author is profoundly grateful to Dr Zoltán Marosi, partner at Oppenheim Law Firm in Budapest, for meticulously reviewing this monograph. Of course, all errors remain the author's own.

The Author

Table of Contents

The Author	3
List of Abbreviations	13
General Introduction	21
§1. GENERAL BACKGROUND OF THE COUNTRY	21
§2. ECONOMIC SYSTEM	21
§3. LEGAL SYSTEM	21
I. History of the Hungarian Legal System	21
II. The Hierarchy of the Sources of Law	23
§4. HISTORICAL BACKGROUND OF ANTITRUST LAW	24
Part I. Structure of Antitrust Law and Its Enforcement	27
Chapter 1. Sources of Antitrust Law	29
§1. EU SOURCES	29
§2. NATIONAL SOURCES	30
I. Constitution	30
II. Statutory Law	30
III. Block-Exemption Regulations	30
IV. Notices, Position Statements and Communications	31
§3. ROLE AND AUTHORITY OF PRECEDENTS	32
Chapter 2. Scope of Application	34
§1. TERRITORIAL REACH	34

Table of Contents

§2. SPECIAL SECTORS	34
§3. STATE-OWNED ENTERPRISES AND PUBLIC UTILITIES	37
§4. SENSIBLE EFFECT AND *DE MINIMIS*	38

Chapter 3. Overview of Substantive Provisions — 39

§1. RESTRICTIVE AGREEMENTS	39
§2. DOMINANT UNDERTAKINGS	40
§3. CONCENTRATIONS	41
§4. OTHER PROHIBITIONS	47
§5. TESTS OF ILLEGALITY	48
I. Per Se Prohibitions and Naked Restraints	48
II. Balancing Tests	49
III. Merger Tests	49

Chapter 4. Overview of Main Notions — 51

§1. UNDERTAKING	51
§2. RELEVANT MARKET	55
§3. MARKET POWER/DOMINANT POSITION	58
§4. AGREEMENTS AND CONCERTED PRACTICES	60
I. *Strictu sensu* Agreements	60
II. Concerted Practices	63
III. Decisions of Associations of Undertakings	67
§5. RESTRICTION OF COMPETITION	68
I. Anti-competitive Object or Effect	68
II. The Inherent Limits of Anti-competitiveness	75
III. Agreements of Minor Importance	76
§6. EXEMPTION	79
I. Individual Exemption	80
II. Block-Exemption Regulations	81
§7. MONOPOLIZATION AND ABUSE OF DOMINANCE	82

Table of Contents

§8. CONCENTRATIONS AND THE DUTY TO NOTIFY		83
I. Company Law Restructuring		85
II. Acquisition of Control		86
III. Joint Control		89
IV. Joint Ventures		91
§9. JOINT VENTURES		91

Chapter 5. Consequences of Violations and Enforcement Institutions   92

§1. ADMINISTRATIVE ENFORCEMENT		92
I. The Competition Authority: The Hungarian Competition Office		92
A. The HCO's Autonomy		92
B. Formation, Composition		92
C. Investigating Powers		94
D. Adjudicating Powers (Ascertaining and Sanctioning)		96
E. Other Institutional Tasks (Consultancy to Parliament/Government)		99
II. Government Direct Enforcement Activities		99
III. Other Administrative Agencies Applying Antitrust Rules		101
IV. Administrative Fines		101
A. Fine in the Merits		101
B. Leniency		106
1. Substantive Issues		108
2. Procedural Issues		111
C. Settlements		113
D. Procedural Fine		115
V. Administrative Injunctions and Other Restrictive Orders		116
VI. Commitment Decisions		117
A. The Purposes of Commitment Procedures		119
B. Cases Where There Is No Place for Commitments		120
C. What Can Be Offered?		121
D. The Legal Consequences of Not Performing the Commitments		123
VII. Interim Measures		124
§2. CIVIL ENFORCEMENT		125
I. Competent Civil Courts		126
II. Sanctions		126
A. Nullity		126
B. Damages		128
C. Hungarian Competition Law's 10% Rule		130
D. Special Rules on Whistle-Blowers in Actions for Damages		132
E. Stand-Alone Actions		134
F. Access to Evidence		135

Table of Contents

	G. Burden of Proof	137
	H. Interim Measures	138

§3. CRIMINAL ENFORCEMENT 139
    I. Criminal Sanctions in Case of Restrictive Agreements in Public
       Procurement and Concession Proceedings 140
    II. Criminal Sanctions on Undertakings 142
    III. Occupational Ban 143
    IV. Role of Prosecutors and Competent Criminal Courts 145

§4. EXCLUSION FROM PUBLIC TENDERS AS A SANCTION (DEBARMENT) ... 145

Part II. Application of the Prohibitions   149

Chapter 1. Restrictive Agreements   149

§1. HORIZONTAL AGREEMENTS 149
    I. Cartels 149
       A. Price-Fixing 149
       B. Market/Client Allocation 149
       C. Production/Innovation Limitation 150
       D. Group Boycott 150
       E. Collusion on Other Objects 150
    II. Information Exchange Practices 151
    III. Cooperation Agreements 153
       A. Research and Development 153
       B. Specialization 154
       C. Joint Production, Joint Purchasing and Joint Selling 155

§2. VERTICAL AGREEMENTS 156
    I. Distribution 156
       A. Resale Price Maintenance 156
       B. Exclusive Distributorship (Territorial Protection) 159
       C. Exclusive Dealing (Non-compete) 161
       D. Selective Distribution 162
       E. Franchising 163
    II. Technology Licensing 163

Chapter 2. Dominant Undertakings' Prohibited Practices   164

§1. EXPLOITATIVE PRACTICES 164
    I. Excessive/Unfair Pricing 164
       A. Calculation of the Necessary Costs and the Reasonable Profit ... 165
       B. Comparative Analyses 166
          1. Territorial Comparisons 167
          2. Temporal/Historical Comparisons 167

Table of Contents

3. Comparison between Product Markets or Customer Groups	168
II. Discrimination	168
§2. EXCLUSIONARY PRACTICES	170
I. Predatory Pricing	170
A. The Relationship between Costs and Price	171
B. Cost Tests in Respect of Multi-product Enterprises	172
C. The Requirement of Recoupment	175
D. Anti-competitive Foreclosure	176
E. Objective Justification	177
II. Bundling/Tying	177
III. Refusal to Deal	178
IV. Price Squeeze	181
V. Exclusivity and Long-Term Agreements	184
A. Anti-competitive Effects	185

Chapter 3. Concentrations — 189

§1. HORIZONTAL MERGERS	191
§2. VERTICAL AND CONGLOMERATE MERGERS	191
§3. PURE CONGLOMERATE MERGERS	192

Part III. Administrative Procedure — 193

Chapter 1. Administrative Investigations before the Antitrust Authority — 193

§1. INITIATIVE	193
I. General Sector Inquiries	193
II. Ex Officio Investigations	194
III. Complaints	195
IV. Informant's Award	196
A. The Conditions of the Informant's Award	197
B. The Amount of the Informant's Award and the Legal Guarantees of the Entitlement	198
C. The Payment of the Informant Award in Case of More Than One Informant; the Exclusion of the Award's Accumulation	199
D. Restraints on the Entitlement to the Informant's Award	200
E. The Protection of the Informant	200
F. The Refund of the Informant's Award	200
V. Limitation Period	201

Table of Contents

§2. Powers	204
I. Requests for Information	205
II. Investigating and Search Powers	205
§3. Right of Defence	210
I. Content and Notification of Opening Decisions	210
II. Proceedings: Hearings, Access to File	212
III. Case-Handler's Report	214
IV. The CC's Preliminary Position	215
V. Final Hearing and Decision	216
VI. Legal Remedies against the HCO's Acts, Orders and Decisions	217

Chapter 2. Voluntary Notifications and Clearance Decisions Merger Control   219

§1. Preliminary Filing Obligations	219
I. Criteria and Thresholds	219
II. Turnover Calculation	225
III. The Notification Duty's Addressee and Deadline	226
IV. The Consequences of the Failure to Notify	226
A. The Consequences of the Failure to Notify before 1 July 2014	226
B. The Consequences of the Failure to Notify after 1 July 2014	229
§2. Structure of Proceedings	231
I. Preliminary Assessment, Simplified Procedure and Full Investigation	231
II. Simplified Procedure	232
III. Time Framework	235
IV. Right of Defence	236
§3. Clearance and Conditional Clearance	239
I. Substantive Merger Analysis	239
II. Conditions and Undertakings	241
III. Ancillary Restraints	242

Chapter 3. Challenging of the Administrative Decision   244

§1. Competent Courts	244
§2. Time limits	244
§3. Standing	244
§4. Scope of Judicial Review	246
I. Questions of Fact	247

Table of Contents

II.	The Abstract Interpretation (Construction) of the Law	249
III.	Application of the Law to a Concrete Case	249
IV.	Expert Questions	250

Selected Bibliography 255

Index 263

Table of Contents

List of Abbreviations

1/2003/EC Regulation — Council Regulation (EC) No 1/2003 of 16 December 2002 on the implementation of the rules on competition laid down in Articles 81 and 82 of the Treaty. OJ [2003] L 1/1.

Act on Administrative Procedure — Act CXL of 2004 on the general rules of the administrative authority procedure and service (in Hungarian: '*A közigazgatási hatósági eljárás és szolgáltatás általános szabályairól szóló 2004. évi CXL. Törvény (Ket.)*')

Act on Consumer Protection — Act CLV of 1997 on Consumer Protection (in Hungarian: '*A fogyasztóvédelemről szóló 1997. évi CLV. törvény (Fgytv.)*')

Act on Credit Institutions — Act CXII of 1996 on Credit Institutions and Financial Enterprises (in Hungarian: '*A hitelintézetekről és a pénzügyi vállalkozásokról szóló 1996. évi CXII. Törvény (Hpt.)*')

Act on Electricity — Act LXXXVI of 2007 on Electricity (in Hungarian: '*2007. évi LXXXVI. törvény a villamos energiáró*')

Act on electronic communications — (in Hungarian: '*Az elektromos hírközlésről szóló 2003. évi C. törvény*')

Act on Public Procurement — Act CVIII of 2011 on Public Procurements (in Hungarian: '*2011. évi CVIII. törvény a közbeszerzésekről*')

Act on Railway — Act CLXXXIII of 2005 on Railway Traffic (in Hungarian: '*A vasúti közlekedésről szóló 2005. évi CLXXXIII. törvény*')

Act on the prohibition of unfair commercial practices — Act XLVII of 2008 on the prohibition of unfair commercial practices (in Hungarian: '*A fogyasztókkal szembeni tisztességtelen kereskedelmi gyakorlat tilalmáról szóló 2008. évi XLVII. törvény (Fttv.)*')

List of Abbreviations

Act on Trade	Act CLXIV of 2005 on Trade (in Hungarian: *'A kereskedelemről szóló 2005. évi CLXIV. törvény (Kertv.)'*)
Advertisement Act	Act XLVIII of 2008 on the fundamental conditions and particular limits of economic advertising activity (in Hungarian: *'A gazdasági reklámtevékenység alapvető feltételeiről és egyes korlátairól szóló 2008. évi XLVIII. törvény (Grt.)'*)
AG	Advocate General
APA	See Act on Administrative Procedure
Article 101	Article 101 of the Treaty on the Functioning of the European Union[1]
Budapest Court	In Hungarian: *'Fővárosi Törvényszék'*, before 1 January 2012: *'Fővárosi Bíróság'*.
CA	Hungarian Competition Act (in Hungarian: *'A tisztességtelen piaci magatartás és versenykorlátozás tilalmáról szóló 1996. évi LVII. törvény (Tpvt.)'*)
CC	Competition Council (in Hungarian: *'Versenytanács'*)
CCP	See Code on Civil Procedure
Civil Code	Act V of 2013 on the Civil Code (in Hungarian: *'2013. évi V. törvény a Polgári Törvénykönyvről'*)
Code on Civil Procedure	Act III of 1952 on Civil Procedure (in Hungarian: *'1959. évi III. törvény a Polgári Perrendtartásról'*)
Code on Criminal Procedure	Act XIX of 1998 on the Criminal Procedure (in Hungarian: *'1998. évi XIX. törvény a büntetőeljárásról'*)
Communication on the Aspects of the Definition of the Relevant Market Concerned by the Concentration	HCO Communication on the Aspects of the Definition of the Relevant Market Concerned by the Concentration (in Hungarian: *'Az összefonódás által érintett piac meghatározásának irányadó szempontjai'*).
Company Court	In Hungarian: *'cégbíróság'*
Constitution	Fundamental Law of Hungary (in Hungarian: *'Magyarország Alaptörvénye'*)
Constitutional Court	In Hungarian: *'Alkotmánybíróság'*
Court of Appeal	In Hungarian: *'Ítélőtábla'*

---

1. In the book, the new numbers introduced by the Treaty of Lisbon will be used, which are applicable as from 1 Dec. 2009. Nevertheless, the original texts of the quotations remain unchanged.

List of Abbreviations

Criminal Code	Act C of 2012 on the Criminal Code (in Hungarian: '*2012. évi C. törvény a Büntető Törvénykönyvről*')
De Minimis Notice	Notice on agreements of minor importance which do not appreciably restrict competition under Article 101(1) of the Treaty on the Functioning of the European Union (De Minimis Notice). OJ [2014] C 291/1.
ECJ	Court of Justice (before 1 December 2009: Court of Justice of the European Communities)
EEA	European Economic Area
EU	European Union
EU courts	Court of Justice of the European Union (including the General Court and the European Court of Justice)
EU Regulation on consumer protection cooperation	Regulation (EC) No 2006/2004 of the European Parliament and of the Council of 27 October 2004 on cooperation between national authorities responsible for the enforcement of consumer protection laws. OJ [2004] L 364/1.
European Commission	Commission of the European Union
GC	General Court (before 1 December 2009: Court of First Instance)
General Methodology: the methodological approach of the analysis of concentrations	HCO's 'General Methodology: the methodological approach of the analysis of concentrations' (in Hungarian: '*Általános módszertan: az összefonódások elemzésének módszertani megközelítése*')
Guidance on Article 102	Guidance on its enforcement priorities in applying Article 82 of the EC Treaty to abusive exclusionary conduct by dominant undertakings. OJ [2009] C 45/7.
Guidelines on Article 101(3)	Guidelines on the application of Article 81(3) of the Treaty. OJ [2004] C 101/97.
Guidelines on Horizontal Cooperation Agreements	Guidelines on the applicability of Article 101 of the Treaty on the Functioning of the European Union to horizontal co-operation agreements. Official Journal [2011] C 11/1.
Guidelines on the assessment of technology transfer agreements	Guidelines on the application of Article 81 of the EC Treaty to technology transfer agreements. OJ [2004] C 101/2.

List of Abbreviations

Guidelines on the effect on inter-state trade	Guidelines on the effect on trade concept contained in Articles 81 and 82 of the Treaty [2004] OJ C 101/81.
Guidelines on Vertical Restraints	Guidelines on vertical restraints. OJ [2010] C 130/1.
HCC	See Civil Code.
HCO	Hungarian Competition Office (in Hungarian: '*Gazdasági Versenyhivatal*')
Hungarian Insurance BER	Gov. Regulation 203/2011 on the exemption from the prohibition of restriction of competition of certain groups of insurance agreements (in Hungarian: '*A biztosítási megállapodások egyes csoportjainak a versenykorlátozás tilalma alóli mentesítéséről szóló 203/2011. (X. 7.) Korm. rendelet*')
Hungarian Motor Vehicle BER	Gov. Regulation 204/2011 on the exemption from the prohibition of restriction of competition of certain categories of vertical agreements in the motor vehicle sector (in Hungarian: '*A gépjármű utópiacra vonatkozó megállapodások egyes csoportjainak a versenykorlátozás tilalma alóli mentesítéséről szóló 204/2011. (X. 7.) Korm. rendelet*')
Hungarian R&D BER	Gov. Regulation 206/2011 on the exemption from the prohibition on restriction of competition of certain groups of research and development agreements (in Hungarian: '*A kutatási és fejlesztési megállapodások egyes csoportjainak a versenykorlátozás tilalma alóli mentesítéséről szóló 206/2011. (X. 7.) Korm. rendelet*')
Hungarian Specialisation BER	Gov. Regulation 202/2011 on the exemption from the prohibition on restriction of competition of certain groups of specialisation agreements (in Hungarian: '*A szakosítási megállapodások egyes csoportjainak a versenykorlátozás tilalma alóli mentesítéséről szóló 202/2011. (X. 7.) Korm. rendelet*')
Hungarian Technology Transfer BER	Gov. Regulation 86/1999 on the exemption from the prohibition on restriction of competition of certain groups of technology transfer agreements was not replaced in 2011 (in Hungarian: '*A technológia-átadási megállapodások egyes csoportjainak a versenykorlátozás tilalma alól történő mentesítéséről szóló 86/1999. (VI. 11.) Korm. rendelet*')

List of Abbreviations

Hungarian Vertical BER	Gov. Regulation 205/2011 on the exemption from the prohibition on restriction of competition of certain groups of vertical agreements (in Hungarian: '*A vertikális megállapodások egyes csoportjainak a versenykorlátozás tilalma alóli mentesítéséről szóló 205/2011. (X. 7.) Korm. rendelet*')
Judiciary Act	Act CLXI of 2011 on the Organisation and Administration of Courts (in Hungarian: '*2011. évi CLXI. törvény a bíróságok szervezetéről és igazgatásáról*')
Jurisdictional Notice	Consolidated Jurisdictional Notice under Council Regulation (EC) No 139/2004 on the control of concentrations between undertakings. OJ [2008] C 95/1.
Merger Control Regulation	Regulation 139/2004 on the control of concentrations between undertakings. OJ [2004] L24/1.
MVBER	Commission Regulation (EU) No 461/2010 of 27 May 2010 on the application of Article 101(3) of the Treaty on the Functioning of the European Union to categories of vertical agreements and concerted practices in the motor vehicle sector. OJ [2010] L 129/52.
new Civil Code	Civil Code
new Criminal Code	See Criminal Code.
Notice 1/2007	HCO Notice 1/2007 on the aspects of setting the fine in case of unfair manipulation of consumer decisions (in Hungarian: '*1/2007. közlemény a bírság meghatározásának szempontjai a fogyasztói döntések tisztességtelen befolyásolása esetén*')
Notice 1/2012	HCO Notice 1/2012 on setting the amount of the fine in case of conducts violating the prohibitions included in Sections 11 and 21 of Act Nr LVII of 1996 on the prohibition of unfair market practice and restriction of competition, as well as Articles 101 and 102 of the Treaty on the Functioning of the European Union (as amended by Notice 5/2014, consolidated version) (in Hungarian: '*1/2012. közlemény az 1996. évi LVVII. törvény (Tpvt.) 11. és 21. §-a, illetve az Európai Unió működéséről szóló szerződés 101. és 102. cikke szerinti tilalmakba ütköző magatartások esetén a bírság összegének megállapításáról (egységes szerkezetben az azt módosító 5/2014. közleménnyel)*')

List of Abbreviations

Notice 1/2014	HCO Notice 1/2014 on the aspects of differentiating between concentrations subject to authorisation in simplified and full procedure (in Hungarian: '*1/2014. közlemény az egyszerűsített és teljes körű eljárásban engedélyezhető összefonódások megkülönböztetésének szempontjairól*')
Notice 2/2014	HCO Notice 2/2014 on the prescription of conditions and obligations in decisions authorizing concentrations (in Hungarian: '*2/2014. közlemény az összefonódást engedélyező határozatokban feltételek, illetve kötelezettségek előírásáról*')
Notice 3/2014	HCO Notice 3/2014 on the application of the simplified decision containing no reasoning and information on legal remedy in procedures of authorizing concentrations (in Hungarian: '*3/2014. közlemény az összefonódás engedélyezése iránti eljárásokban az indokolást és jogorvoslatról való tájékoztatást nem tartalmazó ún. egyszerűsített döntés alkalmazásáról*')
Notice 4/2014	HCO Notice 4/2014 on pre-notification contacts connected to proceedings dealing with the examination of concentrations (in Hungarian: '*4/2014. közlemény az összefonódások vizsgálatával foglalkozó eljárásokhoz kapcsolódó előzetes egyeztetésekről*')
Notice 6/2014	HCO Notice 6/2014 on commitments in proceedings instituted regarding assumed violations of the prohibition of unfair commercial practices against consumers (in Hungarian: '*6/2014. közlemény a fogyasztókkal szembeni tisztességtelen kereskedelmi gyakorlat tilalmának feltételezett megsértése tárgyában indult eljárásokban tett kötelezettségvállalásról*')
Notice on the Relevant Market	Commission notice on the definition of relevant market for the purposes of Community competition law. OJ [1997] C 372/5.
old Civil Code	Act IV of 1959 on the Civil Code (in Hungarian: '*1959. évi IV. törvénya Polgári Törvénykönyvről*')
old Constitution	Act XX of 1949 on the Constitution of the Republic of Hungary (in Hungarian: '*1949. évi XX. törvény a Magyar Köztársaság Alkotmánya*')
old Criminal Code	Act IV of 1978 on the Criminal Code (in Hungarian: '*A Büntető Törvénykönyvről szóló 1978. évi IV. törvény (Btk.)*')

List of Abbreviations

State Supervision of Financial Organisations	In Hungarian: *'Pénzügyi Szervezetek Állami Felügyelete'*. As from 1 October 2013, the State Supervision of Financial Organisations merged in the Hungarian National Bank, which is responsible for the areas covered by the State Supervision of Financial Organisations.
Supreme Court	Supreme Court of Hungary (in Hungarian: *'Kúria'*, before 1 January 2012: *'Magyar Köztársaság Legfelsőbb Bírósága'*)
TEU	Treaty on the European Union. OJ [2012] C 326/13.
TFEU	Treaty on the Functioning of the European Union. OJ [2012] C 326/47.
TTBER	Commission Regulation (EC) No 772/2004 of 27 April 2004 on the application of Article 81(3) of the Treaty to categories of technology transfer agreements. OJ [2004] L 123/11.
UCP Act	Act XLVII of 2008 on the prohibition of the unfair commercial practices against consumers (in Hungarian: *'2008. évi XLVII. törvény a fogyasztókkal szembeni tisztességtelen kereskedelmi gyakorlat tilalmáról'*)
UCP Directive	Directive 2005/29/EC of the European Parliament and of the Council of 11 May 2005 concerning unfair business-to-consumer commercial practices in the internal market and amending Council Directive 84/450/EEC, Directives 97/7/EC, 98/27/EC and 2002/65/EC of the European Parliament and of the Council and Regulation (EC) No 2006/2004 of the European Parliament and of the Council ('Unfair Commercial Practices Directive'). OJ [2005] L 149/22.
VBER	Commission Regulation (EU) No 330/2010 of 20 April 2010 on the application of Article 101(3) of the Treaty on the Functioning of the European Union to categories of vertical agreements and concerted practices. OJ [2010] L 102/1.

List of Abbreviations

General Introduction

§1. GENERAL BACKGROUND OF THE COUNTRY

1. Hungary is a landlocked country in East-Central Europe. It has approximately 10 million inhabitants. Its capital is Budapest, which has approximately 2 million inhabitants. Until 1989, Hungary was a people's republic (People's Republic of Hungary), when the country's name was changed to 'Republic of Hungary'. In 2011, a new constitution (Fundamental Law) was adopted (effective as from 1 January 2012), which changed the country's name to 'Hungary'.

§2. ECONOMIC SYSTEM

2. Until 1989, Hungary was a party to the Warsaw Pact and was a planned economy. After the collapse of the communist regime, the economic system was transformed to a market economy. The majority of the state-owned enterprises were privatized. Hungary's currency is the Hungarian forint (HUF or Ft).

§3. LEGAL SYSTEM

I. History of the Hungarian Legal System

3. The Hungarian legal system belongs to the civil law family. Hungarian private law has Roman law roots, and statutory law plays a central role. The application and interpretation of the law is mainly based on the construction of the statute or other regulation.

4. The first written sources of Hungarian law can be found in the law-books of Saint Stephen (in Hungarian: '*Szent István*'), founder of the Kingdom of Hungary, who was crowned in 1000. Subsequent kings also enacted law-books (e.g., Saint Ladislaus, in Hungarian: '*Szent László*', Coloman I the Book-lover, in Hungarian: '*Könyves Kálmán*', Louis the Great, in Hungarian: '*Nagy Lajos*'). The Golden Bull of 1222 (in Hungarian: '*Aranybulla*'), adopted by Andrew II, is particularly noteworthy as this was the first written constitutional document of Hungary, playing a role in Hungarian legal history similar to the Magna Charta of 1215 in England or the German Golden Bull of 1356 in Germany. It established, among others, the right to personal freedom and fair trial: the first rule of the Hungarian Golden Bull provided that no nobleman could be arrested unless he had been convicted in accordance with the law.

5. In 1514, István Werbőczi wrote a remarkable compilation of Hungarian customary law, entitled '*Tripartitum opus iuris consuetudinarii inclyti regni Hungariae*'. The compilation's abbreviated name was '*Tripartitum*' or '*Triplebook*' (in Hungarian: '*Hármaskönyv*') as it consisted of three books. Though enacted by the parliament and signed by the king, the compilation was never promulgated. Nevertheless, it was applied in judicial practice as the law of the land.

6. In 1848, several laws were adopted (the so-called laws of April) in order to transform Hungary into a constitutional monarchy. Although the revolution and war of independence of 1848 was repressed by the Austrian and Russian armies and the democratic achievements were abolished, in 1867 a settlement (in Hungarian: '*kiegyezés*', in German: '*Ausgleich*') was reached between the Austrian royal court and Hungary, which opened a period of prosperity and development, ended by the First World War. In this period of dualism (Austro-Hungarian Empire) Hungary experienced an economic boom. Legal development also kept pace with this economic progress, entailing the adoption of several modern codes of law, e.g., commercial code of 1875, criminal code of 1878 (Code of Csemegi), code on criminal procedure of 1896, code on civil procedure of 1911.

7. In the twentieth century, Hungary experienced two reverses of fortune. First, as a result of the peace treaty of Trianon, at the end of the First World War, the country lost two-thirds of its territory. Second, after the Second World War, Hungary became part of the Soviet camp and the communist party took power, introducing the system of planned economy (the name of the country was changed to 'People's Republic of Hungary', in Hungarian: '*Magyar Népköztársaság*'). The consequence was that Hungarian law got heavily impregnated with socialist-communist ideology, and this had palpable impact on all fields of law.

8. In 1989, the socialist regime collapsed and several laws were adopted that served the purpose of the transition to a liberal democracy and market-economy. Interestingly, the reform in the domain of private and economic law started some years before the socialist regime collapsed and the 'system change' was accomplished. For instance, the company act was adopted already in 1988 (Act VI of 1988).

9. The history of Hungarian competition law dates back to the first part of the twentieth century. The first unfair competition act was adopted in 1923 (Act V of 1923 on unfair competition), while the first act on cartels was enacted in 1931 (Act XX of 1931 on agreements regulating economic competition).

General Introduction

II. The Hierarchy of the Sources of Law

10. In Hungary, the hierarchy of legal sources is the following. The legal system is headed by the constitution. The old constitution was adopted in Act XX of 1949 and completely amended in 1989.[2] The Hungarian Parliament adopted Hungary's new constitution (Fundamental Law, in Hungarian: '*Alaptörvény*') on 18 April 2011; the new constitution entered into force on 1 January 2012.

11. The acts (statutes) of the parliament follow in rank. The parliament adopts acts normally with simple majority; however, in certain cases a two-thirds majority is required. The Constitution and the amendments of the Constitution have to be adopted with two-thirds of the votes of all the members of the parliament;[3] organic laws have to be adopted with the votes of two-thirds of the members attending the session.[4]

12. Bills submitted by a ministry are accompanied by an 'explanatory memorandum', which sets out the rationale and policy behind the proposal and presents and explains the provisions submitted. Although the explanatory memorandum is not a formal source of law, in practice, it is normally used as an authoritative interpretation of the law; courts use the explanatory memorandum to establish the legislative intent, which provides guidance when interpreting the text.[5]

13. The next layer of the system of legal sources is represented by government regulations, ministerial regulations (regulations issued by individual ministers, the regulations of the president of the Hungarian National Bank, the regulations of the heads of independent regulatory agencies). These regulations normally deal with sectoral issues and execute rules included in acts. Regulations contain, accordingly, rather detailed provisions.[6]

14. The last layer of the legal system consists of the ordinances of the local self-governments (in Hungarian: '*önkormányzat*'). These sources of law deal with local issues.

---

2. Act XX of 1949 on the Constitution of the Republic of Hungary (in Hungarian: '*1949. évi XX. törvény A Magyar Köztársaság Alkotmánya*').
3. Section S(2) of the Fundamental Law.
4. Section T(4) of the Fundamental Law.
5. Law-decrees are also legal sources, which have the same rank in the hierarchy of norms as the Acts of the parliament; in fact, they can be regarded as statutes. Law-decrees cannot be issued anymore; the power to adopt them was utterly abolished in 1989; at the same time, several law-decrees adopted before this date are still in force. Law-decrees were adopted by the Presidential Council of the People's Republic in the period when the Parliament was adjourned; the Presidential Council could regulate any matter with the exception of the amendment of the constitution. This scheme ran counter the principle of separation of power; hence, it was abolished in 1989. At the same time, several important laws were adopted in this form.
6. Section T(2) of the Fundamental Law.

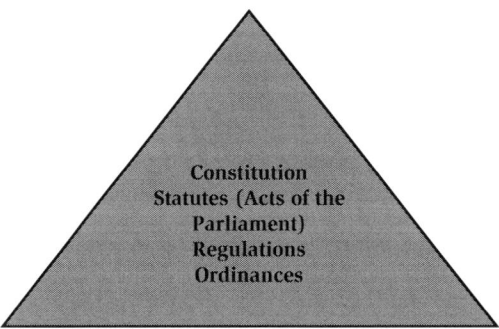

15. It is to be noted that in state of emergency the National Defence Council and the president of the republic are authorized to issue regulations.[7]

§4. HISTORICAL BACKGROUND OF ANTITRUST LAW

16. Hungary has a relatively long history in the field of competition law, including antitrust. The first competition act was adopted in 1923,[8] which, however, dealt solely with unfair competition law. The first act in the field of antitrust was Act XX of 1931 on agreements regulating economic competition.[9] This, as its title suggests, dealt exclusively with restrictive agreements; however, restrictive agreements as such were prohibited only if they were contrary to the public interest. Restrictive agreements were to be registered at the competent ministry.

17. Following the communist party's taking power in Hungary after the Second World War, Hungary was converted into a state-planned economy, making antitrust law unnecessary. However, as from 1968, an economic reform was introduced in Hungary (entitled new economic mechanism), which gave some room for free market, enabling the creation of small and medium-size enterprises. This process resulted in the doubling of the economy. The 'state' sector (public enterprises) contained the country's big enterprises and was managed according to the rules of state planning, while the private sector contained SMEs, which could operate on a relatively free market. The gradual extension of the free market made economic regulation necessary, including the status of the entrepreneurs, company law and antitrust law. As part of this process, a competition act was adopted in 1984, long before the collapse of the communist regime.

---

7. Section T(2) of the Fundamental Law.
8. Act V of 1923 on unfair competition (in Hungarian: '*1923. évi V. törvénycikk a tisztességtelen versenyről*').
9. In Hungarian: '*1931. évi XX. törvénycikk a gazdasági versenyt szabályozó megállapodásokról*'.

General Introduction

18. After the socialist regime collapsed in 1989, a new competition act was adopted in 1990 (Act LXXXVI of 1990 on the prohibition of unfair market conduct), which established the Hungarian Competition Office. The latter was the successor of the Material and Price Office. This act essentially followed the mainstream legislation practice, addressing restrictive agreements, abuse of dominant position and mergers. Perhaps the most important shortcoming of the act was that, with the exception of resale price-fixing, it did not prohibit vertical restrictive agreements.[10]

19. In 1996, the Hungarian parliament adopted a new competition act (Act LVII of 1996), which entered into force on 1 January 1997. This act replaced the Act of 1990 and is still effective, albeit it has been amended several times. The last comprehensive amendment of the CA was introduced by Act CCI of 2013, the provisions of which, for the most part, entered into force on 1 July 2014.

---

10. Section 14 of Act LXXXVI of 1990 on the prohibition of unfair market conduct.

Part I. Structure of Antitrust Law and Its Enforcement

20. Hungarian competition law was designed in accordance with EU competition law. Substantive rules and their interpretation are highly influenced by EU competition law and policy, albeit there are numerous points where Hungarian competition law diverges from the EU regime. On the other hand, as to procedural provisions, this parallelism is less close.

21. The Competition Act regulates most fields of competition law in wider sense. Besides antitrust, it contains rules on unfair competition law and on the prohibition of unfair manipulation of business decisions (unfair commercial practices in a business-to-business context). Under Hungarian law, competition law, in its widest sense, also covers the law of unfair commercial practices against consumers, which is regulated in a separate act (Act Nr XLVII of 2008 on the prohibition of unfair commercial practices).[11] This act implements the UCP Directive and provides that matters substantially affecting competition come under the HCO's competence. Initially, the CA contained a separate chapter on unfair manipulation of consumer decisions (the prohibition of misleading consumers), which had a roughly similar regulatory aim as the UCP regime; with the implementation of the UCP Directive, this chapter was amended to address the unfair manipulation of business decisions (misleading communication in a business-to-business context), leaving the prohibition of unfair commercial practices in a business-to-consumer context to the UCP Act. However, as noted, this field is supervised primarily by the HCO.

22. Hungarian antitrust substantive law has three fields: the rules on restrictive agreements, abuse of dominant position and merger control (concentrations). Sections 11-20 CA deal with restrictive agreements and are the equivalent of Article 101 TFEU. They equally apply to horizontal and vertical agreements. Section 11 contains a general prohibition on restrictive agreements, in line with 101(1) TFEU, distinguishing between agreements anti-competitive by object and by effect. Section 17 CA contains the rules of individual exemption, which converge with the requirements embedded in Article 101(3) TFEU. Section 16 CA empowers the government to adopt block-exemption regulations; these regulations, as a rule of thumb, are in line with EU block-exemption regulations. Section 21 CA prohibits the abuse

---

11. In Hungarian: *'2008. évi XLVII. törvény a fogyasztókkal szembeni tisztességtelen kereskedelmi gyakorlat tilalmáról'*.

of dominant position, containing a general prohibition and an illustrative list of interdicted conducts, while section 22 CA defines economic dominance essentially in accordance with EU competition law. Sections 23-32 CA contain the rules of merger control: concentrations over a certain size have to be notified to the HCO for clearance.

23. The rules of competition law enforcement are partly included in the CA and partly in the Administrative Procedure Act (APA). The latter is subsidiary to the CA, i.e., only those rules of the APA are applicable in competition law enforcement proceedings that are not expressly excluded by the exchaustive list contained in the CA. The rules on the judicial review of HCO decisions are included in the CA, the APA, and the Code on Civil Procedure and the Act on Civil Summary Proceedings in Administrative Matters. As a rule of thumb, the HCO's decisions in the merits can be attacked before the court in an action ensuring full-blown review. Procedural decisions, e.g., imposition of a procedural fine, refusal to institute a proceeding, can be attacked before the court in a 'summary proceeding' ('*nemperes eljárás*'), which is a simplified documentary procedure.

24. Due to the HCO's idiosyncratic structure, the administrative competition procedure is split. The competition investigation is done by the case-handlers, who work in one of the HCO's bureaus and are part of the hierarchy controlled by the head of the HCO. The results of the investigation – in the form of a report – are submitted to the Competition Council (CC), which has exclusive competence to decide in the merit of the case. The status of the CC is controversial: while from an institutional and budgetary perspective, it is part of the HCO, the CA declares that its members have independence in making their decisions and they act as quasi-judges. The decision of the CC – which is, legally speaking, the decision of the HCO, as the CC has no legal personality – can be attacked before the Budapest Administrative and Labour Court,[12] the judgment of which can be appealed before the Budapest Court.[13] The parties may submit a plea of supervision against the latter's judgment to the Supreme Court ('*Kúria*').[14] This is an extraordinary appeal restricted to points of law.[15]

25. The above procedural rules are applicable also in case the HCO applies EU competition law.[16] Furthermore, although the UCP Act contains some special procedural provisions,[17] the above rules are, in principle, also applicable in cases when the HCO applies the UCP Act.

---

12. Sections 22(2) and 326(1) CCP.
13. Sections 10(2) and 340(2) CCP.
14. Sections 10(3) CCP.
15. Section 270(2) CCP.
16. Section 1(2) CA.
17. Sections 25-27 UCP Act.

Chapter 1. Sources of Antitrust Law

§1. EU SOURCES

26. Hungary joined the European Union on 1 May 2004. As from this date, EU law, including the competition rules, are directly applicable in Hungary. Due to the decentralized application of EU competition law, the HCO is responsible for applying EU rules on restrictive agreements (Article 101 TFEU) and abuse of dominant position (Article 102 TFEU) in matters affecting interstate trade.

27. It is to be noted that, in essence and in theory, EU competition law (i.e., the prohibition of anti-competitive agreements and the abuse of a dominant position) has been applicable to matters affecting the trade between the EU and Hungary even before Hungary's accession, as Hungary's Association Treaty reproduced the then-effective EU instruments and provided that these were applicable to such cases (this provision, however, was rarely applied in practice).[18]

28. EU competition law is relevant not only as to cases affecting inter-state trade but also when applying Hungarian antitrust law. As stated above in part I, Hungarian antitrust law complies at most points with EU competition rules, and in cases of first impression EU rules and judicial and decisional practice have a persuasive authority and are normally followed in practice. Nonetheless, there are several points (both substantive and procedural) where Hungarian competition law departs from its EU counterpart: e.g., the treatment of resale price-fixing, predatory pricing, the general policy towards abuses of dominant position, merger notifiability of acquisition of joint control, the admissibility of evidence, etc.

29. It is noteworthy that in *Allianz*[19] the Hungarian Supreme Court submitted preliminary questions in a purely Hungarian competition matter (one which was based on facts arising before Hungary's accession to the EU), considering that 'the concepts referred to in Paragraph 11(1) of the (...) [CA] must in fact be interpreted in the same way as the equivalent concepts in Article 101(1) TFEU and that it is bound in that regard by the interpretation of those concepts provided by the Court'.[20] Accordingly, the CJEU held that section 11(1)-(2) CA, as the national equivalent of Article 101 TFEU, 'faithfully reproduces Article 101(1) TFEU. It is clearly apparent, moreover, from the preamble to and the explanatory memorandum for the CA that the Hungarian legislature sought to harmonize domestic competition law with that of the European Union'.[21] Although the statement related specifically to section 11 CA, in principle, it may be extrapolated to the substantive rules of Hungarian competition law at large, provided certainly that such rules do not contain an express deviation from the EU rules (such as, for example, in case of *de minimis* agreements as detailed below).

---

18. Article 62 of Hungary's Association Agreement of 1991 (entered into force in 1994).
19. Case C-32/11, not published yet.
20. Paragraph 22.
21. Paragraph 21.

§2. National Sources

30. The relevant national sources of Hungarian substantive competition law are the Constitution (Fundamental Law), the Competition Act (CA), the block-exemption regulations issued by the government of Hungary and the notices and other guidances issued by the HCO. The sources of the competition procedure are included in the CA, the APA, and the Code on Civil Procedure and the Act on Civil Summary Proceedings in Administrative Matters.

I. Constitution

31. The Fundamental Law of Hungary, in Article M(2), contains a specific rule on antitrust, providing that 'Hungary ensures the conditions of fair economic competition. Hungary acts against the abuse of dominant position and protects the rights of consumers.'

II. Statutory Law

32. The most important piece of legislation is Act LVII of 1996 on unfair market practices and restraints of competition (CA), which is supplemented by a set of block-exemption regulations (see below). As regards procedural issues, the questions not regulated in the CA are governed by Act CXL of 2004 on the general rules of administrative procedure and service (APA). The Code on Civil Procedure and the Act on Civil Summary Proceedings in Administrative Matters contain rules on judicial review.

III. Block-Exemption Regulations

33. Section 16 of the CA authorizes the government to exempt certain categories of agreements from the prohibition on restrictive agreements as embedded in section 11 CA, taking into account the conditions of individual exemption as defined in section 17 CA.

34. With the exception of technology transfer agreements, the currently effective block-exemption regulations were adopted on 7 October 2011 and entered into force on 22 October 2011, in line with the EU block-exemption regulations:

– Gov. Regulation 202/2011 on the exemption from the prohibition on restriction of competition of certain groups of specialisation agreements;
– Gov. Regulation 203/2011 on the exemption from the prohibition of restriction of competition of certain groups of insurance agreements;
– Gov. Regulation 204/2011 on the exemption from the prohibition of restriction of competition of certain categories of vertical agreements in the motor vehicle sector;

Part I, Ch. 1, Sources of Antitrust Law

- Gov. Regulation 205/2011 on the exemption from the prohibition on restriction of competition of certain groups of vertical agreements;
- Gov. Regulation 206/2011 on the exemption from the prohibition on restriction of competition of certain groups of research and development agreements.
- Gov. Regulation 86/1999 of the Government on the exemption from the prohibition on restriction of competition of certain groups of technology transfer agreements (which was not replaced in the course of the revision in 2011).

IV. Notices, Position Statements and Communications

35. Though formally not legal sources, the HCO's notices ('*közlemény*') and position statements ('*elvi állásfoglalás*') have a pivotal role in the interpretation and application of Hungarian competition law. The notices summarize the fundamental principles of the HCO's decisional practice and ascertain its policy and interpretation of the law.[22] 'Position statements' summarize the CC's interpretation of the CA's provisions and are essentially excerpts from various significant decisions (each statement contains a reference to the case where the interpretation was established). The HCO also issues 'information communications' ('*tájékoztató*'). These are issued when the conditions of adopting a notice are not met and are meant to provide information on the way the HCO interprets the CA's provisions as well as on practical matters concerning the HCO's proceedings.

36. Notices in the domain of antitrust:

- Notice 1/2012 on setting the amount of the fine in case of conducts violating the prohibitions included in sections 11 and 21 of Act Nr LVII of 1996 on the prohibition of unfair market practice and restriction of competition, as well as Articles 101 and 102 of the Treaty on the Functioning of the European Union;
- Notice 1/2014 on the aspects of differentiating between concentrations subject to authorization in simplified and full procedure;
- Notice 2/2014 on the prescription of conditions and obligations in decisions authorizing concentrations;
- Notice 3/2013 on the application of the simplified decision containing no reasoning and information on legal remedy in procedures of authorizing concentrations;
- Notice 4/2014 on pre-notification discussions connected to proceedings dealing with the examination of concentrations.

37. Notices in the domain of unfair commercial practices:

- Notice 6/2014 on commitments in proceedings instituted regarding assumed violations of the prohibition of unfair commercial practices against consumers;
- Notice 1/2007 on the aspects of setting the fine in case of unfair manipulation of consumer decisions.

---

22. Section 36(6) CA.

38. The HCO regularly publishes (information) communications, which summarize the authority's practice and provide, for the sake of transparency, information to the public.

– Communication on the application of the leniency rules of sections 78/A and 78/B CA;
– Communication on preliminary consultations connected to procedures for the assessment of concentrations;
– The aspects of determining the relevant market concerned by the concentration;
– The aspects of the assessment of non-coordinated horizontal effects of concentrations;
– The principles applied by the HCO to the elaboration and quality of the data used in the quantitative analysis of concentrations;
– General methodology (concentrations);
– Communication on the analytical methods applied by the HCO in procedures for the authorization of concentrations, as well as on the circle of data necessary for these and on the requirements against these data.

§3. ROLE AND AUTHORITY OF PRECEDENTS

39. Case law is, formally, not a source of law in Hungary. Hungarian law does not recognize the concept of *stare decisis*: formally, courts are not bound by earlier judgments and the decisions of higher courts, in principle, do not bind lower courts. Nevertheless, in practice, judicial decisions do have a *quasi*-binding nature, and the judgments and judicial practice of higher courts are followed by the lower level judiciary.[23]

40. It is to be noted that, according to Hungarian law, judgments can be published only after having been anonymized; hence, individual judgments are identified through the case number and not through the name of the parties.

41. The Supreme Court has four statutorily regulated tools to ensure the uniformity of the judicial practice: it may adopt 'law-unification decisions' ('*jogegységi határozat*'), conduct an analysis on the judicial practice in conclusively settled matters, publish rulings of principle ('*elvi bírósági határozat*') and decisions of principle ('*elvi bírósági döntés*').[24]

42. The 'law-unification procedure' (in Hungarian: '*jogegységi eljárás*') is a special mechanism aimed at ensuring the consistency and uniformity of the judicial practice; at the end of the procedure, a 'law-unification decision' (in Hungarian: '*jogegységi határozat*') is adopted.[25] It is very important to note that these decisions

---

23. *See* Tamás Lábady, *A magyar magánjog (polgári jog) általános része* 171 (Dialóg Campus Kiadó 2002).
24. Section 25 CA.
25. Sections 32-41 CA.

Part I, Ch. 1, Sources of Antitrust Law   43–44

are not judgments in the sense that they do not adjudicate a particular matter; but they decide on questions of interpretation of the law. 'Law-unification decisions' are binding on courts,[26] albeit the scope of the 'law-unification decision' does not cover the parties of the individual case that gave rise to the institution of the 'law-unification procedure'.[27]

43. Rulings of principle are Supreme Court judgments that are rendered in a matter that has a great social significance or an outstanding significance from the perspective of the public interest and concern questions of principle. Decisions of principle are lower court judgments that meet the foregoing requirements.[28]

44. Until 1997, the different colleges of the Supreme Court (divisions responsible for different branches of law, for instance, civil law, criminal law, labour law) could adopt positions; by way of example, civil college positions (in Hungarian: '*polgári kollégiumi állásfoglalás*', abbreviated as '*PK*'), criminal college positions (in Hungarian: '*büntető kollégiumi állásfoglalás*', abbreviated as '*BK*'), administrative college positions (in Hungarian: '*közigazgatási kollégiumi állásfoglalás*', abbreviated as '*KK*'). Although these positions are formally not binding on courts, they are followed in practice. Several such positions are still in force and shape the interpretation of the law.

Currently, colleges have no power to adopt positions; however, the colleges can opine on debated questions of law-application. These college opinions are not binding.[29]

---

26. Section 41 CA.
27. Section 42(1) CA.
28. Section 31 CA.
29. Section 27(1) CA.

Chapter 2. Scope of Application

§1. Territorial Reach

45. Under the CA, in the domain of antitrust law, a conduct falls within the HCO's competence if it occurs on the territory of Hungary or it occurs outside of Hungary but may have an effect on the territory of Hungary. The CA thus follows the 'effects-principle' as to the determination of the antitrust rules' territorial scope.[30] The 'effects principle' has normally been applied in merger cases. Other provisions of the CA, i.e., the rules on unfair competition and on the prohibition on unfair manipulation of business decisions, come under the effects-principle only if the act was committed in the European Economic Area: these provisions apply to market practices carried out on the territory of Hungary and to market practices carried out on the territory of the European Economic Area, provided the practice has a potential effect on the Hungarian market.

46. Since cases having a cross-border element are governed by EU competition law, provided the effect on inter-state trade is appreciable,[31] the 'effects-principle' may have relevance mainly in two cases: first, in matters that – notwithstanding the cross-border intra-EU element – have no appreciable effect on inter-state trade; second, in cases that involve non-EU countries (or Hungary and one or more non-EU countries) and are too small to have an appreciable effect on EU inter-state trade.[32] Furthermore, it is to be noted that contrary to restrictive agreements,[33] the application of EU competition law is not fully harmonized in cases concerning an abuse of dominant position: Member States are not 'precluded from adopting and applying on their territory stricter national laws which prohibit or sanction unilateral conduct engaged in by undertakings'.[34]

§2. Special Sectors

47. Special rules apply to agricultural produces. These provisions depart from general competition rules at two points. First, the minister of agriculture is authorized to grant individual exemption to certain agreements, under conditions different from those of individual exemption. Second, the CC cannot impose a fine in respect of agreements and concerted practices concerning agricultural produces on the first occasion: it has to call the parties to bring their conduct in conformity with the law; it can impose a fine only if the parties fail to obey the order within the time-limit set by the CC.

---

30. Section 1 CA.
31. *See* Guidelines on the effect on inter-state trade.
32. Csongor István Nagy, *Kartelljogi Kézikönyv. A közösségi és a magyar kartelljog kézikönyve* 225 (Budapest: HVG-Orac 2006).
33. Article 3 of Regulation 1/2003; Case 14/68 *Walt Wilhelm and others v. Bundeskartellamt* [1969] ECR 1.
34. Article 3(2) of Regulation 1/2003. *See* Recital 8 of Regulation 1/2003.

Part I, Ch. 2, Scope of Application 48–51

48. First, section 18/A of Act CXXVIII of 2012 on inter-professional organizations and on certain questions of the regulation of the agricultural market, which entered into force on 28 November 2012, provides that in respect of agricultural produces, the violation of the prohibition embedded in section 11 CA cannot be established, if the distortion, restriction or prevention of competition accruing from the agreement as defined in section 11 CA does not exceed the extent necessary for ensuring an economically justified, equitable income (fair income) and no market actor is precluded from joining it, furthermore, Article 101 TFEU has not been applied.[35] The decision on whether the agreement meets the foregoing conditions comes under the competence of the minister of agriculture.[36] When investigating the infringement of section 11 CA in respect of agricultural produces, the HCO has to request a position statement from the minister of agriculture and is bound by that statement. The minister has sixty days to issue the position statement, and during this time the HCO's competition proceeding has to be suspended.[37]

49. Second, in case of restrictive agreements and concerted practices concerning agricultural produces (irrespective of whether they violate section 11 CA or Article 101 TFEU), the CC has to suspend the imposition of the fine, and to call the parties concerned to bring their conduct in conformity with the law; the CC has to set a time-limit for this purpose. If the parties do not bring their conduct in conformity with the law within this time-limit, the CC can impose a fine.[38]

50. It is important to note the wider context of the second set of provisions above, namely that this legislation was adopted amidst Case *Vj-62/2012 Watermelon*, where various Hungarian supermarkets and agricultural organizations, under the auspices of the Hungarian Ministry for Rural Development, fixed the prices of watermelons and agreed not to market imported watermelons. The parliament, during the course of the competition investigation, enacted the above amendment to Act CXXVIII of 2012 on inter-branch organizations and on certain issues of the regulation of agricultural markets; the amendment's rules entered into force with immediate effect, i.e., also as to pending proceedings.

51. After the adoption of the above legislation, the HCO terminated its proceedings, notwithstanding the clear fact that the immunizing rules obviously appeared to go counter to EU competition law. Although the HCO did find EU law to be applicable to the underlying arrangements, it did not put aside conflicting Hungarian rules and did not impose any sanctions on the undertakings concerned.

---

35. 18/A(1) of Act CXXVIII of 2012 on inter-professional organizations and on certain questions of the regulation of the agricultural market.
36. 18/A(2) of Act CXXVIII of 2012 on inter-professional organizations and on certain questions of the regulation of the agricultural market.
37. 18/A(3) of Act CXXVIII of 2012 on inter-professional organizations and on certain questions of the regulation of the agricultural market.
38. 18/A(4) of Act CXXVIII of 2012 on inter-professional organizations and on certain questions of the regulation of the agricultural market.

52. In its decision, the HCO established that the Ministry for Rural Development does not come under the scope of the CA, since it does not qualify as an undertaking and pursues no economic activity. Hence, it cannot condemn it for organizing the cartel.

53. The HCO approached the Ministry for Rural Development for its assessment on whether the watermelon cartel met the requirements embedded in the amendment. The Ministry came to the conclusions that the watermelon cartel did meet these requirements and, hence, was exempted. The HCO established that, due to the Ministry's assessment, it could not apply the prohibition embedded in section 11 of the CA.

54. The HCO considered that the cartel affected inter-state trade and, hence, it was caught in the net of Article 101(1) TFEU. However, the HCO held that, due to the amendment's provision, as to agricultural products it can impose a fine only after having called the participating undertakings to bring their conduct in conformity with the law and set a deadline. Taking into account that the incriminated conduct ceased (the watermelon is an in-season fruit and the administrative decision was adopted after the season), it held that it could impose no fine; it noted that it could have imposed a fine only if the undertakings had continued the violation, while in fact the violation was terminated in the meantime.

55. The HCO made it clear that in case of conduct violating Article 101(1) TFEU the exclusion of the possibility to impose a fine may go counter to Article 5 of Regulation 1/2003, which provides that national competition authorities shall have the power to impose fines. However, it held that it had no competence to lift the tension between Article 5 and the amendment, since this could be adjudicated only in a preliminary ruling by the CJEU and the HCO had no power to submit a preliminary question to the CJEU.

56. Finally, the HCO examined whether it should proceed to establish the illegality of the conduct. Under Hungarian competition law, the HCO has to institute a competition proceeding solely if this is in the public interest. The HCO came to the conclusion that the mere establishing of the conduct's illegality, deprived of the possibility to impose a fine, would not be in the public interest, since it would have no deterrent effect. Furthermore, it also considered that the legislator, through the adoption of the amendment, made the interpretation of the public interest doubtful as to the agricultural sector.

57. On the basis of the above grounds, the HCO terminated the competition proceeding.

58. This case is a good example on how national legislation may block the investigation and sanctioning of a cartel that goes counter to the core principles of EU competition law. The argument that the HCO has no competence to disapply national rules that infringe EU competition law seems to be, put it mildly, odd, especially because the contradiction between Article 5 of Regulation 1/2003 and the amendment's exclusion of the possibility

Part I, Ch. 2, Scope of Application 59–62

to impose a fine is blatant. Furthermore, the argument that the continuation of the competition proceeding would not be in the public interest because the HCO could merely establish the violation of the law but could not impose a fine seems to be flawed. First, a decision on illegality could have sent a clear message to the market. Second, it could have assisted follow-on actions for damages: the HCO could have helped the victims of the cartel with establishing the legal base of such actions. However, the HCO considered that this is not in the public interest.

59. It is to be noted that, in April 2014, the Commission launched an infringement procedure against Hungary on the basis that the above rules go counter to Article 5 of Regulation 1/2003 and Article 4(3) TEU.[39] In 2015,[40] after the closing of the present manuscript, the Hungarian parliament repealed the above provisions of Act CXXVIII of 2012 and inserted them into section 93/A CA; however, with the important qualification that these rules can be applied only if the necessity of applying Article 101 TFEU does not emerge.

§3. STATE-OWNED ENTERPRISES AND PUBLIC UTILITIES

60. The CA contains no general rule exempting state-owned enterprises or public utilities from competition law. However, the activity of certain public entities, depending on the nature of the activity, may not qualify as market conduct and, hence, may not be caught in the net of competition law.

Obviously, the exercise of pure public power is not covered by the rules of competition law.[41]

61. The provision of public service may qualify as non-market conduct in case the service provided does not amount to a market service, even if the users are required to pay some remuneration; e.g., the service provider's operation is exhaustively regulated and it has only a limited autonomy in determining its market conduct, the service (under the conditions and in the structure established by the law) would not be viable under market circumstances.

62. In Case *Vj-190/2001 Diákhitel Központ Rt. (DHK)*, the CC scrutinized the conduct of the Student Loan Centre, which was a non-profit organization established by the state to provide student loan. The Centre's activity was exhaustively regulated; the applicable rules provided that the interest rate and other costs of the student loan have to be set on a level that covers the Centre's expenditures; however, the Centre could not strive for profit. A complaint was lodged against the Student Loan Centre because it required students to have a bank account at Postbank, a state-owned bank, if they wanted to receive the loan. The CC came to the conclusion that

---

39. http://europa.eu/rapid/press-release_MEMO-14-293_en.htm.
40. Act LXXVIII of 2015. The amendment entered into force on 1 Sep. 2015.
41. *See* Case *Vj-164/2000 Balatonfenyves Község Önkormányzata*, Case *Vj-192/2000 Szekszárd Megyei Jogú Város Önkormányzata*, Case *Vj-126/2001 Budapest Főváros Önkormányzata*.

the student loan, as provided by the Centre, did not qualify as market conduct (it was not a market product) and was, hence, not covered by the CA.

63. The CC considered that an entity comes under the scope of the CA only if it engages in market activities.[42] It came to the conclusion that the state student loan, in the form and under the conditions set out by the respective regulation, was not a market product and could not be provided under market conditions.

64. The Centre had no autonomy as to the provision and distribution of the student loan. The CC held that those entities that are the instruments of a state policy pursuing the general good and are covered by close and continuous state regulation and supervision, and have powers similar to the institutions of public power, pursue a public purpose. Such entities do not qualify as undertakings in the application of the CA, because they do not pursue market activity.

65. After characterizing the Centre's activity as non-market in nature, the CC examined whether the distribution of this non-market service, that is, its payment and the related bank account service, shares the legal fate of the student loan itself.

66. In this respect, it came to the conclusion that the payment of the student loan cannot be detached from the product (student loan) itself. The CC approached the question from the perspective of the final users and found that the provision and the payment of the student loan are not two separate markets. The production and the trade of the product are not two separate markets but are the two phases of the same production-distribution chain, which are closely related and interdependent. Distribution and trade are not only separate services but also part of a product's supply system; as such, they do not qualify as an independent product market but they are simply a segment of the vertical production-distribution chain. Accordingly, since the CC regarded the student loan as a non-market product, not covered by the CA, it established that the distribution of the student loan does not qualify as a market product either. The CC also referred to the circumstance that the Student Loan Centre's operations were heavily regulated and the Centre had no real autonomy as to its decisions.[43]

§4. Sensible Effect and *De Minimis*

67. The CA, as to the scope of application, contains no rule embedding an appreciability requirement, albeit there are such provisions among the substantive rules on restrictive agreements.

---

42. Paragraph 340.
43. Section 15(2) CA.

Chapter 3. Overview of Substantive Provisions

§1. RESTRICTIVE AGREEMENTS

68. In Hungarian antitrust law, in line with EU competition law, the regulation of restrictive agreements has two conceptual layers: the general prohibition on restrictive agreements and the exemption.[44]

69. The general prohibition on restrictive agreements is established in section 11(1) of the CA (the national equivalent of Article 101(1) TFEU): every agreement, concerted practice and decision of an association of undertakings violates the general prohibition, if either by object or by actual or potential effect prevents, restricts or distorts competition. Section 11(2) contains an illustrative list of prohibited practices.

70. In a long line of cases including, prominently, *Vj-21/2005 Albacomp, Synergon and others*, the CC held that the competition law assessment of agreements and concerted practices proceeds from the requirement that undertakings have to make their decisions autonomously and independently, avoiding any collusion with competitors as regards market conduct. Market operators have to adopt their business policy independently from each other, and this requirement prevents all direct and indirect contacts between independent market players.[45]

71. The general prohibition on restrictive agreements has its inherent limits. For instance, there is no anti-competitiveness (prevention, restriction or distortion of competition), apart from certain exceptions, if the agreement is of minor importance (*de minimis*), or if the agreement has both anti-and pro-competitive effects, and the balance of these effects is pro-competitive: the anti-competitive repercussions are outweighed by the pro-competitive merits. Furthermore, in very limited circumstances, public interest arguments can also be considered when examining the competition law compliance of the decisions of professional associations (bars, chambers, etc.).

72. In sum, Hungarian competition law's general prohibition on restrictive agreements may be boiled down to the following conceptual elements:

– the concept of agreement (*strictu sensu* agreements, concerted practices, decisions of associations of undertakings);
– anti-competitive object or effect;

---

44. *See* Csongor István Nagy, *Kartelljogi Kézikönyv. A közösségi és a magyar kartelljog kézikönyve* 267 (HVG-Orac 2006); Csongor István Nagy, *III. Rész: Antitröszt jog*, in *Magyar versenyjog* 179-180 (Kinga Pázmándi ed., HVG-Orac 2012).
45. Paragraph 88.

– the immanent limits of the general prohibition on restrictive agreements (agreements of minor importance, economic reasonableness test and public interest reasonableness test).[46]

73. The second layer of the rule on restrictive agreements consists of the notion of exemption, which may be either individual[47] or block exemption.[48] The reason for this second layer is that in certain cases, the most efficient pattern of economic operation is not rivalry but cooperation. Accordingly, competition law establishes an exception, albeit rather strict, to the requirement of non-collusive competition.

§2. Dominant Undertakings

74. In line with EU competition law, under Hungarian antitrust law dominant position as such is not prohibited; however, undertakings in a dominant position must not abuse their market power. The legal test on the abuse of dominant position has two conceptual elements: existence of a dominant position and abusive conduct.

75. Dominant position is defined in section 22(1) CA; this definition is generally in line with EU competition law's grasp and was inspired by the CJEU's judgment in *United Brands*.[49] Accordingly, an undertaking has a dominant position in the relevant market, if it can pursue its economic activity to a large extent independently from other market participants, without the need to substantially take into account what market conduct its competitors, suppliers and business partners pursue in relation to it.

76. Section 22(2) CA contains an illustrative list of factors that are to be examined in order to establish whether there is a dominant position in the market:

– entry barriers: the costs, risks and technical, economic and legal conditions of market entry and exit;
– the property, financial and income situation of the undertaking and group of undertakings, and its change;
– the structure of the relevant market, the market shares of the undertakings present on the market (both in absolute terms and comparatively), the conduct of the market participants, the undertaking's and the group's economic influence on the development of the market.

---

46. Csongor István Nagy, *Kartelljogi Kézikönyv. A közösségi és a magyar kartelljog kézikönyve* 269 (HVG-Orac 2006); Csongor István Nagy, *III. Rész: Antitröszt jog*, in *Magyar versenyjog* 200-201 (Kinga Pázmándi ed., HVG-Orac 2012).
47. Section 17 CA.
48. Section 16 CA.
49. Case C-27/76 *United Brands v. Commission* [1978] ECR 207, para. 65.

Part I, Ch. 3, Overview of Substantive Provisions 77–81

77. According to section 22(3) CA, a dominant position may be held by an undertaking or a group of undertakings (individual dominance), or by more than one undertaking or more than one group of undertakings (collective or joint dominance).

§3. CONCENTRATIONS

78. Section 23 CA defines the concept of concentration, while section 24 CA establishes the turnover threshold over which transactions are to be notified to the HCO and establishes the duty to notify.

According to section 23(1) CA, a concentration between undertakings occurs if:

– two or more undertakings independent of each other amalgamate (they amalgamate creating a new legal person) or one of them merges into another one (incorporation: the former becomes part of the latter and loses its legal personality), or part of an undertaking becomes part of another undertaking independent from the one containing the part of undertaking;
– an undertaking or more undertakings jointly acquire direct or indirect control over an undertaking that is independent from the former undertaking(s), or over more undertakings that are independent from it (them) but not independent from each other;
– more than one undertaking independent from each other jointly establish an undertaking controlled by them that is capable of pursuing, on a lasting basis, all the functions of an independent undertaking (full-function joint venture).

79. According to section 23(2) CA, an undertaking has direct control over another undertaking if:

– it disposes of business shares (in case of a limited liability company) or shares (in case of shareholding companies) that ensure the majority of the voting rights or it has more than 50% of the voting rights;
– it is entitled to appoint, elect or recall the majority of the undertaking's executives;
– it is entitled to exercise decisive influence on the undertaking's decisions on the basis of a contract;
– it becomes, in fact, able to exercise decisive influence on the undertaking's decisions (de facto control).

80. According to section 23(3) CA, an undertaking has indirect control over another undertaking if one or more undertakings controlled by it, whether together with the controlling undertaking or not, individually or jointly, control the other undertaking.

Section 23(4) CA establishes an exception to the above definition of concentration: the activity of a liquidator or receiver (irrespective of whether it acts in a winding-up or insolvency proceeding) does not qualify as a concentration.

81. According to section 23(5) CA, the term 'part of undertaking' encompasses assets and rights, including the undertaking's clientele, the acquisition of which, in

themselves or together with the assets and rights the acquiring undertaking already has, is sufficient for the pursuance of the market operation.

Section 24 CA determines the turnover thresholds over which the concentration necessitates the HCO's permission and establishes the duty to notify.

82. Section 29 CA provides that notifiable concentrations cannot be implemented without the HCO's authorization, in particular the voting rights and the rights as to the appointment or election of the executive officers cannot be exercised; in the course of the business relations between the acquirer and the target, the pre-merger situation has to prevail. This prohibition does not apply to the conclusion of the contract serving as the basis of the concentration or to the issuance of the public offer, as well as to such legal acts and declarations that are necessary for creating the concentration but do not entail that the acquirer can exercise controlling rights. Section 29/A empowers the HCO to authorize, upon request, the acquirer of the right of control to exercise its right before the final decision on the concentration, in particular, if this is necessary for the preservation of the investment's value; in this case, the HCO may adopt a control-restricting provision, qualifying the exercise of control or establishing obligations in this regard.[50]

83. According to section 29/A(4) CA, if the HCO does not authorize the concentration, all legal acts and declarations that infringe the prohibition of implementation embedded in section 29 CA or a control-restricting provision adopted under section 29/A(2) CA are automatically invalid. However, the undertaking violating the prohibition of implementation or the control-restricting provision cannot refer to the foregoing provision, and this undertaking may be held responsible for the damages emerging from the application of the legal consequence of automatic invalidity.

84. According to section 29/A(5) CA, in case of concentrations created during the insolvency proceeding of an enterprise having a special significance for the national economy as defined in section 65 of Act XLIX of 1991 on the reorganization and insolvency proceedings that resulted in the acquisition or change of control over the undertaking or part of undertaking having a special significance for the national economy, the HCO's permission is not necessary for the exercise of the controlling rights. This provision, however, does not concern the application of the rules on control-restricting provisions.

85. According to section 25 CA, the temporary acquisition of control (for a period not longer than one year) of certain organizations (insurance companies, credit institutions, financial holding companies, holding companies with mixed operation, investment companies, trustee organizations etc.) does not entail a notification duty, if the purpose of the acquisition of control is to prepare the resale of the enterprise, and the undertaking acquiring control does not exercise its controlling rights or it does only to the extent inevitably necessary. The HCO, upon the request of the enterprise acquiring control

---

50. Section 29/A(1)-(2) CA.

Part I, Ch. 3, Overview of Substantive Provisions

submitted before the end of the one-year-long transitory period, can prolong the transitory period on one occasion by, at most, one year, if the enterprise proves that the sale, for a reason it is not responsible for, was not possible within one year.

86. According to section 24 CA, the HCO's permission is to be requested for the concentration, if the joint net turnover realized in the preceding business year by all the groups of undertakings concerned (as defined in section 26(5) CA) and by the undertakings jointly controlled by the members of the groups of undertakings concerned and other undertakings exceeds HUF 15 billion and among the groups of undertakings concerned there are at least two groups of undertakings the individual net turnover of which, including the undertakings jointly controlled by the members of the groups of undertaking and other undertakings, exceeds HUF 500 million. Section 24(2) CA provides that when calculating the individual turnovers for the purpose of applying the HUF 500 million threshold the non-notifiable concentrations between the acquiring group and the group of undertakings losing its controlling rights that occurred within a period of two years preceding the concentration are to be taken into account. The message of section 24(2) CA is clear: if the acquiring group of undertakings, in the preceding two years, purchased one or more undertakings or parts of undertakings from the selling group and these concentrations were not notifiable due to their remaining under the turnover threshold, these turnovers are to be counted in.

87. Sections 24(3) and 27 CA contain provisions on how to calculate the turnover in the application of section 24 CA.

88. According to section 24(3) CA, in case of concentrations between insurance companies, instead of the net turnover, the value of the gross insurance fees is to be taken into account; in case of the concentration of investment service providers the relevant figure is the income from the investment services, in case of funds the relevant figure is the value of the contributions. In case of credit institutions and financial undertakings, the sum of the following income elements is to be taken into account: (a) interests and interest-like income, (b) income from investment papers (securities in stock corporations, other investment papers yielding a variable return, income from shares, income from shares in connected undertakings), (c) commissions, (d) the net profit of financial operations, and (e) income from other business activities.

89. Section 24/A CA authorizes the government to deprive the HCO of its competence and to exempt a concentration from the notification duty: the government – if this is justified by the public interest, especially the preservation of the workplaces for the sake of the security of supply – may qualify a concentration as having a national strategic significance; such concentrations, contrary to section 24 CA, do not have to be notified to the HCO. Although a relatively short time period has elapsed since the entry into force of this provision, there have already been several examples, where the Government availed itself of this possibility, notably in case of acquisitions by Government-controlled entities in the energy and telecommunications sectors. The

above provision was inserted into the CA by Act CXCI of 2013. Between this provision's entry into force (on 22 November 2013) and 31 December 2014, the government adopted a dozen of regulations on the basis of section 24/A CA.[51]

90. According to section 27(1) CA, in the application of section 24(1) CA, when calculating the net turnover, the turnover between undertakings belonging to the same group and between their parts has to be disregarded.

91. According to section 27(2) CA, when calculating the turnover of undertakings of foreign domicile, the net turnover realized from the products sold on the territory of Hungary in the preceding business year shall be taken into account.

92. According to section 27(3) CA, when calculating the net turnover of undertakings the majority owner of which is the state or the local self-government (municipality), the turnover of the undertaking shall be taken into account that forms an economic unit and has autonomous decision-making power as to its market conduct.

---

51. *See* 338/2014. (XII. 18.) Korm. rendelet az MVM Magyar Villamos Művek Zártkörűen Működő Részvénytársaságnak a Fővárosi Gázművek Zártkörűen Működő Részvénytársaságban fennálló részesedése MFB Magyar Fejlesztési Bank Zártkörűen Működő Részvénytársaság és MFB Invest Befektetési és Vagyonkezelő Zártkörűen Működő Részvénytársaság általi megszerzése nemzetstratégiai jelentőségűnek minősítéséről; 330/2014. (XII. 16.) Korm. rendelet az MFB Magyar Fejlesztési Bank Zártkörűen Működő Részvénytársaságnak a Fővárosi Gázművek Zártkörűen Működő Részvénytársaságban történő részesedésszerzése nemzetstratégiai jelentőségűnek minősítéséről; 282/2014. (XI. 14.) Korm. rendelet a WELT 2000 Szolgáltató és Kereskedelmi Korlátolt Felelősségű Társaság társasági üzletrészének a Magyar Állam javára történő megszerzése nemzetstratégiai jelentőségűnek minősítéséről; 254/2014. (X. 2.) Korm. rendelet a Magyar Gáz Tranzit Zártkörűen Működő Részvénytársaság társasági részesedéseinek állam javára történő megszerzésére irányuló ügylet nemzetstratégiai jelentőségűnek minősítéséről; 235/2014. (IX. 18.) Korm. rendelet a Magyar Államnak a Bombardier MÁV Hungary Kft.-ben történő részesedés szerzése társasági összefonódásának közérdekből történő nemzetstratégiai jelentőségűnek minősítéséről; 218/2014. (VIII. 28.) Korm. rendelet a Fővárosi Gázművek Zártkörűen Működő Részvénytársaság Fővárosi Önkormányzat tulajdonában lévő társasági részesedésének állam javára történő megszerzése nemzetstratégiai jelentőségűnek minősítéséről; 190/2014. (VII. 30.) Korm. rendelet a Magyar Államnak az MKB Bank Zrt.-ben történő részesedés szerzése társasági összefonódásának közérdekből történő nemzetstratégiai jelentőségűnek minősítéséről; 142/2014. (IV. 30.) Korm. rendelet a Nemzedékek Tudása Tankönyvkiadó Zártkörűen Működő Részvénytársaság és az Apáczai Kiadó és Könyvterjesztő Korlátolt Felelősségű Társaság társasági üzletrészének a Magyar Állam javára történő megszerzése nemzetstratégiai jelentőségűnek minősítéséről; 106/2014. (III. 26.) Korm. rendelet az "Antenna Hungária" Magyar Műsorszóró és Rádióhírközlési Zártkörűen Működő Részvénytársaság 100%-os társasági részesedése állami tulajdonban álló társaság általi megszerzése nemzetstratégiai jelentőségűnek minősítéséről; 51/2014. (II. 28.) Korm. rendelet a WELT 2000 Szolgáltató és Kereskedelmi Korlátolt Felelősségű Társaság társasági üzletrészének a Magyar Állam javára történő megszerzése nemzetstratégiai jelentőségűnek minősítéséről; 48/2014. (II. 26.) Korm. rendelet a Magyar Takarékszövetkezeti Bank Zártkörűen Működő Részvénytársaság és a Magyar Takarék Befektetési és Vagyonkezelő Zártkörűen Működő Részvénytársaság összefonódása közérdekből nemzetstratégiai jelentőségűnek minősítéséről; 14/2014. (I. 29.) Korm. rendelet a Fővárosi Gázművek Zártkörűen Működő Részvénytársaság 49,83%-os társasági részesedése MVM Magyar Villamos Művek Zártkörűen Működő Részvénytársaság általi megszerzése nemzetstratégiai jelentőségűnek minősítéséről.

Part I, Ch. 3, Overview of Substantive Provisions

93. According to section 27(4) CA, in case of a part of undertaking, the net turnover realized in the preceding business year through the utilization of the assets and rights sold is to be taken into account.

94. According to section 27(5) CA, the net turnover of the undertaking under joint control shall be divided equally between the controlling undertakings; undertakings being part of the same group of undertakings are, from this perspective, to be regarded as one unit. The net turnover has to be established on the basis of the turnover in the annual report or simplified annual report of the last authentically closed business year preceding the earlier from the following: publication of the public offer, conclusion of the contract or the acquisition of the right of control.[52] When converting the amounts in foreign currency to HUF, the Hungarian National Bank's exchange rate valid at the time of the closing of the undertaking's business year has to be applied.[53]

95. According to section 26 CA, the undertakings concerned are the undertakings that directly or indirectly participate in the concentration.
The direct participants are the undertakings between which the concentration occurs. According to section 26(2) CA, the following qualify as direct participants:

– in case of amalgamation: the amalgamating undertakings;
– in case of incorporation: the incorporating and the incorporated undertaking;
– in case a part of an undertaking becomes part of another undertaking: the receiving undertaking;
– in case of acquisition of control: the undertaking(s) acquiring direct control, the undertaking(s) acquiring indirect joint control (undertaking(s) controlling the first undertaking jointly with one or more members of another group of undertakings), and the undertaking(s) getting under control; and
– in case of establishing a joint venture: the founding parties of the joint venture (founders).

96. The indirect participants are the further members of the group of undertakings the direct participants are part of. When determining the circle of indirect participants, the undertaking that loses the right of control due to the concentration and the undertaking controlled by this undertaking, provided it does not qualify as a direct participant, have to be disregarded. The 'group of undertakings concerned' (or by way of shorthand: the 'group concerned') is the totality of a direct participant and the indirect participants connected to it.

97. Section 28 CA identifies the entity that is under the duty to notify (the applicant). The concentration has to be notified, in case of amalgamation, incorporation and the foundation of a joint venture, by the direct participant, in all other cases, by

---

52. Section 27(6) CA.
53. Section 27(7) CA.

the acquirer of the part of undertaking or the acquirer of the direct right of control or the undertaking having direct control over the acquiring undertaking.

98. As from 1 July 2014, the CA sets no deadline for the submission of the merger application.[54] However, section 28(3) CA provides that in case of the concentration of credit institutions and insurance companies, the merger application has to be submitted at the same time when the application for the permission of the Hungarian National Bank is submitted.

99. Section 30(1) CA provides that when deciding on the merger application, the concentration's advantages and disadvantages are to be considered. In particular, the following factors are to be examined:

– the structure of the relevant market, the actual and potential competition in the relevant markets, the procurement and marketing possibilities, the costs, risks, as well as the technical, economic and legal conditions of market entry and market exit, the concentration's expected impact on the competition in the market;
– the market position and strategy, the economic and financial abilities, business conduct, the competitiveness in the domestic and foreign markets of the undertakings concerned and the expected change of these;
– the concentration's effect on the suppliers and the business partners.

100. As to the substantive test, the CA applies a test essentially identical to the European regime (although the wording is slightly different, this should not entail any difference in assessment). Section 30(2) CA provides that the HCO has to authorize the concentration if it does not lessen competition substantially in the relevant market, especially as a consequence of creating or strengthening a dominant position. If the purpose or effect of the joint venture is to coordinate the founders' market conduct, the concentration is to be assessed on the basis of the provisions governing individual exemption (i.e., section 17 CA).

101. In respect of remedies, according to section 30(3) CA, if the substantial lessening of competition in the relevant market resulting from the concentration can be eliminated in case of the occurrence of a particular preliminary or posterior condition – especially the sale of certain parts of undertaking or certain assets, the termination of control over an indirect participant – or in case of complying with certain behavioural rules, and the undertakings concerned in this regard undertake to appropriately amend the concentration according to such conditions, as well as during the concentration's implementation will act accordingly, the CC, instead of prohibiting the merger, authorizes

---

54. Earlier, the CA provided that the merger application had to be submitted within thirty days of the publication of the public offer, the conclusion of the contract or the acquisition of the right of control; if more than one of these occurred, the deadline started from the one that occurred earlier. In case of agreements concluded during the insolvency proceeding of an enterprise having a special significance for the national economy as defined in s. 65 of Act XLIX of 1991 on the reorganization and insolvency proceedings that resulted in the acquisition or change of control over the undertaking or part of undertaking having a special significance for the national economy, the deadline was fifteen days. With the introduction of the express prohibition of implementation, the foregoing deadlines were repealed.

Part I, Ch. 3, Overview of Substantive Provisions 102–106

the concentration with the prescription of the preliminary or posterior condition or obligation.

102. Ancillary restraints are expressly addressed by section 30(5) CA: the merger permission covers all those restrictions of competition that are necessary for implementing the concentration.

103. If in the competition procedure the HCO establishes that a concentration covered by the notification duty established in section 24 CA was implemented without a merger permission and it could not have been permitted (if notified), it may prescribe in a decision, setting an appropriate deadline, that the merged undertakings, assets or shares are to be separated, sold, the joint control is to be terminated and it may establish also other obligations for restoring effective competition.[55]

104. According to section 31 CA, if it is established during the competition proceedings that the notifiable concentration implemented without a permission could not have been cleared, the CC, in its decision, prescribes the dissolution of the merged undertakings or assets (or shares of business) or the termination of the joint control within a particular deadline, or may establish any other obligation for reinstating efficient competition.

§4. OTHER PROHIBITIONS

105. The Act on Trade introduced special prohibitions as to large commercial retailers (retail chains) with significant market power, not amounting to a dominant position. The Act entered into force on 1 June 2006. It prohibits abusive practices on the part of retailers with significant market power against suppliers. The purpose of the Act was to provide legal protection to suppliers dealing with large retailers (normally retail chains), which, notwithstanding the lack of dominant position, have a strong bargaining power vis-à-vis small suppliers. The Act extended the HCO's remit to such abusive practices; when applying the rules of the Act on Trade, the HCO's procedure is governed by the CA's rules applied in dominant position matters.[56]

106. The Act on Trade defines significant market power as 'a market situation as a consequence of which the dealer becomes or has become a contracting partner for the supplier the latter is unable to reasonably evade at forwarding its goods and services to the customers and which is able, due to the size of its share in the turnover, to influence regionally or all over the country the market access of a product or a group of products'.[57] The Act also sets out certain cases where the existence of significant market power has to be irrebuttably presumed. There is significant market power against the supplier, if the net income of the group of undertakings acquired from

---

55. Section 31 CA.
56. Section 9(3) of the Act on Trade.
57. Section 2(7) of the Act on Trade.

commercial operations in the previous year exceeds HUF 100 billion.[58] Under this turnover threshold, the trader has significant market power, if the trader, group of undertakings or purchasing association has or acquires a unilaterally beneficial bargaining position against the supplier on the basis of the structure of the market, entry barriers, market share, financial strength and other resources, the width of its commercial network, the size and location of its shops and the entirety of its commercial and other operations.[59]

107. The Act on Trade prohibits all abuses of significant market power and contains an illustrative list of abusive practices (unjustified discrimination, unilaterally beneficial share of risks, unjustified alternation of the contractual terms, charging of unjustified fees, etc.).[60]

108. Special rules apply to unfair distributor practices vis-à-vis suppliers of agricultural products and foodstuffs.[61]

109. The HCO has already initiated proceedings against several retailers under the Act on Trade and has already imposed fine for abuses of significant market power, *inter alia*, due to the use of rebate schemes that were regarded as detrimental to suppliers.[62]

§5. Tests of Illegality

I. Per Se Prohibitions and Naked Restraints

110. Hungarian competition law follows the pattern of EU law as to the competition analysis of restrictive agreements. Accordingly, in principle, all agreements that have an anti-competitive object or effect are prohibited (under section 11 CA, the national equivalent of Article 101(1) TFEU); however, agreements violating this general prohibition may benefit from an exemption under section 17 CA (the national equivalent of Article 101(3) TFEU).

111. Agreements having an anti-competitive object violate section 11 CA per se, while all other agreements fall foul of this provision only if they have anti-competitive effects; such effects can be proven only on the basis of a market-analysis. Although there is a list of agreements that in the decisional practice are

---

58. Section 7(3) of the Act on Trade.
59. Section 7(4) of the Act on Trade.
60. Section 7(1)-(2) of the Act on Trade.
61. Section 7(6) of the Act on Trade. Act XCV of 2009 on the prohibition of unfair distributor practices applied against suppliers as to agricultural products and foodstuffs (in Hungarian: '2009. évi XCV. törvény a mezőgazdasági és élelmiszeripari termékek vonatkozásában a beszállítókkal szemben alkalmazott tisztességtelen forgalmazói magatartás tilalmáról').
62. *See* e.g. Case *Vj-47/2010 SPAR*.

Part I, Ch. 3, Overview of Substantive Provisions 112–117

regarded as having an anti-competitive object, the CC normally grasps this concept broadly.

112. Theoretically, all agreements going counter to section 11 CA may meet the requirements of section 17 CA.[63] Nonetheless, similarly to EU competition law, it is rather unlikely that an agreement having an anti-competitive object may qualify for an individual exemption.

II. Balancing Tests

113. If an agreement has no anti-competitive object, it is to be examined whether it has anti-competitive effects. Detailed effects-analysis is conducted only in the minority of the matters, since most prosecuted cases involve hard-core agreements, where such an analysis is not necessary.

114. In the frame of the effects-analysis, the HCO assesses the agreement's impact on competition in the market and compares it with the would-be situation without the agreement (i.e., the plight in the absence of the agreement). This analysis has to identify both actual and potential effects. Accordingly, if the agreement involves the risk of a particular anti-competitive repercussion, it has a potential anti-competitive effect and, hence, may go counter to section 11 CA. That is, it is sufficient if the anti-competitive effects are possible (in case of ongoing or future arrangements), they do not have to be actual.

115. The existence of some anti-competitive repercussions cannot be decisive as to the agreement's legal fate: an agreement may entail both anti-competitive and pro-competitive effects; the balance of the agreement's effects has to be anti-competitive.

III. Merger Tests

116. Until 2009, Hungarian merger law followed the dominance test. As from 1 June 2009,[64] this has been replaced with the 'effect on competition test', which is similar to EU merger control law's 'significant impediment to effective competition' (SIEC) test.

117. The rationale and legislative consideration behind the new test is that a concentration may be detrimental to competition not only in case it creates or strengthens a dominant position, but also the increase of market concentration may, by way

---

63. In *Matra Hachette SA v. Commission* the General Court held that 'in principle, no anti-competitive practice can exist which, whatever the extent of its effects on a given market, cannot be exempted, provided that all the conditions laid down in Article 85(3) of the Treaty are satisfied and the practice in question has been properly notified to the Commission'. Case T-17/93 *Matra Hachette SA v. Commission* [1994] ECR II-595, para. 85.
64. Act XIV of 2009.

of example, ease cartelization and collusion and may enhance the undertaking's ability to engage in such strategies. Accordingly, the relevant question is whether the concentration lessens competition substantially.[65]

---

65. HCO's 'General Methodology: the methodological approach of the analysis of concentrations', para. 1.1.

Chapter 4. Overview of Main Notions

§1. Undertaking

118. Hungarian competition law essentially follows EU competition law's 'economic unit' concept but uses a conceptual system different from that of EU law. Under the latter, the term 'undertaking' is mainly used as the equivalent of 'economic unit', and, put it roughly, the competition rules of the TFEU apply to undertakings and not to individual legal subjects. Under Hungarian competition law, the term 'undertaking' designates a legal subject (legal or natural persons), while the counterpart of the concept of 'economic unit' is the term 'group of undertakings'.

119. Partnerships (general partnership, in Hungarian: '*közkereseti társaság*', in short: '*kkt.*',[66] and limited partnership, in Hungarian: '*betéti társaság*', in short: '*bt.*'[67]) and companies (limited liability company, in Hungarian: '*korlátolt felelősségű társaság*', in short: '*kft.*',[68] publicly held stock corporation, in Hungarian: '*nyilvánosan működő részvénytársaság*', in short: '*nyrt.*', closely held stock corporation, in Hungarian: '*zártkörűen működő részvénytársaság*', in short: '*zrt.*'[69]) are legal persons.

120. An important (though rather academic) difference between EU and Hungarian competition law is that while under EU law on restrictive agreements and dominant position there are no specific and concrete rules on how to determine which entities belong to an undertaking (in terms of 'economic unit') and such a strict definition is to be found only in the Merger Control Regulation, Hungarian competition law contains a clear statutory definition on the delimitation of the group of undertakings, which is used in all fields of competition law (i.e., restrictive agreements, abuse of dominant position and merger control).

121. Under EU competition law, it is up to an individual assessment in a given case whether the subsidiary is regarded as belonging to the same undertaking as the parent company. Although in case the parent company has the majority of the voting right, it is presumed that it has control over the subsidiary; this is a rebuttable presumption. This is true even if it appears to be particularly difficult to find CJEU cases, where this presumption was successfully rebutted.[70] Under Hungarian competition law, an undertaking (or more undertakings together) has direct control over another undertaking if it has the majority of the voting rights, it is entitled to appoint the majority of the executives, is empowered by contract to exercise decisive influence on the controlled

---

66. 'Kkt.' is generally equivalent to the German '*offene Handelsgesellschaft*', in short: '*OHG*', and of the French '*Société en nom collectif*', in short: '*SNC*'.
67. 'Bt.' is generally equivalent to the German '*Kommanditgesellschaft*', in short: '*KG*', and of the French '*Société en commandite simple*', in short: '*SCS*'.
68. 'Kft.' is generally equivalent to the German '*Gesellschaft mit beschränkter Haftung*', in short: '*GmbH*', and of the French '*Société à Responsabilité Limitée*', in short: '*SARL*'.
69. Zrt. and Nyrt. are generally equivalent to the German '*Aktiengesellschaft*', in short: '*AG*', and of the French '*Société Anonyme*', in short: '*S.A.*'.
70. See Case 75/84 *Metro v. Commission* [1986] ECR 3021.

undertaking or has de facto control over it.[71] Accordingly, if the parent disposes of the majority of the voting rights in the subsidiary, the two entities belong to the same group of undertakings; this is not a rebuttable presumption.

122. According to section 15(1) CA, undertakings forming part of the same group and undertaking that are controlled by the same undertakings are not independent from each other. section 15(2) CA defines the concept of 'group of undertakings' as follows: undertaking 'A' is part of the same group of undertakings as undertaking 'B':

– if 'A', individually, directly or indirectly, controls 'B';
– if 'B', individually, directly or indirectly, controls 'A';
– if the undertaking controlling 'A', individually, directly or indirectly, controls 'B';
– if two or more from the undertakings that are in a controlling relationship with 'A' as specified in the preceding points and undertaking 'A' control 'B' jointly.

123. Although the addressees of the Hungarian competition rules are undertakings (natural and legal persons), the concept of economic unit ('group of undertakings') is taken into account during the substantive competition assessment. Since – contrary to EU competition rules – the provisions of Hungarian competition law are addressed to persons (natural and legal) and not economic units, the CA contains numerous rules that endeavour to correct this and implement the doctrine of economic unit. Furthermore, it is to be noted that the HCO, in its decisional practice, always bears in mind the principle that the final addressees of the competition rules should be economic units and in its balancing normally takes the economic reality of economic units into consideration.[72] Hence, even in the absence of a specific rule, the HCO takes the concept of economic unit into account in its balancing.

124. As noted, section 1 CA provides that it applies to natural and legal persons pursuing a market activity; in other words, the act applies to all persons (i.e., all subjects of law) and the addressees of the substantive provisions and prohibitions are the persons and not the group of undertakings. However, at different parts the CA provides that the entire group of undertakings is to be taken into account when applying the competition rules.

125. When examining whether an undertaking is in a dominant position, the group of undertakings it is part of shall be taken into account. Section 22(3) CA provides that economic dominance may be held by an individual undertaking or an

---

71. Section 23(1) CA.
72. For instance, in Case *Vj-174/2007/332*, the defendant was part of a group another member of which had already been condemned for a similar violation; the HCO considered this as recidivism and regarded it as an aggravating circumstance. Furthermore, when setting the fine, the HCO considered the group's characteristics and not those of the perpetrator undertaking in order to ascertain the financial bearing capacity. This decision was subsequently upheld by the Supreme Court.

Part I, Ch. 4, Overview of Main Notions 126–128

individual group of undertakings, as well as by more than one undertaking or more than one group of undertakings jointly.[73] Furthermore, section 22(2) CA, when defining the factors to be taken into account when establishing the existence of a dominant position, refers to the features of both the undertaking and the group.[74]

126. There is no such provision of general application in the field of restrictive agreements. However, in the decisional practice and in the scholarship, the doctrine of economic unit is also part of the effects-analysis.[75] The HCO 'maps' the group of undertakings concerned also in case of restrictive agreements, and assesses the impact on competition on the basis of the features of the group. Section 11(1) CA expressly provides that agreements between undertakings belonging to the same group do not come under the scope of application of the rules on restrictive agreements. Furthermore, when applying the rule on agreements of minor importance[76] and the block-exemption regulations,[77] the entire group's market share has to be taken into account.

127. Although the addressees of the CA are natural and legal persons and the competition fine in the merits may be imposed on the defendant, who is a natural or legal person, there are two special rules that enable the HCO to take the concept of economic unit into consideration when setting the fine. First, the HCO may launch the proceeding against both the parent company and the subsidiary and may establish that both of them violated the competition rules and may impose a fine on both of them. Second, section 78(5) CA provides that if the undertaking that committed the violation does not pay the fine and the enforcement measures for the collection of the fine are unsuccessful, any member of the group the undertaking is part of may be enjoined to pay the fine, provided, this member was 'named' in the administrative decision.

128. In Case *Vj-199/2005/246*, the Supreme Court, in the context of section 78(6) CA (which deals with the scenario when the association of undertakings cannot pay the fine and provides that those members of the association that participated in adopting the incriminated decision shall have subsidiary liability), held that the

---

73. The explanatory memorandum of the Amendment that inserted the institution of 'group of undertakings' into the CA in respect of the abuse of dominant position makes it clear that the HCO had followed the principle of economic unit well before its statutory introduction (remarks on s. 4 of Act LXVIII of 2005) and the Amendment simply codified the prevailing decisional practice.
74. Sections 22(2)(b)-(c) and s. 22(3) CA.
75. Csongor István Nagy, *Kartelljogi Kézikönyv. A közösségi és a magyar kartelljog kézikönyve* 175-180 (HVG-Orac 2006).
76. Section 13 CA.
77. Section 1(6) of Gov. Regulation 202/2011 on the exemption from the prohibition on restriction of competition of certain groups of specialisation agreements; s. 1(4) of Gov. Regulation 203/2011 on the exemption from the prohibition of restriction of competition of certain groups of insurance agreements; s. 1(2) of Gov. Regulation 205/2011 on the exemption from the prohibition on restriction of competition of certain groups of vertical agreements; s. 1(7) of Gov. Regulation 206/2011 on the exemption from the prohibition on restriction of competition of certain groups of research and development agreements. *See also* s. 1(5), 2(2), 5(2)(a) of Gov. Regulation 86/1999 of the Government on the exemption from the prohibition on restriction of competition of certain groups of technology transfer agreements.

undertaking has to be named in the operative part of the decision.[78] In Case *Vj-147/2007 Railway Construction Companies*,[79] the Supreme Court confirmed this line of interpretation also as to section 78(5) CA. As to whether it is justified to apply the interpretation of section 78(6) CA in Case *Vj-199/2005/246* by analogy to section 78(5) CA, it can be argued that these provisions, notwithstanding the use of the same term ('named'), base the member undertaking's liability on different grounds. In case of a group member, the member's subsidiary liability is strict, automatic and unconditional, that is, it subsists independent of the undertaking's conduct and it rests merely on the undertaking's membership. On the contrary, the member of the association of undertakings has subsidiary liability only if it did take part in the decision-making, that is, if with its own conduct it made itself involved in the mischief. These differences could have warranted the differential interpretation of the term 'named' in section 78(5) CA and section 78(6) CA. However, as noted above, in Case *Vj-147/2007 Railway Construction Companies*,[80] the Supreme Court held that the two provisions have to be interpreted in the same way.

129. In Case *Vj-73/2001 Holcim and others*, the CC established, on the basis of section 55 of the then-effective Company Act,[81] that the legal successor is generally liable for the legal predecessor's violation of competition law. It advanced that the legal successor has the same status as the legal predecessor, so the competition proceeding may be instituted also against it.[82] The CC's decision also stressed that there was continuity not only as to the economic activity but also as to the owners and the control of the undertaking; hence, the CC found that the restructuring, from a competition law perspective, entailed no new market participant and referred to the concept of economic unit.[83] The CC's interpretation was confirmed by the Supreme Court.[84] The Civil Code, which contains the currently effective rule of company law, contains a similar provision;[85] there is no reason to assume that the above approach would not be applied under it.

130. The doctrine of economic unit is taken into account also when determining the amount of the fine in the merits. Section 78(1) CA provides that the fine in the merits cannot be higher than 10% of the net turnover realized in the preceding calendar year by the group of undertakings the defendant is part of, provided the group is identified in the CC's decision. It is to be noted that the term 'group' covers the entire concern, i.e., in case of transnational enterprises the entire global group.[86]

---

78. Case *Kfv.III.37.557/2009/18*. (Supreme Court).
79. Case *Kfv.III.37.690/2013/9* (Supreme Court).
80. Case *Kfv.III.37.690/2013/9* (Supreme Court).
81. Act CXLIV of 1997 on economic companies.
82. Paragraph 113.
83. Paragraph 115.
84. Case *Kfv.II.39.262/2006/10-II*. (Supreme Court).
85. Sections 3:39(1), 3:44(1) and 3:45-46 of the Civil Code.
86. Paragraph 41 of Notice 1/2012 on setting the amount of the fine in case of conducts violating the prohibitions included in ss 11 and 21 of Act Nr LVII of 1996 on the prohibition of unfair market practice and restriction of competition, as well as Arts 101 and 102 of the Treaty on the Functioning of the European Union.

Part I, Ch. 4, Overview of Main Notions 131–135

131. Furthermore, the CC takes the concept of economic unit into account in its balancing concerning the amount of the fine. Although section 78(3) CA, which enumerates the factors to be taken into account when establishing the amount of the fine, makes no express mention to the group of undertakings, the CC has a wide margin of appreciation in interpreting these provisions[87] and it normally takes the doctrine of economic unit into account.[88]

132. The HCO's Notice on the Setting of Fines provides that recidivism can be established also in case the prior violation was committed by the legal predecessor or by another member of the group of undertakings named in the decision.[89]

133. This approach was followed in Case *Vj-174/2007/332 CELLVASÚT and others*, where the CC, when setting the fine in the merits, took 'intra-group recidivism' into account: although the undertaking committing the violation was not recidivist, another member of the company group had already been condemned for violating the CA. The HCO held that it was an aggravating circumstance that the undertaking was part of a company group, which had violated the CA on different occasions, committing similar infringements. Earlier, the HCO condemned and fined another member of the company group twice for bid-rigging. This approach was affirmed by the Supreme Court in Case *Kfv.III.37.690/2013/29*.

134. In this case, the CC also held: when establishing the condemned undertaking's financial situation (in the process of determining the fine), not only the perpetrator enterprise but also the entire group can be taken into account.[90] When assessing the preventive effect of the fine, the entire group of undertakings may be taken into consideration; in other words, it is not the undertaking but the group that is to be deterred from future violations.[91] The CC established that the group of undertakings is responsible for making the member undertakings observe the rules of competition law. It advanced that the rationale behind taking not only the direct perpetrator but also the entire group into account in respect of recidivism is that the group, which operates in the market in a rational and uniform manner, is expected to ensure that each and every undertaking forming part of the group complies with the rules of competition law and to ensure that none of the group members commits a violation of a similar kind.[92]

§2. RELEVANT MARKET

135. Hungarian competition law's test on the definition of the relevant market largely converges with that of EU competition law. The Commission's Notice on

---

87. *See* Case *Kf. V. 39.361/2001/4. Büki Üdítő Kft. v. GVH* (Supreme Court); Case 2. *Kf. 27.484/2008/7.* (Budapest Court of Appeal), published under nr VEF 2007.60.
88. Case *Vj-174/2007/332 CELLVASÚT and others*, para. 286.
89. Paragraph 35.
90. Paragraph 286.
91. Paragraph 286.
92. Paragraph 284.

the Relevant Market is frequently cited in the CC's decisions. This convergence is strengthened by the fact that economic analysis and balancing has a pivotal role in the definition of the relevant market.

136. The definition of the relevant market is a key concept of competition law, which is central to all three antitrust fields (restrictive agreements, dominant position and mergers). The determination of the relevant market enables the delimitation of the competing products and undertakings; that is, it delimitates the 'arena' of competition. The relevant market gives the framework, within which the conditions of competition can be evaluated and the market position of the undertaking or undertakings concerned can be ascertained and assessed. The definition of the relevant market has a central role also as to the calculation of the market share, since an undertaking's share can be ascertained only after the relevant market has been delimited. As competition law's most rules of thumb hinge on market share, the calculation of which presupposes the definition of the relevant market, the latter's practical relevance is pivotal.

137. Put it simple, the starting point of the definition of the relevant market is the following: a separate relevant market exists if a hypothetical monopolist could profitably increase the prices (Small but Significant and Non-transitory Increase in Price, SSNIP test). A price increase impacts the undertakings profit in two ways: sales at increased prices entail a higher rate of return per unit, while some of the customers switch to other products or stop consuming the product and this reduces the quantity sold. The relevant question is whether the increase of the margin outweighs the loss in quantity. If it does, other products are not sufficiently interchangeable with the product at stake; hence, these are not part of the same market. These alternative products put no competitive pressure on the sale of the products at stake; hence, they do not discipline the undertaking's market conduct. On the other hand, if the price increase were not profitable, the product at stake (product 'A') and the alternative product consumers would switch to (product 'B') are substitutes in the eyes of the consumers and, thus, they are competing with each other; accordingly, the analysis has to be extended to the alternative product. In the next step, the exercise is to be accomplished as to products 'A' and 'B' as an independent product group; that is, the relevant question is whether a hypothetical monopolist in products 'A' and 'B' could profitably increase the prices. Once the competing products are delimited and they are distinguished from products that trigger no competitive pressure, the real arena of competition is delimited.

138. In the CC's decisional practice, the definition of the relevant market is not an end but a means to assess the situation of competition in the market.[93] The fundamental purpose of the definition of the relevant market is to systematically identify the restraints the undertakings concerned face; the aim is to single out those actual competitors of the undertakings investigated that are capable of restricting the latter's market conduct

---

93. Communication on the Aspects of the Definition of the Relevant Market Concerned by the Concentration, para. 1.2.

Part I, Ch. 4, Overview of Main Notions

and preventing them from acting independently from the forcing power of actual competition.[94]

139. The definition of the relevant market is a functional concept, and it hinges on the characteristics of the investigated market conduct.[95]

140. The definition of the relevant market has, in its widest sense, three coordinates: relevant product market, relevant geographical market and temporal market. The practical relevance of the temporal market is negligible. The CA, in line with the Commission's Notice on the relevant market, makes no mention of this facet, providing that the market definition has two elements: the product market and the geographical market.[96] The HCO issued a Communication on the Aspects of the Definition of the Relevant Market Concerned by the Concentration,[97] summarizing its decisional practice. This document applies only to merger procedures but may indicate the HCO's general understanding of the relevant market.

141. The relevant product market encompasses those goods between which there is a reasonable demand-side or supply-side substitutability, taking into account the purpose of use, the price, the quality and the conditions of performance. Demand-side substitutability has to be realistic; mere physical similarity does not suffice, and it is required that the products are interchangeable in the eyes of the consumers. As the CA's explanatory memorandum advances, the consumer, when choosing between different products, considers not only physical similarity or dissimilarity but also other features, such as use, price, quality and conditions of performance.[98]

142. Supply-side substitutability did not appear in the CA's original text; this aspect of marker definition was inserted in the Act in 2000.[99] According to the explanatory memorandum of the Amendment of 2000, in respect of supply-side substitutability the HCO has to examine whether there are undertakings that are not producing or providing the product or service in question but are essentially capable of switching to this immediately, without incurring any significant costs or risks and thus entailing a competitive pressure of a similar intensity as those undertakings that are actually producing or providing the product or service. The explanatory memorandum also notes that supply-side substitutability has to be distinguished from potential competition; the latter aspect is not part of the definition of the relevant market but has to be taken into account when assessing the market effects of the agreement, market conduct or concentration. The explanatory memorandum's distinction between supply-side

---

94. Notice on the Relevant Market, para. 2.
95. Notice on the Relevant Market, para. 12.
96. *See* Péter Miskolczi-Bodnár, *A versenytörvény magyarázata* 184 (KJK-Kerszöv 2002); Lennart Ritter & W. David Braun, *European Competition Law: A Practitioner's Guide* 26–42 (Kluwer Law International 2005). On the other hand, some authors treat the temporal market as an independent dimension of the relevant market. *See* Csongor István Nagy, *Kartelljogi Kézikönyv. A közösségi és a magyar kartelljog kézikönyve* 252 (HVG-Orac 2006).
97. In Hungarian: '*Az összefonódás által érintett piac meghatározásának irányadó szempontjai*'.
98. CA's Explanatory memorandum, remarks on ss 11-20 CA.
99. Act CXXXVIII of 2000. The Amendment entered into force on 1 Feb. 2001.

substitutability and potential competition is essentially in line with EU competition law and the Commission's Notice on the Relevant Market.

143. The relevant geographical market is the area outside which the consumer cannot acquire the products or can acquire them only under significantly less favourable conditions or the seller cannot sell the products or can sell them only under significantly less favourable conditions. The CA's explanatory memorandum advances that taking into account the size of the domestic (i.e., Hungarian) market, in most cases, the geographical market is the entire territory of Hungary; however, in case of certain special products and in particular in case of services, the relevant geographical market may be narrower,[100] while in quite a few cases the geographical market defined by the CC is wider than Hungary.

144. The definition of the relevant market raises interesting questions in case of bid-rigging cartels (cartels concerning public tenders).[101] In Case *Vj-138/2002 Alterra Kft. and others*, the CC defined a narrow relevant market. The CC considered that since the collusion occurred in the frame of a public tender (covered by the Act on Public Procurement), the geographical market was the area delimited in the call and the product market comprised the goods or services the buyer identified in the call (since interchangeability was to be examined from the perspective of the customer). The CC underpinned this proposition with the principle that the definition of the relevant market is a means and not an end, which serves as a tool to identify the competitors of the undertakings, whose market conduct is investigated. It considered that reasonable substitutability cannot be interpreted in a way that it covers all undertakings that could potentially submit an offer to such a tender and to cover the entire territory of Hungary.[102]

§3. MARKET POWER/DOMINANT POSITION

145. Section 22(1) CA defines the term 'dominant position' as follows:

> a person is in a dominant position on the relevant market (section 14), if it can pursue its economic activity to a large extent independently from other market participants without the need to take into account, when determining its own market conduct, the market conducts of its competitors, suppliers and business partners.

---

100. CA's Explanatory memorandum, remarks on ss 11-20 CA.
101. *See* Pál Szilágyi, *Versenyeztetési eljárások hatása az érintett piac meghatározására és a versenyfeltételekre a közösségi jogban versenypolitikai szemszögből*, 64(5) Jogtudományi Közlöny 220 (2009); Pál Szilágyi, *Bidding Markets and Competition Law in the European Union and the United Kingdom. Part I*, 29(1) Eur. Com. Law Rev. 16 (2008); Pál Szilágyi, *Bidding Markets and Competition Law in the European Union and the United Kingdom. Part II*, 29(2) Eur. Com. Law Rev. 89 (2008).
102. Paragraph 28.

146. This definition was apparently inspired by EU competition law's concept of dominant position, especially the one adopted by the CJEU in *United Brands*.[103]

147. The concept of economic unit appears also in the definition of dominant position: a dominant position may be held by an undertaking or a group of undertakings.[104]

148. The key conceptual element of dominant position is the independence from other market participants, that is, the insufficient level of competitive pressure. In economic terms, an undertaking has a dominant position, if it can act, due to its status, independently from other market participants, thus increasing its prices profitably: the incremental profit entailed by the price increase is not offset or outweighed by the decrease in the quantity sold.

149. Section 22(2) CA provides that the following factors are to be taken into consideration when examining the existence of a dominant position:

– entry barriers: the costs, risks and technical, economic and legal conditions of market entry and exit;
– the property, financial and income situation of the undertaking and group of undertakings, and its change;
– the structure of the relevant market, the market shares of the undertakings present on the market (both in absolute terms and comparatively), the conduct of the market participants, the economic influence on the development of the market by the undertakings and groups of undertakings.

150. Besides the factors expressly enumerated in section 22(2) CA, the CC also takes into account the following circumstances:

– access to the input and sales markets;
– connections between undertakings (e.g., cross-ownerships);
– competition induced by partially interchangeable products or services; and
– general evaluation of the conditions of competition.

151. The existence of a dominant position cannot be connected to the possession of a particular market share, as there are numerous other factors that affect the undertaking's market position. However, in Hungarian competition law, in accordance with international practice, certain rules of thumb are used when establishing the undertaking's dominant position or its absence. Accordingly, under 25%–30% market share, it is normally unlikely that the undertaking has a dominant position,[105] between 25/30% and 40%, this depends on the circumstances, while above 40% market share the existence of dominant position is probable.

---

103. Case C-27/76 *United Brands v. Commission* [1978] ECR 207, para. 65.
104. Section 22(1) CA.
105. Notice 1/2014, para. 13.

152. Section 22(3) CA recognizes not only individual but also collective (joint) dominance: a dominant position may be held by an individual undertaking or group of undertakings, as well as by more than one undertaking or group of undertakings jointly. Collective (or joint) dominance exists when two or more independent undertakings can be regarded as acting as one dominant undertaking,[106] without having agreed on that; this may be traced back to the tacit parallelism peculiar to oligopolistic markets.

§4. AGREEMENTS AND CONCERTED PRACTICES

153. The term 'agreement' has a twofold meaning in Hungarian competition law. In narrower sense, it covers agreements in colloquial sense: actual and tacit concurrence of wills, irrespective of its form or expression. In its widest sense, the term 'agreement' covers all conducts prohibited by the law on restrictive agreements, including *strictu sensu* agreements, concerted practices and decisions of associations of undertakings. This dual meaning appears in section 11(1) CA.

154. It is to be stressed that it is completely irrelevant whether an undertaking breaches competition law via an agreement or a concerted practice; both are governed by the same prohibitions and rules. In Case *Vj-145/2001 Restaurants near lake Balaton*, the CC established that the assessment of a conduct does not hinge on whether it was committed through an agreement or a concerted practice, or both.[107] The CC adopted a similar approach in Case *Vj-154/2002 Baucont, Klíma-Vill. and Középületépítő*, establishing that a conduct may fall foul of the prohibition on restrictive agreements irrespective of whether it is an agreement in narrower sense or a concerted practice. The distinction between the two categories has no relevance in cases where the illegal conduct contains the elements of both, and the concerted practice can be established without doubt, but the conclusion of a *strictu sensu* agreement cannot be ascertained.[108] The CC followed a similar approach also in Case *Vj-102/2004 ABB Power Technologies Management Ltd. and others* and in Case *Vj-21/2005 Albacomp, Synergon, Kivitelező and others*.

I. *Strictu sensu* Agreements

155. The concept of agreement is a wide notion embracing all concurrences of wills irrespective of form. It covers all plights where two or more undertakings reach an understanding as to their market conduct, irrespective of whether the agreement is valid under civil law, legally enforceable and executed.[109]

---

106. Discussion paper on the application of Art. 82 of the Treaty to exclusionary abuses. 2005, para. 44. Available: http://ec.europa.eu/competition/antitrust/art82/discpaper2005.pdf.
107. Paragraph 35. This proposition was adopted by Position Statement No. 11.1, providing that a conduct's adjudication does not hinge on whether it is the result of an agreement or a concerted practice, or both.
108. Paragraph 75.
109. Case *Vj-89/2003 Vadászkartell*, para. 20; Case *Vj-74/2003 Magyar Gabonafeldolgozók*,

Part I, Ch. 4, Overview of Main Notions 156–158

156. According to the HCO's Position Statement No. 11.3: from a competition law perspective, an agreement comes into existence also in case it is invalid under civil or company law; the undertaking's participation in the agreement can be established if the person attending the meetings does not have the right to sign declarations on behalf of the company (no right of representation) but the others attending the meeting assume with good reason that the undertaking will act in accordance with the agreement. It is to be noted that this Position Statement is based on Case *Vj-145/2001*, which reveals that the impression on the persons attending the meeting is, in itself, not sufficient for establishing an agreement but it is to be demonstrated that there was a genuine concurrence of wills, and this may be proved also through the undertaking's subsequent behaviour. The impression on the participants of the meeting is, in itself, not sufficient for proving the agreement and the undertaking's participation. The central question is whether the person having no right of representation did, as a matter of practice, actually represent the undertaking. In this regard, the impression on the participants of the meeting is one of the factors that are to be taken into account.[110]

157. An agreement may be established also in case it was not implemented. In Case *Vj-154/2002 Baucont and others*, the CC held that the violation can be established also in case the undertakings did not implement the illegal agreement. A reference to the circumstance that the agreement was not implemented does not exempt the party from the liability for infringing competition law.[111] In the absence of actual implementation, the agreement has to be judged according to its object and potential effects. In Case A *Vj-74/2003 Magyar Gabonafeldolgozók, Takarmánygyártók és - Kereskedők Szövetsége*, the CC considered that for the application of the prohibition on restrictive agreements it is sufficient that it is possible that the effects emerge; the effects may be direct or indirect, actual or potential. Accordingly, the announcement of a target price may affect competition because this enables the undertakings to use this information when predicting the pricing policy the competitor will follow.[112] The CC adopted a similar approach in Case *Vj-102/2004 ABB Power Technologies Management Ltd. and others*.

158. The standard of proof as to the participation in an agreement is low and the burden of proof may easily shift. If it is proved that the representative of an undertaking attended an anti-competitive meeting or received a call for an anti-competitive cooperation, the burden shifts onto the defendant to prove that it did not actually take part in the collusion. That is, the attendance at the meeting and the reception of the anti-competitive proposal, in themselves, shift the burden of proof: it is the undertaking that has to prove that it did not become part of the anti-competitive cooperation.

Takarmánygyártók és -Kereskedők Szövetsége, para. 75; Case *Vj-21/2005 Albacomp, Synergon és Kivitelező*, para. 89; Case *Vj-145/2001 Restaurants near lake Balaton*, paras 41–42.
110. Csongor István Nagy, *Kartelljogi Kézikönyv. A közösségi és a magyar kartelljog kézikönyve* 309-311 (HVG-Orac 2006).
111. Paragraph 60.
112. Paragraph 74.

What is more, in line with EU competition rules,[113] Hungarian antitrust law requires public distancing on the part of the undertaking, that is, silence infers consent: in the absence of public distancing, the addressee of the anti-competitive proposal is to be regarded as part of the unlawful agreement.

159. In Case *Vj-74/2003 Magyar Gabonafeldolgozók, Takarmánygyártók és - Kereskedők Szövetsége*, the CC established that in case it is proved that the undertaking participated in a meeting having an anti-competitive agenda, the undertaking is required to prove unequivocally that its participation in the meeting was free from all anti-competitive elements, and its attendance was based on grounds different from those of the competitors. If the undertaking fails to prove this, it is liable for the violation even if afterwards it does not follow the agreement concluded on the meeting (e.g., it does not follow the pricing policy systematically), provided it did not distance itself officially from the meeting's content, e.g., through reporting the meeting to the competent authority. It does not prevent the establishing of the violation, if the undertaking remains passive during the meetings and discussions. Failing this, other participants may reasonably infer that the undertaking applauds the meeting's results and assents to the agreement. [114]

160. The above approach was followed by the CC in Case *Vj-102/2004 ABB Power Technologies Management Ltd. and others*.[115]

161. If the undertakings conclude more than one agreement (e.g., they regularly divide public tenders), their acts may be regarded not simply as a series of individual agreements but also as a general framework-agreement aimed at colluding as to the public tenders (institutionalized cartels, single and continuous infringement). In such cases, the HCO investigates the institutionalized cartel (i.e., the framework agreement) and not the individual agreements. This interpretation was adopted in Case *Vj-154/2002 Baucont and others*. Although the institutionalized cartel could not be established in this case, the decision defines this notion clearly. The CC held that during the competition procedure, the investigated acts, which are illegal also in themselves, are to be examined not separately but in their entirety, taking into account the connections between them. A 'unitary violation' can be established if it can be demonstrated that the same anti-competitive aim to manipulate the operation of the relevant market lied behind the various acts. In accordance with the concept of 'unitary violation', not only the conducts at the individual tenders are to be examined but it is also to be taken into consideration how the undertakings acted on other tenders.[116]

---

113. Case T-141/89 *Tréfileurope Sales SARL v. Commission* [1995] ECR II-791, paras 85–86 and 118; Case T-310/94 *Gruber + Weber GmbH & Co. KG v. Commission* [1998] ECR II-1043, para. 130; Case T-317/94 *Moritz J. Weig GmbH & Co. KG v. Commission* [1998] ECR II-1235, para. 87; Case T-56/99 *Marlines SA v. Commission* [2003] ECR II-5225, paras 30, 34–35, 56 and 41.
114. Paragraph 76.
115. Paragraph 275.
116. Paragraph 76.

Part I, Ch. 4, Overview of Main Notions 162–166

162. In Case *Kfv.II.37.076/2012/28*, the Supreme Court interpreted the doctrine of single and continuous infringement in a comprehensive manner. It held that the establishment of a single and continuous infringement has a legal and two factual prerequisite. The acts have to have the same purpose and be congenial (legal condition). Furthermore, it has to be proven that there was a comprehensive plan and it was implemented continuously (factual conditions).

This issue was examined by the CC also in Case *Vj-102/2004 ABB Power Technologies Management Ltd. and others*.

163. The establishing of an 'institutionalized cartel' may be favourable for the competition authority in several respects. First, the term of limitation (since the 'institutionalized cartel' qualifies as a continuous infringement) starts only when the violation ends;[117] hence, the events at the outset of the collusion may also be investigated. Second, the competition authority need not prove that a particular cartel member actively took part in each and every agreement: if an undertaking is proved to be part of an institutionalized cartel, it is liable for the entire cooperation.

164. In a vertical context, the concept of 'agreement' raises peculiar questions of interpretation. In this regard, the notion of agreement is rather vague and goes beyond the colloquial sense of the term. It is not rare that unilateral or seemingly unilateral acts of the producer qualify as an agreement. In competition law practice, there are two theories explaining how unilateral producer behaviour may qualify as an agreement. The first is the concept of 'preliminary authorization': the framework contract between the producer and the distributor empowers the former to adopt unilateral measures. The second is the 'tacit acquiescence' theory: the distributors may assent to the producer's call even tacitly, thus the producer's call becomes an agreement.[118]

II. Concerted Practices

165. The concept of concerted practice may be defined by distinguishing it from parallel behaviour. Enterprises may act in line under certain market conditions. This parallelism may have numerous legitimate grounds. First, market circumstances may change (e.g., increase of input costs, inflation), and these developments may have the same or similar impact on all market actors. Second, parallel conduct may also be caused by oligopolistic interdependence: the enterprises determine their market conduct taking into account the expected conduct of their competitors.[119]

166. In Hungarian competition law, the concept of concerted practice is applied mainly in two scenarios.

---

117. Section 67(4) CA.
118. *See* Csongor István Nagy, *A vertikális megállapodás mint a kartelltilalom küszöbfogalma: összehasonlító jogi elemzés és értékelés*, 7(1) Versenytükör 20 (2011).
119. Case *Vj-17/2001/89 Holcim, Breitenburger and CeBeK*, paras 126–127.

167. First, it is a concerted practice if the enterprises do not simply take into account the expected conduct of their competitors but enter into a tacit agreement, which, however, does not reach the level of a *strictu sensu* agreement, as the parties express their wills only tacitly or indicate them through their actual market conduct. If the explicit call of one of the parties were accepted tacitly by the addressee, this would amount to an agreement and not a concerted practice. The notion of concerted practice covers mutually conscious, mutually shaped acts, which are based on tacit consensus; if the parties' behaviour goes beyond tacit consensus, the arrangement is an agreement.

168. The borderline between concerted practice and parallel behaviour is thin. Hungarian competition law does not prohibit enterprises from taking into account the expected behaviour of the rivals, and from shaping their market conduct accordingly. Thus, it is not contrary to the law, if in a concentrated market of three undertakings, the enterprises consider that it would be irrational to cut prices, as their rivals would follow suit and, thus, none of the enterprises would increase its market share, while their profits would diminish due to the price-cutting. In this case, although market participants act in accordance with the expected behaviour of their competitors, this does not amount to a concerted practice. Namely, the element of mutual consciousness is missing. In case of concerted practice, there is some kind of a collusion or contact between the enterprises, which converts the parallel behaviour into a concerted practice.

169. Second, the concept of concerted practice also has an evidentiary function: it helps competition law to cope with cases where the agreement cannot be proved but can be inferred from the circumstances. In other words, it is the extension of the *strictu sensu* agreement, where market behaviour serves as circumstantial evidence. If there is no reasonable explanation to the market participants' parallel behaviour but collusion, the competition authority may find that they engaged in a concerted practice.[120] However, this inference requires a market analysis. This strand of concerted practice can be applied only exceptionally, due to the uncertainties related to proof.

170. In Case *Vj-154/2002 Baucont, Klíma-Vill. és Középületépítő*, the CC defined concerted practice as follows. Concerted practice, contrary to *strictu sensu* agreements, does not contain the 'concurrence of wills' element. Concerted practice covers the alignment of market conduct aiming at the avoidance or mitigation of the entrepreneurial risks emerging from market competition. Concerted practice enables the undertakings to eliminate or lessen the risks of failure due to the future conduct of rivals, which is present in the absence of coordination.[121]

171. In Case *Vj-21/2005 Albacomp, Synergon and others*, the CC stressed that competition law prohibits not only anti-competitive agreements but also restrictions

---

120. Case *Kf. II. 29. 324/1999/14.* (Supreme Court) (judicial review in Case *Vj-185/1994 Coffee Cartel*).
121. Paragraph 61.

Part I, Ch. 4, Overview of Main Notions

of competition entailed by concerted practice, so it extends to those arrangements that do not reach the level of an agreement but contain a conscious restriction of competition. Accordingly, competition law interdicts the level of coordination between the undertakings that does not qualify as an agreement, though, it implies, in practice, a cooperation dangerous to competition, because the undertakings replace the risks attached to competition (or part of them) with the comfort of cooperation. The concerted practice, by nature, does not contain all the elements of the agreement.[122]

172. The concept of concerted practice was interpreted in Case *Vj-114/2002 Taxi cartel* as well where the CC combined the two strands of concerted practice: concerted practice based on contact and concerted practice inferred from market behaviour (as circumstantial evidence). However, in this case there was documentary evidence proving that the undertakings agreed that the prices are low, should be increased and a uniform action is needed for this purpose.[123] Although there was no evidence supporting that the undertakings agreed to a specific price, the CC established that it is contrary to competition law if the undertakings discuss the necessity a price increase, mutually express their intention to increase the price, they regard this as a common target, especially if afterwards they or a substantial part of them increase the prices in the same proportion or to the same amount.[124] This cooperation amounts to concerted practice, even if no agreement comes into existence. In accordance with European practice, the CC defined concerted practice as follows: two or more undertakings cooperate consciously without concluding an agreement in order to or with the effect that they get away or mitigate the compelling pressure of competition. A detailed action plan is not a pre-condition of concerted practice. It is sufficient that there is a contact between the undertakings that aims at or results in influencing the competitors' future conduct. Similarly to an agreement, in case of a concerted practice, the undertakings exclude or considerably lessen the uncertainties entailed by the competitive process, which is, however, the inducement of effective competition.[125] Since the concerted practice could be established on the basis of the contacts between the undertakings and in this regard documentary evidence was available, the CC found that there was no need to deduce the collusive nature of the parallel price increase from the characteristics of the relevant market. However, the CC noted that it is unlikely that in a market with numerous enterprises having different sizes and different costs, the same fees and fee elements emerge, and are maintained in case market competition is working.[126] The concurrence of wills behind the price increase is not refuted by the fact that the fees were not increased on the dame say but at different times within a certain period. Although market players often follow suit after the market leader increases the

---

122. Paragraph 90.
123. Paragraph 53.
124. Paragraph 54.
125. Paragraph 55. This proposition was adopted in the HCO's Position Statement No. 11.10.
126. Paragraph 56.

price, the evidence and the fact that the base fee was exactly the same refuted this interpretation of the market trends. In case of real and intensive competition, it is not reasonable for the competitors to increase the base fee exactly to the same level.[127] As the concerted practice was based on inter-firm contacts, those enterprises were part of the violation that were proved to have expressed their intention to increase the price, for instance, through actively or passively participating in the meetings and, afterwards, increasing the price accordingly.[128]

173. As to the price increases in 2001, no evidence was available concerning the contacts between the undertakings, hence, the CC had to examine whether the only reasonable explanation of the fee increase was collusion. In this respect, the CC came to the conclusion that the price increases could be explained with the market leader enterprise's price increase, which the competitors might have followed spontaneously. The timing of the fee increases was not uniform; as there was no evidence concerning inter-firm contacts, there was not sufficient evidence to establish that the enterprises colluded in 2001.[129]

174. Likewise, the CC established the violation of section 11 CA on the basis of both direct and indirect evidence in Case *Vj-154/2002. Baucont and others.*

175. In Case *Vj-96/2002 Európa-Pék Export and others*,[130] the CC dealt with concerted practice based on inter-firm contacts. The undertakings, albeit not entering into an agreement, intimated to each other that a price increase would be needed, and afterwards they increased the prices accordingly, even if to various degrees. The CC also took into account that the market had an oligopolistic structure.[131]

176. In Case *Vj-13/2002 Deko-Apple and others*,[132] the CC dealt with the consequences of the failure to reject an anti-competitive proposal and established that an apparently unilateral conduct may also amount to a concerted practice, e.g., if the addressee fails to reject a proposal to an anti-competitive cooperation.[133]

177. This principle was confirmed in the HCO's Position Statement No. 11.4. Accordingly, it may amount to a concerted practice if an undertaking on an inter-firm meeting expresses its business policy relevant from the perspective of market competition that it wishes to pursue in the future. In such a case, all undertakings are part of the anti-competitive collusion that took part in the meeting or learned the competitor's announcement, unless it is proved that the undertaking expressly rejected the anti-competitive proposal.

---

127. Paragraph 57.
128. Paragraph 58.
129. Paragraphs 60–61.
130. Case *Vj-96/2002 Európa-Pék and others.*
131. Paragraph 20.
132. Case *Vj-13/2002 Deko-Apple and others.*
133. Paragraph 80.

Part I, Ch. 4, Overview of Main Notions

III. Decisions of Associations of Undertakings

178. Section 11 CA, besides agreements and concerted practices, also covers the decisions of associations of undertakings (social organizations, chambers, associations, etc.). These decisions may be caught in the net of section 11 CA even if they are non-binding or informal. The term 'decision' is a functional and embracing concept, which encompasses formal decisions, recommendations, position statements, ordinances and codes of conduct.[134]

179. One of the central questions related to the decisions of associations is the relationship between the liability of the association and that of the members. While the association's liability for its decisions is autonomous and independent from the liability of the members, conduct by the members may also be caught in the net of the prohibition of restrictive agreements in parallel with the association's decision. This may be the case, when an undertaking takes part in the decision-making resulting in the condemned decision or it engages in concerted practice during the decision's implementation. Nevertheless, the association's conduct is to be distinguished from the behaviour of the members. The undertakings may use the institutional framework of the association to conclude or implement an anti-competitive agreement or to carry out a concerted practice. In such a case, it is the undertakings and not the association that commit the violation. The undertakings, inspired by the anti-competitive decision of the association, may, in parallel to the association, act in a way that falls foul of the competition rules. In such a case, both the association and the members may be liable; however, these are to be distinguished. The illegality of the association's decision does not imply the liability of the members; and *vice versa*, the fact that the members used the association's institutional framework to organize meetings, discussions, to conclude agreements or to carry out a concerted practice, in itself, does not imply that the association violated competition law.

180. In Case *Vj-13/2002 Deko-Apple and others*, the CC advanced that it is often difficult to decide whether the violation was committed by the association alone, by the member undertakings or some of them, or by both the association and the member undertakings. The session of the association may provide an opportunity to the undertakings to engage in collusive practices. The undertakings whose representatives participate in the meeting of the association's steering committee may be liable also in case the committee adopted no decision or recommendation. The director of the member undertaking cannot argue that he took part in the work of the steering committee as a private person, *pro bono*.[135]

---

134. Péter Miskolczi-Bodnár, *A versenytörvény magyarázata* 154–155 (KJK-Kerszöv 2002); Csongor István Nagy, *Kartelljogi Kézikönyv. A közösségi és a magyar kartelljog kézikönyve* 338–341 (HVG-Orac 2006).
135. Paragraphs 78–79.

§5. Restriction of Competition

181. Once it is established that the undertakings entered into an agreement, engaged in a concerted practice or the association of undertakings adopted a decision, the next question to be inquired is the content of the prohibition of restrictive agreements (anti-competitiveness); that is, what is the substance that cannot be agreed to. The concept of anti-competitiveness can be boiled down to three conceptual elements, although these elements hardly appear in the HCO's relevant decisions in such a clear form:

– the distinction between anti-competitive object and effect;
– anti-competitiveness; and
– the immanent limits of the general prohibition on restrictive agreements (test of reasonableness).

182. The analysis under the general prohibition on restrictive agreements is to be distinguished from the concept of exemption (individual and group/block exemption). If a seemingly restrictive agreement does not violate the general prohibition, this may be due to the fact that it is of minor importance or it promotes competition more than it deteriorates it. On the contrary, through the concept of exemption, Hungarian competition law accepts that the agreement holds back competition, but it also recognizes that the social surplus entailed by the agreement outweighs the detriments caused by the restriction of competition.

183. Although conceptually the issue to be examined first is whether the agreement falls foul of the general prohibition on restrictive agreements and the analysis of whether the conditions of exemption are met needs to be accomplished afterwards, as a matter of practice, the competition law check-list often starts the other way around. Since the general prohibition on restrictive agreements contains vague terms, legal counsels first endeavour to ascertain whether the agreement comes under one of the safe harbours of Hungarian competition law: the rule on agreements of minor importance or one of the block-exemption regulations.

I. Anti-competitive Object or Effect

184. Section 11 CA distinguishes between agreements anti-competitive by object and agreements anti-competitive by effect. Object type agreements are restrictive of competition by nature and, hence, necessitate the investigation of the context and the arrangement's repercussions; such agreements violate the general prohibition on restrictive agreements per se.

185. The CA's explanatory memorandum makes clear the automatic condemnation (at least as to section 11 CA) of object type agreements, stating that in case the

Part I, Ch. 4, Overview of Main Notions 186–190

anti-competitive purpose/object is established, it need not be inquired whether the arrangement is in fact susceptible of attaining the wished end.[136]

186. In Case *Vj-74/2003 Magyar Gabonafeldolgozók, Takarmánygyártók és - Kereskedők Szövetsége*, the CC held that when applying section 11 CA the actual effects need not be demonstrated, and it suffices if the arrangement's intention or suitability is proved. This implies that it is needless to examine the conduct's actual effect, if it aims to restrict, prevent or distort competition.[137]

187. When inquiring whether the agreement is anti-competitive by object, not the parties' subjective intentions but the agreement's characteristics (objective purpose) are relevant.[138]

188. The concept of agreements anti-competitive by object has a pivotal role in the HCO's investigation practice, since this enables the authority to condemn an agreement without a full-blown market analysis, which is required in case of agreements that are not anti-competitive by object but are to be adjudicated on the basis of an effects-analysis. Object type agreements can be condemned on the basis of what was agreed to (i.e., the text of the agreement); that is, it is to be proved what the parties agreed to but the agreement's market context (definition of the relevant market, the parties' market position, the structure of the market, entry barriers, etc.) and its actual and potential consequences need not be discovered. Of course, the legal and economic context may still be relevant as to the interpretation and assessment of the stipulations. However, the examination of the context does not extend to the investigation of the actual and potential effects the agreement may entail.

189. On the other hand, in case of agreements to be judged by their effects, a market analysis is needed. Although the effects may be actual or potential, direct or indirect, the agreement's market context is to be explored, otherwise it could not be established whether it may entail the prevention, restriction or distortion of competition or not.

190. In Case *Vj-180/2004 Magyar Ügyvédi Kamara*, in the context of a decision of an association of undertakings (the Hungarian Bar), the CC described the difference between anti-competitive object and effect. A conduct that involves the potential of restricting competition has an anti-competitive object. The decision's purpose can be deduced from its text, the objective endeavours of the decision-makers, the legal and economic environment and from the parties' behaviour; it does not depend on the parties' subjective intentions. The decision's method of implementation may also reveal the anti-competitive object. If the anti-competitive object cannot be established, it is to be examined whether the conduct has anti-competitive effects. The latter involves

---

136. Explanatory memorandum, remarks on ss 11-20 CA.
137. Paragraph 73.
138. *See* Case *Vj-180/2004 Magyar Ügyvédi Kamara*, para. 22; Csongor István Nagy, *Kartelljogi Kézikönyv. A közösségi és a magyar kartelljog kézikönyve* 349–350 (HVG-Orac 2006).

both the actual and potential anti-competitive effects. A decision has anti-competitive effects, if on the basis of the impact on actual or potential competition it can be reasonably expected that in the relevant market it will have a negative effect on prices, output and innovation, the supply of the products and services, and quality. The negative effects need to be perceivable.[139]

191. In most cases, it can be relatively easily ascertained on the basis of the agreement's content and characteristics whether the agreement has an anti-competitive object or has to be subjected to an effects-analysis. The anti-competitiveness embedded in the agreement determines whether it is regarded as anti-competitive by object or its effects are to be examined. Although, as a matter of principle, there are certain contents that make the agreement anti-competitive by object, in Hungarian competition law the borderline between object and effect type agreements is, unfortunately, blurred. Although the characterization of the agreement does not depend on the parties' subjective intentions, it depends on the context. Hence, although, as a rule of thumb, it is possible to draw a list of agreements that are anti-competitive by object, the CC follows a case-by-case approach.

192. The CC's approach can be boiled down to three principles. First, restrictions regarded as hardcore under EU competition law, as a rule of thumb, are also automatically condemned under section 11 CA. Second, the CC considers the restraints included in the illustrative list of section 11 CA as 'presumably illegal'; this is a notion peculiar to Hungarian competition law, which has no counterpart in EU antitrust law. Third, the circle of agreements anti-competitive by object is not definite; the CC can examine on a case-by-case basis whether the agreement is anti-competitive by nature and as such qualifies as anti-competitive by object.

193. As to horizontal agreements, the CC considers horizontal price-fixing[140] and market-sharing[141] to be anti-competitive by object. In Case *Vj-28/2003 Baucont and others*,[142] the CC characterized 'mirror contracts' between undertakings participating in the same tender as anti-competitive by object: here, the enterprises agreed that the winner will hire the unsuccessful bidders as sub-contractors.[143]

194. As to vertical agreements, Hungarian competition law, in line with EU law, regards the fixing of a minimum resale price, as well as the fixing of a specific resale price and the prohibition of passive sales (absolute territorial protection) as anti-competitive by object. In Case *Vj-171/2002/15 MOL*, the CC held that the fixing of the resale price or of a minimum resale price is, according to competition law practice, evidently anti-competitive.[144] This decisional practice has not changed; in Case *Vj-7/2008/178 Castrol Hungária*, the CC confirmed that it is anti-competitive by object and violates section 11 CA if the enterprise fixes the minimum or concrete

---

139. Paragraph 22.
140. Case *Vj-64/2000 Délhús and others*; Case *Vj-92/2003 Mentők és Betegszállítók Országos Egyesülete*.
141. Case *Vj-74/2004 Construm és Royal Bau*, para. 89.
142. See Case *Vj-154/2002 Baucont, Klíma-Vill. és Középületépítő*.
143. Paragraphs 81 and 83.
144. Paragraph 52. See Case *Vj-47/2004 Magyar Könyvkiadók és Könyvterjesztők Egyesülése*, para. 101.

Part I, Ch. 4, Overview of Main Notions 195–197

final or consumer price; namely, in this case the trader, due to the restraints on pricing policy, is restricted in using the most important tool of competition.[145]

195. It is to be noted that in Case *Vj-164/2006 Büki Ásványvíz* the CC considered a vertical price-fixing scheme not to infringe section 11 CA. Here, the producer fixed no generally applicable resale price but agreed with the distributors individually. The decision's reasoning suggests that resale price-fixing does not violate competition rules automatically and without exception. The CC held that although it regards horizontal price-fixing as the most serious restriction of competition, this case centred around vertical price-fixing, which required a more complex analysis, due to the potential efficiency arguments. The CC found that in this matter it was probable that the enterprise's conduct did not aim at switching-off price competition and had no such effects, either. First, only a few of the contracts contained resale price-fixing clauses. Second, the supplier established no uniform resale price of general application; the resale price was determined on an individual basis, taking into account the market circumstances and there were huge differences between the individual prices (the lowest price was HUF 260, while the highest was HUF 850). The CC found that the enterprise did not intend to influence the uniform market price. It happened that within the same settlement one of the traders had a fixed price, while the rest did not. The CC noted that although selective resale price-fixing may fall foul of competition law, as, for instance, it may be susceptible of driving rivals out of the market, no anti-competitive consequences were proved in the proceeding.[146] It is to be noted that in this case the CC examined the arrangement of resale price-fixing under the general prohibition on restrictive agreements (section 11 CA) and not under the individual exemption (section 17 CA) and came to the conclusion that it did not violate the law.

196. The decision in Case *Vj-164/2006 Büki Ásványvíz* clearly suggests a more lenient approach towards resale price-fixing, as the CC in fact regarded this arrangement as not being anti-competitive by object and considered that an effects-analysis would be warranted. However, this trend was not followed subsequently, and in Case *Vj-7/2008/178 Castrol Hungária*, as noted above, the CC reiterated the old rule that resale price-fixing per se violates the general prohibition on restrictive agreements (i.e., section 11 CA).

197. It is to be noted that notwithstanding the CC's above decisional practice, Hungarian competition law's treatment of resale price-fixing is not fully in line with EU competition law. While under EU competition law, resale price-fixing falls out of the scope of the *de minimis* rule (as stated in the Commission's *de minimis* notice), under Hungarian competition law vertical price-fixing is still covered: if the market share of the parties is less than 10%, vertical price-fixing falls outside the scope of the prohibition of anti-competitive agreements.[147]

---

145. Paragraph 47.
146. Paragraph 75.
147. Section 13(2) CA.

198. In Case *Vj-156/2004 Unilever and others*, the CC held, referring to EU competition law, that the exclusion of passive sales (absolute territorial protection) is, in fact, per se anti-competitive: it violates the general prohibition on restrictive agreements automatically and cannot benefit from an individual exemption.[148] The adoption of the *Consten and Grundig* doctrine in Hungarian competition law is criticized in the scholarship; in EU competition law the most important argument behind the harsh treatment of absolute territorial protection is the purpose of market integration (single market imperative[149]), while this purpose is not part of Hungarian national competition law.[150] Furthermore, under EU competition law, absolute territorial protection falls out of the scope of the *de minimis* rule, as it is regarded as hardcore. On the contrary, under Hungarian competition law absolute territorial protection is covered by the safe harbour of agreements of minor importance: if the market share is less than 10%, vertical absolute territorial protection falls outside the scope of the prohibition of anti-competitive agreements.[151]

199. In its decisional practice, the CC worked out the doctrine of 'presumably anti-competitive agreements'. This is a peculiar Hungarian competition law concept, which has no counterpart in EU competition law.[152] Section 11(1) CA, as a general principle, prohibits all anti-competitive agreements, while section 11(2) CA contains an illustrative list. In Case *Vj-21/2005 Albacomp, Synergon and ORACLE*, the CC established: the legislator presumed that the agreements listed in section 11(2) CA were illegal, thus, in such cases no detailed demonstration is required to establish anti-competitiveness.[153] This proposition was confirmed in Case *Vj-7/2008/178 Castrol Hungária*.[154] Accordingly, the following agreements are presumed to be anti-competitive:

– direct and indirect fixing of the purchase or sales prices or other business conditions;
– limitation or control of the production, distribution, technical development or investments;
– division of input sources, restriction of the choice from them, and exclusion of a particular circle of business partners from purchasing a particular product;
– division of the market, exclusion from sales, restriction of the choice between marketing possibilities;
– hindering of market entry;
– discrimination between business partners as to transactions of the same value or character, including the application of prices, payment deadlines, discriminatory sales or purchase conditions or methods that may cause a competitive disadvantage to certain business customers; and

---

148. Paragraphs 88 and 93–94.
149. Richard Whish & David Bailey, *Competition Law* 51 (OUP 2012).
150. Csongor István Nagy, *Kartelljogi Kézikönyv. A közösségi és a magyar kartelljog kézikönyve* 241. (HVG-Orac 2006); Csongor István Nagy, *EU and US Competition Law: Divided in Unity?* 163–164 (Ashgate Publishing 2013).
151. Section 13(2) CA.
152. Csongor István Nagy, *Kartelljogi Kézikönyv. A közösségi és a magyar kartelljog kézikönyve* 352–353 (HVG-Orac 2006).
153. Paragraph 106.
154. Paragraph 45.

– making the conclusion of the contract subject to the acceptance of obligations that, by their nature or due to customary contractual practice, do not belong to the contract's subject-matter.

200. As noted above, if an agreement is neither hardcore, nor listed in section 11(2) CA, the CC will examine on a case-by-case basis whether it is anti-competitive by nature and as such anti-competitive by object. Hungarian competition law's grasp of object type agreements seems to be considerably wider and more obscure than its counterpart in EU law and the category of per se illegal agreements in US antitrust law. This seems to be unfortunate, since the character of having an anti-competitive object has serious repercussions. The wide grasp of object type agreements may also go counter to the logic and *raison d'être* of this concept. Competition effects-analysis is time-consuming, costly and, last but not least, uncertain. Competition law cannot provide a more predictable standard in any of the leading competition law regimes of the globe. However, as a general principle, it tries to distinguish clear-cut cases from the uncertain ones. Agreements of minor importance and those covered by a block exemption are the ones that are clearly not contrary to the law. Agreements anti-competitive by object are those agreements that are clearly contrary to the general prohibition on restrictive agreements (albeit theoretically even these agreements may benefit from an exemption).

201. The merit of the concept of agreements anti-competitive by object is that market context need not be examined. Of course, the context is relevant from the perspective of the agreement's interpretation; however, this is the maximum function it may have. If the in depth analysis of the market context (definition of the relevant market, calculation of the market shares, etc.) cannot be saved because it can be established only on the basis of this context whether the agreement has an anti-competitive object, the essence of this concept is lost.

202. The HCO's endeavour is understandable: the competition authority is tempted to regard as many agreements as possible as anti-competitive by object, since in such cases it does not have to bother itself with proving that the agreement has anti-competitive effects. However, if the definition of object type agreements is too wide and obscure, leaving the competition authority a very wide playing field, the function of this concept becomes frustrated and the enterprises will not be able to identify those agreements that will be automatically condemned.

203. This problematic decisional practice culminated in Case *Vj-51/2005/184 Allianz, Generali and others*,[155] where the HCO investigated, among others, agreements concluded by two Hungarian leading insurance companies (Allianz and Generali) with motor

---

155. For a detailed overview of the case, *see* Katalin J. Cseres & Pál Szilágyi, *The Hungarian Car Insurance Cartel Saga*, in Landmark Cases in Competition Law – around the World in Fourteen Stories 145 (Barry Rodger ed., Wolters Kluwer 2013).

vehicle insurance brokers. Albeit the contracting practice of the two insurance companies was similar, apart from this parallel behaviour, there was no evidence indicating any horizontal collusion between them. The agreements provided that if the insurer's products made up a certain proportion of the policies the insurance broker sold, the broker received a higher remuneration. Under Hungarian insurance law, there are three types of insurance mediators: brokers, multiple agents and agents. Agents (whether simple or multiple) act on behalf of the insurance company, while brokers are the advisors of the client and not the agents of the insurer. Brokers are independent insurance counsels, who have to give impartial and professional advice to the client. However, according to general industry practice, brokers' remuneration is paid by the insurer and not by the client. Since the remuneration paid by the insurers may vary, it is not easy to reconcile this practice with the circumstance that the broker is the client's adviser and not the insurer's agent. Linking the level of remuneration to the number of insurance products sold catalyses this problem and raises serious issues of conflict of interest.

204. In some of the agreements, the insurers specified a minimum number or percentage of car insurance policies to be sold over a given period of time and linked the remuneration to this target. In other agreements, concluded with repair shops, the remuneration was paid in the form of a higher hourly repair charge. Repair shops have a twofold function. First, they repair cars, a part of which are covered by an insurance policy; the reparation of these vehicles is financed by the insurance companies. Second, they also act as insurance brokers, intermediating between clients and insurance companies. In the agreements between the insurers and the repair shops, the hourly repair charge depended on the number of insurance products sold by the repair shop. The CC held that both above groups of agreements were anti-competitive by object because they caused a serious conflict of interest and interfered with the requirement of impartial and professional advice imposed by Hungarian insurance law on insurance brokers.

205. The Supreme Court requested a preliminary ruling from the CJEU[156] under the Treaty on the Functioning of the European Union solely concerning the agreements with the repair shops.[157] Although the question related to EU competition law, the Supreme Court advanced that section 11 CA and Article 101(1) TFEU had to be given the same interpretation, because they were substantially connected and section 11 adopted the provision of Article 101(1) almost verbatim. Hence, the application of section 11 CA made the interpretation of Article 101(1) TFEU necessary.

206. AG Cruz Villalón came to the conclusion[158] that the bilateral agreements between the insurers and the repair shops were not anti-competitive by object, unless there was a horizontal agreement or concerted practice.[159] The CJEU, however, did

---

156. Case *Kfv.IV.37.077/2010/11.* (Supreme Court).
157. Case C-32/11 *Allianz, Generali and others v GVH*, not published yet.
158. Opinion of AG Cruz Villalón in Case C-32/11 *Allianz, Generali and others v GVH*, not published yet.
159. Paragraph 100.

Part I, Ch. 4, Overview of Main Notions

not accept AG Cruz Villalón's opinion and ruled that the agreements between the insurance companies and the repair shops (stipulating that the degree of the remuneration paid by the insurer depends on the number and percentage of insurance products the dealer-broker sells as intermediary) can be considered to be a restriction of competition 'by object' within the meaning of that provision, where, following a concrete and individual examination of the wording and aim of those agreements and of the economic and legal context of which they form a part, it is apparent that they are, by their very nature, injurious to the proper functioning of normal competition on one of the two markets concerned.[160]

The ruling in *Allianz, Generali and others v. GVH* endorses the CC's decisional practice blurring the line between clear-cut per se rules and evaluation based on effects-analysis.[161]

II. The Inherent Limits of Anti-competitiveness

207. The content of anti-competitiveness is mainly determined by its limits. The general prohibition on restrictive agreements covers all agreements, concerted practices and decisions of associations of undertakings that, actually or potentially, restrict the undertakings' independent and autonomous decision-making. In case of object type agreements, this condemnation is automatic (albeit theoretically such agreements might benefit from an exemption), while in case of effect type agreements illegality can be established only if the arrangement is capable of entailing anti-competitive effects (irrespective of whether these anti-competitive repercussions have already emerged or not).

208. The first inherent limit of the general prohibition on restrictive agreements is the concept of agreements of minor importance (*de minimis*). Since these agreements have no (perceivable) anti-competitive consequences, it is unnecessary to extend the general prohibition to them. The second inherent limit is the test of reasonableness. Theoretically, all voluntarily agreed restrictions on an enterprise's future conduct may qualify as anti-competitive, albeit they may still benefit from an exemption; however, this would make the application of the general prohibition excessive. According to the test of 'economic reasonableness', an arrangement is not covered by the general prohibition if it gives more to competition than it takes away, that is, its pro-competitive effects outweigh the anti-competitive ones. According to the test of 'public interest reasonableness', under limited circumstances, the undertakings may argue that their agreement serves the public interest.[162]

---

160. Paragraph 51.
161. For an analysis of the case *see* Csongor István Nagy, *The Distinction between Anti-competitive Object and Effect after Allianz: The End of Coherence in Competition Analysis?*, 36(4) World Comp. Law & Eco. Rev. 541 (2013).
162. *See e.g.*, Case *Vj-180/2004 Magyar Ügyvédi Kamara*.

III. Agreements of Minor Importance

209. Due to its utmost practical importance, the decisional practice on *de minimis* agreements merits a detailed analysis. The essence of this concept is that agreements between enterprises having a weak market position are not prohibited, since these cannot affect competition substantially; however, hardcore arrangements are not covered by this safe harbour, these are prohibited irrespective of market share.[163] The rationale of this rule is that such agreements do have the potential of restricting competition, while they never (or almost never) have a redeeming virtue; for the sake of predictability and procedural economy, it is warranted to treat them as per se violating the general prohibition on restrictive agreements. At most, the net of the prohibition may catch also agreements that – notwithstanding their anti-competitive potential and purpose – in fact cannot produce these negative effects.

210. According to section 13 CA, agreements of minor importance are not covered by the general prohibition on restrictive agreements enshrined in section 11 CA. An agreement is of minor importance if the parties' joint market share in the relevant market (including connected undertakings, which are not independent from them) is not higher than 10%. However, this safe harbour is not applicable to horizontal price-fixing (direct and indirect fixing of the purchase or sales prices between competitors) and to horizontal market-sharing (the sharing of the market by competitors). The market share has to be less than 10% in each calendar year; if the contract is concluded for a shorter term, this condition has to be met during the entire period of time. Nonetheless, an agreement where the parties' market share is less than 10% may still fall foul of competition law if there are cumulative effects, i.e., where competition is significantly prevented, restricted or distorted by the cumulative effects of the agreements in question and of further similar agreements operating in the relevant market. If the CC considers that there are such cumulative effects and, hence, the safe harbour of *de minimis* is not applicable, it establishes the illegality without imposing a fine.

211. It is to be noted that Hungarian competition law uses a uniform market share threshold (10%) as to agreements of minor importance, contrary to the Commission's Notice on Agreements of Minor Importance, which applies differential market share thresholds (10% to horizontal and 15% to vertical agreements).[164] Another crucial difference between the two regimes comprises in the list of hardcore restraints, which excludes the agreement from the safe harbour. While section 13(2) CA enumerates only horizontal hardcore restraints, the Commission's Notice on Agreements of Minor Importance excludes quite a few vertical restraints and the agreements containing them (fixing of concrete or minimum resale prices, absolute

---

163. *See* Case *Vj-58/2004 Metőtech-Ért, Huntraco, McCormick and Laverda*, para. 34; Case *Vj-141/2004 Dow AgroSciences*, para. 43; Case *Vj-162/2004 SAP, International Business Machines Corporation, Synergon, ORACLE and International System House*, para. 434.
164. Paragraph 7.

Part I, Ch. 4, Overview of Main Notions

territorial protection, certain restraints in selective distribution agreements and restraints on the supplier of spare parts) from the benefit of the safe harbour.[165]

212. The application of the 10% market share cap normally raises no special complications in case of agreements between competitors; the interpretation of this rule is, however, uncertain as regards vertical agreements. Unfortunately, the CC has no uniform method for calculating the relevant market share.

213. In *Case Vj-57/1998 Henkel Magyarország Kft. and others*, the CC advanced that in case of vertical agreements the calculation method of the joint market share is not so obvious as in case of horizontal agreements, where the parties' market shares are to be simply added together. Namely, the sum of the producer's and the distributor's market share contains duplications, since the products sold by the reseller are also included in the producer's sales. According to the CC, the purpose of defining the joint market share is to single out those products and services the agreement may have a restrictive effect on. Accordingly, after adding together the parties' market shares, the overlapping sales are to be deduced; these are the products the supplier sold to the distributor for the purpose of resale, as these elements appear in the turnover of both parties.[166] This approach will be called 'corrected accumulation', since it adds together the turnover of both parties and, in order to correct this figure, deduces the overlaps.

214. The CC followed a different approach in *Case Vj-31/2000 Interusz Külkereskedelmi Kft* concerning an exclusive distribution agreement. Here, the CC took solely the market share of the party into account whose market share could be regarded as a proxy of the potential anti-competitive effects; this was the party operating on the level of the production-distribution chain where the anti-competitive effects might emerge.[167] This approach was confirmed in *Vj-12/2003 Bobájka Kereskedelmi és Szolg. Kft*, which also followed the principle of the 'place of the restrictive effect' when, calculating the relevant market share.[168]

215. Contrary to the above decisional practice, in Case *Vj-81/2003 MB-Auto Magyarország Kft. and others*, the CC departed from both above principles ('corrected accumulation' and 'place of the restrictive effect'). Here, the CC took the bigger market share into account. Accordingly, it established the market shares of both parties and used the higher figure.[169]

Section 13 CA establishes two exceptions to the application of the 10% cap: horizontal price-fixing and horizontal market-sharing.

---

165. Paragraph 11(2).
166. This problem was highlighted by the CC also in Case *Vj-64/2000 Délhús and others*, holding that in case of vertical agreements the purchasers' market share does not have to be added up, because this would entail cumulation.
167. Paragraphs 17–18.
168. Paragraph 22.
169. Paragraph 15.

216. Horizontal price-fixing can be easily established, if the agreement aims directly at fixing or influencing the prices charged by the enterprises. However, problems of interpretation may emerge, if the agreement does not aim directly at fixing the prices but has such an indirect consequence. In Case *Vj-195/2001 REÁL Hungária and TEMPO Szupermarket*, the CC gave the exclusion of horizontal price-fixing a narrow definition; accordingly, it does not amount to a price-fixing if the agreement does not aim directly at fixing the prices, although it does entail uniform prices. The CC noted: albeit that the joint purchasing arrangement obviously results in uniform purchase prices, the exception embedded in section 13(2)(a) CA applies solely to agreements that aim exclusively at the fixing of the prices. The restriction of competition pertains to those agreements, which have no redeeming virtue. Obviously, a joint purchasing agreement has no such character; hence, it may benefit from the safe harbour of *de minimis* agreements.[170]

217. This approach was followed also in Case *Vj-176/2003 METRO, SPAR and PRAKTIKER*.[171]

218. While vertical territorial restrictions are not excluded from the safe harbour of *de minimis*, exclusive supply agreements between competitors qualify as horizontal market-sharing, which amounts to a hardcore restriction.[172]

219. In Case *Vj-74/2004 Construm and Royal Bau*, the CC established that it qualifies as market-sharing if two bidders of a public tender agree on which of them will submit the better offer.[173]

220. In Case *Vj-162/2004 SAP Hungary*, the CC interpreted section 13 CA again in the context of a public tender. Here, the enterprises cooperated in order to win jointly on public tenders: they agreed to submit offers in parallel, jointly influenced the drafting of the calls and conducted anti-competitive negotiations.[174] The CC held that taking into account that this occurred in connection with a public tender,

---

170. Paragraph 22.
171. The CC examined whether the agreement was excluded from the *de minimis* safe harbour. In this matter, the parties concluded a joint purchasing agreement. The CC considered that although this may entail uniform purchase prices, s. 13(2)(a) CA excludes such agreements from the benefit of the *de minimis* rule that aim solely at the fixing of the prices and, hence, it is only the restriction of competition that appears in their object and effect, without any redeeming virtue. A joint purchasing agreement is obviously not of such a nature, hence, under s 13(2)(a) CA it is not excluded from the safe harbour established for agreements of minor importance. Para. 26.
172. *See* Case Vj-120/2004 Nógrádi Béke Mezőgazdasági Ipari és Szolgáltató Szövetkezet and Berkenye Faluszövetkezet, paras 45–46.
173. Paragraph 89.
174. Paragraph 1. In this case, the agreements had two layers. The undertakings concerned concluded a cooperation framework agreement (teaming agreement). However, the CC established that the competition investigation addressed not solely the teaming agreement, in particular the issue whether this arrangement qualifies as a common research and development entailing a new product. It was not the teaming agreement the decision pronounced illegal but the cooperation between the defendants based on the teaming, aiming at jointly winning on public tenders published by the universities, that violated s 11 CA. para. 367.

it qualified as horizontal market-sharing and excluded competition between team members and restricted the possibilities of outsider undertakings.[175]

221. Section 13(2)(a)-(b) CA makes no express mention of quantity cartels (restriction of output) and quota cartels. However, in the CC's decisional practice, these arrangements amount to market-sharing, thus they cannot benefit from the safe harbour of agreements of minor importance. This is a reasonable interpretation, since quantity and quota cartels are the functional equivalents of horizontal price-fixing and market-sharing. When the cartelist enterprises set a price higher than the market price, this entails the decrease of the demand and leads to the decrease of the output. The purpose of higher prices may be reached also through restricting the output, since this causes shortage in the market, which, in turn, leads to higher prices. The three types of horizontal hardcore arrangements go hand in hand. By way of example, the administering of a price cartel often requires the control of the output and demands the determination of individual quotas. Quantity and quota cartels come under the notion of market-sharing in wider sense: when the undertakings set quotas, in fact, they indirectly divide the customers and, thus, the market. This is why the CC characterizes quantity and quota cartels as market-sharing.

222. In Case *Vj-74/2003 Magyar Gabonafeldolgozók, Takarmánygyártók és - Kereskedők Szövetsége*, a Hungarian agricultural association proposed output reduction and recommended prices. The CC established that this qualified as market-sharing and price-fixing.[176]

§6. EXEMPTION

223. Although the starting point of Hungarian competition law is that competition in terms of rivalry is normally more efficient that cooperation, it also recognizes that in certain cases cooperation is socially more beneficial. Accordingly, in line with EU competition law, it establishes an exception to the general prohibition on restrictive agreements (exemption).

224. Section 17 CA provides that if an agreement meets the four conditions of individual exemption, it is exempted from the general prohibition on restrictive agreements enshrined in section 11 CA. Since the interpretation and application of these conditions are rather uncertain, section 16 CA authorizes the government to adopt block-exemption regulations, which concretize the conditions included in section 17 and exempt certain groups of agreements from the general prohibition on restrictive agreements. The block-exemption regulations adopted by the government are, with some minor differences, in line with EU block-exemption regulations. This holds true also for earlier block-exemption regulations.

---

175. Paragraph 435.
176. Paragraph 115.

225. Section 16/A CA provides that the block exemption granted by a regulation does not apply if due to the cumulative effects of the agreement and similar other agreements in the relevant market, the conditions set out in section 17 CA are, in fact, not met. However, the HCO may withdraw the block exemption only *pro futuro* and in such cases it can impose no fine.

I. Individual Exemption

226. The test of individual exemption embedded in section 17 CA is fully in line with Article 101(3) TFEU.

227. The first (and principal) condition of individual exemption is the production of an efficiency benefit; this implies that the arrangement is required to entail a more efficient result than the situation that would prevail in the absence of the agreement (counter-factual). In other words: the cooperation's efficiency benefits are to be compared to the production, distribution, technical and economic development in the absence of the cooperation.

228. The second condition is that an equitable part of the benefit or surplus emerging from the agreement is passed on the final business partners. This requirement is normally met if the cooperation does not cover the marketing of the goods or services produced as a result of the cooperation, and the enterprises compete with each other when selling them. This is the case if the undertakings cooperate in developing a new technology or production process, but the cooperation does not extend to the marketing of the products manufactured on the basis of this new technology or process. The consumers will receive an equitable share from the efficiency benefits resulting from the new technology, the degree of which will depend, among others, on the flexibility of the demand in the selling market. The same holds true for the case when the undertakings achieve a cost-saving due to specialization.

229. The third condition of individual exemption is that the arrangement may contain only restrictions that are inevitable for achieving the efficiency benefits in question. The extent of the restriction cannot go beyond what is necessary for achieving the efficiency benefits.

230. According to the fourth condition, the agreement cannot exclude competition in respect of a substantial part of the products concerned. The cooperation may exclude competition only in a limited circle.

231. Section 20 CA provides that the burden of proof as to the conditions of individual exemption rests on the undertaking invoking it.[177]

Agreements anti-competitive by object have only a negligible chance to meet the requirements of individual exemption, albeit this possibility (at least theoretically) cannot be excluded.

---

177. Section 20 CA.

Part I, Ch. 4, Overview of Main Notions

232. For instance, in Hungarian competition law practice, resale price-fixing is regarded as anti-competitive by object; there has been a single case (Case *Vj-150/ 1995 Kontavill Kontakta*) where the CC granted an individual exemption to such a restriction. The decision was rendered under the old CA and was rather exceptional; hence, its precedential value is questionable. The case concerned agreements for the resale of electricity spare parts. The CC established that economic competition is not an aim but merely a tool to facilitate efficient economic activities serving the public interest and the interests of consumers. In this context, the CC regarded price competition between market operators as desirable only if price competition does not force market operators to deteriorate the conditions of marketing (or the product's quality) to such an extent that is harmful to consumers. In case of luxury products, technically complex and widely diversified commodities, and in case of merchandise where a huge inventory is needed, the producer is interested in the distributor's selling its products under appropriate conditions and proper standards. The CC argued that resale price-fixing can serve the interests of consumers, provided it is in accordance with the costs necessary for complying with the required standards, as resale price-fixing, in terms of financing, enables the distributor to provide high level marketing services. The HCO concluded that the agreement in fact enabled wholesalers not to cut relevant expenses (emerging from maintaining a full range of products, the conditions of serving the customers, storage, advertisements and related services), what would deteriorate the quality of the service to the detriment of consumers.

II. Block-Exemption Regulations

233. Section 16 CA authorizes the Government to issue block-exemption regulations, exempting particular categories of agreements. The block exemptions have to be based on the requirements of individual exemption as enshrined in section 17 CA.

234. Section 16/A authorizes the HCO to withdraw the benefit of a block exemption if by the cumulative effects of the agreement(s) at stake and similar other agreements the requirements of individual exemption as set out in section 17 are not satisfied. However, this withdrawal applies only for the future and no fine can be imposed. The HCO has never made use of this provision in its decisional practice.

235. Currently, the following block-exemption regulations are in force:

– Gov. Regulation 86/1999 on the exemption from the prohibition on restriction of competition of certain groups of technology transfer agreements;
– Gov. Regulation 202/2011 on the exemption from the prohibition on restriction of competition of certain groups of specialization agreements;
– Gov. Regulation 203/2011 on the exemption from the prohibition of restriction of competition of certain groups of insurance agreements;

– Gov. Regulation 204/2011 on the exemption from the prohibition of restriction of competition of certain categories of vertical agreements in the motor vehicle sector;
– Gov. Regulation 205/2011 on the exemption from the prohibition on restriction of competition of certain groups of vertical agreements; and
– Gov. Regulation 206/2011 on the exemption from the prohibition on restriction of competition of certain groups of research and development agreements.

236. The above block-exemption regulations are essentially in line with their EU competition law counterparts; the regulation on technology transfer is in line with (since then repealed) Regulation 240/96 on the application of Article 85 (3) of the Treaty to certain categories of technology transfer agreements.[178]

§7. Monopolization and Abuse of Dominance

237. Section 21 CA prohibits abuses of dominant position, while section 22 CA defines economic dominance. These provisions are the national equivalents of Article 102 TFEU. Accordingly, the concept of abuse of dominant position has two constituent elements: the notion of dominant position and the concept of abuse.

238. The statutory provisions, as well as the decisional and judicial practice on abuse of dominant position are, for the most part, in line with EU competition law. For instance, under Hungarian competition law, both exploitative and exclusive (exclusionary) abuses are prohibited. However, the practice of Hungarian competition law departs in numerous important questions from EU antitrust law. For instance, the Hungarian practice on predatory pricing is less interventionist and more influenced by Chicago economics (see below). Furthermore, in Hungarian competition policy, dominant position cases have received a more relaxed treatment. It is noteworthy that no fine was imposed in dominance matters between 2007 and 2010.

239. The various types of abuses are addressed below in Part 2 Chapter 2 on 'Dominant undertakings' prohibited practices'. At this point, the general principles governing the abuse of dominant position are summarized.

240. In Hungarian law, as noted above, abusive conducts can be grouped into two categories: exploitative and exclusionary (exclusive) practices. In the first case, the undertaking endeavours to exploit the demand side of the market, through maximizing its extra-profit. Normally, this is achieved through charging a supra-competitive price, which is higher than the would-be price in case of workable competition. Exclusionary abuses aim at driving competitors out of the market, weakening their market position or preventing their entry, that is, at the acquisition, preservation or extension of market power. The two groups of abuses are interlinked

---

178. OJ [1996] L 31/2.

Part I, Ch. 4, Overview of Main Notions   241–242

in a certain sense: the purpose of the exclusionary abuses is to acquire or stabilize market power, which, in turn, enables the undertaking to earn extra-profit.[179]

241. Section 21 CA prohibits all abuses of dominant position at large (general prohibition) and gives an illustrative list of the most important types of abuses. The following abuses are specified in section 21 CA:

– one-sided contractual stipulations, especially excessive prices: in business relations, including the application of standard contractual terms, charging unfair purchase or sales prices, stipulating in any other manner unjustified advantages, forcing the other party to accept disadvantageous conditions;
– limitation of the output, distribution or technical development to the prejudice of final business partners;
– refusal to deal: refusing, without justification, to establish or maintain a business relation conformable with the transaction's characteristics.
– influencing the other party's economic decisions in order to acquire an unjustified advantage;
– withdrawing or holding back, without justification, the product from circulation before the increase of the price or with the purpose of causing the increase of the price, or in a manner capable of producing an unjustified advantage causing a competitive disadvantage;
– tying/bundling: making the supply or taking of the products subject to the supply or taking of other goods, furthermore making the conclusion of the contract subject to the acceptance of obligations that, by their nature or according to commercial usage, do not belong to the subject of such contracts;
– discrimination: discriminating, without justification, between business partners in case of transactions of equivalent value or character, including the application of prices, payment deadlines, sales and purchase conditions or methods that cause the business partners a disadvantage in the competition;
– predatory pricing: applying excessively low prices capable of driving competitors out of the relevant market or hindering their market entry that are not based on a higher level of efficiency as compared to competitors;
– hindering, without justification, market entry in any other manner; and
– creating, without justification, a market situation that is detrimental to competitors or influencing their economic decisions with the purpose of acquiring an unjustified advantage.

§8. CONCENTRATIONS AND THE DUTY TO NOTIFY

242. Under Hungarian competition law, a transaction is notifiable (i.e., the HCO's merger permission has to be requested), if it qualifies as a concentration and the CA's turnover thresholds are exceeded.

The CA establishes certain exceptions to the duty to notify.

---

179. *See* Csongor István Nagy, *III. Rész: Antitröszt jog*, in *Magyar versenyjog* 229–230 (Kinga Pázmándi ed., HVG-Orac 2012).

243. Conceptually, the first case is not an exception to the notification duty but an exclusion from the notion of concentration. Section 23(4) CA establishes an exception to the definition of concentration: the activity of a liquidator or receiver (irrespective of whether it acts in a winding-up or insolvency proceeding) does not qualify as a concentration.

244. Furthermore, the CA provides in respect of certain transactions that even if it qualifies as a concentration under section 23(1) CA, it need not be notified to the HCO. According to section 25 CA, the temporary acquisition of control (for a period not longer than one year) of certain organizations (insurance companies, credit institutions, financial holding companies, holding companies with mixed operation, investment companies, trustee organizations etc.) does not entail a notification duty, if the purpose of the acquisition of control is to prepare the resale of the enterprise, and the undertaking acquiring control does not exercise its controlling rights or it does only to the extent inevitably necessary. The HCO, upon the request of the enterprise acquiring control submitted before the end of the one-year-long transitory period, can prolong the transitory period on one occasion by, at most, one year, if the enterprise proves that the sale, for a reason it is not responsible for, was not possible within one year.

245. Finally, section 24/A CA authorizes the government to exempt a concentration from the notification duty, if this is warranted by the public interest: the government – if this is justified by the public interest, especially the preservation of the workplaces for the sake of the security of supply – may pronounce a concentration to have a national strategic significance; such concentrations, contrary to section 24 CA, do not have to be notified to the HCO.

246. In line with international practice, only concentrations above a certain threshold are notifiable to the competition authority; mergers under this size are presumed not to raise competition concerns.

247. As a general consideration, the quantitative measure established in this regard has to fulfil two requirements. First, it has to screen out those concentrations that, due to their small size, are not susceptible of substantially affecting competition. Second, it has to establish clear criteria that can be applied easily. Since market share data, which would probably be the best proxy of the potential of competition problems, do not meet the latter requirement, taking into account the uncertainties related to the definition of the relevant market and the availability of market data, the merger threshold is based on the undertakings' turnover, which is, however, a rather imperfect filter. The excessive width of the scope of the notification duty is corrected in the merger procedure: if the concentration, obviously, raises no competition concerns, the CC will clear it in a simplified procedure.[180],[181]

---

180. *See* s. 63(3) CA.
181. Csongor István Nagy, *III. Rész: Antitröszt jog*, in *Magyar versenyjog* 261–262 (Kinga Pázmándi ed., HVG-Orac 2012).

Part I, Ch. 4, Overview of Main Notions

248. A concentration is notifiable if the joint net turnover of the groups of undertakings concerned (i.e., the sum of the net turnover of the groups between which the concentration occurs) is higher than HUF 15 billion, and each of at least two of the groups concerned have (severally) a net turnover higher than HUF 500 million. If only two groups are involved in the concentration, both groups have to have a net turnover higher than HUF 500 million.[182] In this context, the term 'net' refers to the income excluding sales taxes (VAT, excise tax and similar taxes).

249. Section 23(1) CA distinguishes between three categories of concentrations: restructuring under company law, change of control and full function joint-ventures. In each case, it is a fundamental requirement that the transaction occurs between undertakings that are independent from each other. Section 15(1) CA defines when two undertakings cannot be regarded as independent from each other: undertakings belonging to the same group of undertakings and undertakings controlled by the same undertakings are not independent from each other. The notion of 'group of undertakings' is defined in section 15(2) CA, while the concept of control is defined in section 23(2)-(3) CA.

I. Company Law Restructuring

250. A concentration may occur when the entities concerned unite from a company law perspective. Section 23(1) CA distinguishes between the following three types of corporate restructuring.

- Amalgamation: two or more previously independent undertakings amalgamate; the undertakings concerned dissolve and are converted into the new entity, which will be the legal successor of these undertakings.
- Incorporation: one of the undertakings merges into the other one; the former ceases to exist and merges into the latter, which will be the legal successor of the former.
- Part of an undertaking becomes part of another undertaking that is independent of the first one.

251. Section 23(5) defines the term 'part of undertaking': assets and rights, including the undertaking's clientele, qualify as a 'part of undertaking', if their acquisition, in their own or together with the assets and rights the acquirer already has, is sufficient for pursuing the market operation. Accordingly, merger control rules cannot be avoided through selling the assets of the undertaking instead of the undertaking itself; this may equally qualify as a concentration.

252. It is to be noted that since the CA, *ratione personae*, is applicable not only to companies but to all natural and legal persons, the above rules are applicable to the amalgamation and incorporation of all types of organizations that come under the CA's scope.

---

182. Section 24(1) CA.

II. Acquisition of Control

253. A concentration may occur in cases where the control changes: an undertaking or more than one undertaking jointly may acquire direct or indirect control over another undertaking that has been independent from the acquiring undertaking (or undertakings) or over more undertakings that are independent from it (them) but not independent from each other.[183]

254. Control implies that an undertaking is able to exercise decisive influence over the decisions of another undertaking. Control may be sole or joint, and direct or indirect.

255. Sole control means that an undertaking is, by itself, able to exercise decisive influence over the decisions of another undertaking; in case of joint control, more than one undertaking acquires this position. The core element of joint control is that the controlling undertakings have to reach an agreement concerning all considerable issues regarding the controlled undertaking's market conduct. This interdependence may rest on objective circumstances or on the shareholders' agreement. By way of example, if the enterprise has four shareholders and each of them has 25% shares, there is no joint control, since the consensus of three shareholders is sufficient for arriving at a (majority) decision, and this majority may be built up from different combinations of shareholders.[184]

256. In case of direct control, the undertaking is capable of influencing the decisions of another undertaking directly. In case of indirect control, the undertaking influences the conduct of another undertaking through a third enterprise. If undertaking 'A' controls undertaking 'B', which, in turn, controls undertaking 'C', 'A' has direct control over 'B' and indirect control over 'C'.

257. Both direct and indirect control may be sole or joint. For instance, it amounts to sole indirect control, if undertaking 'A' has sole direct control over undertaking 'B', which, in turn, has sole direct control over undertaking 'C'. It amounts to joint indirect control if undertaking 'A' has sole control over undertaking 'B', which has, with undertaking 'C', joint control over undertaking 'D'. In this case, 'A' has joint indirect control over 'D'.

258. Section 23(2) CA lists those cases when an undertaking has direct (sole or joint) control over another. An undertaking by itself (or more undertakings together) has direct control over another undertaking:

– if it has the majority of the voting rights;
– if it is entitled to appoint the majority of the executive officers;
– if it is empowered by contract to exercise decisive influence over the controlled undertaking; or

---

183. Section 23(1)(b) CA.
184. Position Statement No. 23.9, *see* Case *Vj-80/2003 Baucont and others*.

Part I, Ch. 4, Overview of Main Notions 259–263

– if it has de facto control over it.

259. It is to be noted that the change of the mode of control does not amount to a concentration; that is, there is no concentration if an undertaking has control in the sense of one of the categories listed in section 23(2) CA and acquires control also under another rule listed here. Accordingly, by way of example, it is not a concentration if undertaking 'A' has de facto control over the company and, subsequently, becomes entitled to appoint the majority of the executive officers; or undertaking 'A' has the right to appoint the majority of the executive officers and, afterwards, acquires the majority of the voting rights.[185]

260. As noted above, the first mode of control listed in section 23(2) CA is disposal over the majority of the voting right. There is direct control if an undertaking has the majority of the voting rights in another. This is normally due to the fact that the controlling undertaking is the owner of the majority of the shares. However, a minority shareholder may also be the holder of the majority of the voting rights, if it has, by way of example, priority shares ensuring voting rights that are higher than the capital share (equity) they embed.

261. The second mode of control comprises the right to appoint the executive officers. An undertaking acquires direct control if it becomes entitled to appoint, elect or recall the majority of the executive officers of another undertaking. Again, this right may be based on priority shares. The term 'executive officer' (in Hungarian: '*vezető tisztségviselő*', literally 'leading officer') is defined in the Civil Code and includes the manager (managing partner) in respect of partnerships, the managing director in respect of limited liability companies and the member of the board of directors in respect of shareholding companies;[186] that is, the executive officers are the top company officers who are responsible for the management of the company and have an independent decision-making power.

262. Third, the right of control may be based also on contract. An undertaking has direct control over another, if the former is, by contract, entitled to exercise decisive influence over the decisions of the latter. This may be a syndicate contract.

263. The fourth category of direct control is de facto control, where the undertaking becomes in fact able to exercise decisive influence over the decisions of another undertaking. The CC has established the existence of de facto control in numerous cases.[187]

---

185. Position Statement No. 23.3, *see* Case *Vj-31/1998 RWE Energie AG and Energie Baden-Württemberg AG*. In this matter, the undertaking had already had the right to appoint the majority of the executives when it acquired the majority of the voting rights.
186. Sections 3:144, 3:196 and 3:282 of the Civil Code.
187. Besides the cases analysed below, the HCO faced the issue of de facto control also in the following cases, where, nevertheless, no question of interpretation emerged and, hence, no detailed guidance was provided: Case *53/2005 Dél-Magyarországi Húsipari Rt. and Pick Szeged Rt.*, Case *Vj-12/2004 Átalános Értékforgalmi Bank and Lasselsberger*, Case *141/2002 Triász-Perry and Stollwerck*, Case *51/2002 Arago*, Case *131/1997 Orosházi Üveggyár és Sajószentpéteri Üveggyár*.

264. In Case *Vj-101/1999 Renault and Nissan*, the CC examined the issue of de facto control at large. It held that it is not possible to give a general definition on the level of minority shares that triggers de facto control; this may be established only on a case-by-case basis, through the investigation of the circumstances and taking into account the distribution of the shares among the shareholders. Only a very high minority share may establish de facto control; de facto control is the more probable, the higher the biggest minority shareholder's shares are as compared to the second biggest minority shareholder. Furthermore, the more dispersed the shares of the rest of the shareholders are, the more likely it is that de facto control exists.[188]

265. In Case *Vj-100/2001 MOL and TVK (2)*, the CC established the existence of de facto control in the context of the following fact pattern. MOL had 34.48% of the shares in TVK and an option to purchase over 17.85 % of the shares. The CC held that the option to purchase does not establish control, but it may have such an effect if combined with additional circumstances.[189]

266. The majority of TVK's board of directors were the employees of MOL and were nominated by MOL at the general assembly, which elected them. According to the CC, this circumstance entailed that MOL could exercise decisive influence over TVK's decisions.[190] The CC noted that the existence of de facto control may be established only if this plight exists on a lasting basis;[191] and cannot be established automatically, since the general assembly can dismiss any board member with simple majority and MOL was not able to prevent this with its shares of 34.48%. Nevertheless, the CC took the position that it was unlikely that the shareholders concerned by MOL's call option (i.e., MOL's option to purchase their shares) would vote against MOL. The CC noted that, in fact, these shareholders had systematically voted with MOL on the general assembly, including the election of the directors.[192]

267. On the basis of the above circumstances, the CC came to the conclusion that MOL had de facto control over TVK.

268. The above case is very interesting in the context of the CC's earlier decision in Case *Vj-29/2001 MOL and TVK (1)*. This matter involved the same parties and roughly the same fact pattern with the difference that at this time MOL had not

---

188. Paragraph 15.
189. Paragraph 49.
190. Paragraph 52.
191. In Case *Vj-196/2005 Tate & Lyle and Eastern Sugar*, the CC held that the fact that the directors nominated by undertaking 'A' have a majority in the board of directors of undertaking 'B' entails that undertaking 'A' can exercise decisive influence over the operations of undertaking 'B'; however, de facto control can be established only if this situation persists permanently (on a lasting basis). In this matter, the relevant period was two years and the CC found that this is sufficient to establish de facto control. paras 20–21.
192. Paragraphs 53–54.

acquired the call options it had in Case *Vj-100/2001 MOL and TVK (2)*. Here, the CC came to the conclusion that MOL had no de facto control over TVK. MOL had 32.98% of the shares; the second biggest shareholder was BorsodChem, which had 14.98%. The CC noted that these two entities had conflicting interests and the rest of the shareholders, who had small shares and were fundamentally financial investors, had no motivation to support MOL's proposals with their votes.[193]

269. In Case *Vj-93/2001 Hachette and Hungaropress*, the CC stated that it reinforced the existence of de facto control that the person who was elected as the limited liability company's (sole) managing director was nominated by Hachette.

270. In Case *Vj-33/2003 Sanpaolo and Inter-Europa Bank*, the CC held that veto rights may in themselves establish de facto control.[194]

271. In Case *Vj-178/2001 Arago and PICK*, Arago had 41.34% of the shares and 44.64% of the voting rights in PICK and on PICK's general assembly nominated persons to directorship. Six out of eight members of the newly elected board of directors and two out of three members of the supervisory board had been in contact with Arago or had held top manager positions there.[195] The CC came to the conclusion that with this Arago acquired de facto control over PICK.[196]

272. In Case *Vj-78/2008 Apáthy and others*, the CC held that the shareholder having 50% of the shares (voting rights) has de facto (negative) control over the undertaking, provided that no special rule applies to the decision-making on the shareholders' meeting. The CC considered that if a shareholder has 50% of the voting rights, the shareholders' meeting cannot reach a decision without this shareholder's assent; consequently, this shareholder may exercise de facto decisive influence over the undertaking's decisions.

273. It is to be emphasized that in this case the 50% related to the voting rights on the shareholders' meeting and not to the shareholder's influence in the board of directors; nevertheless, the approach of negative control may be *mutatis mutandis* applicable to cases where the undertaking has the right to appoint 50% of the executive officers.

III. Joint Control

274. The acquisition of joint control is equally notifiable as that of sole control. Hungarian competition law defines the scope of the notification duty very broadly,

---

193. Paragraph 12.
194. Paragraph 8.
195. Paragraph 10.
196. Paragraph 15.

and in this regard, it slightly departs from EU merger control law in respect of the acquisition of joint control.

275. It qualifies as a concentration if an undertaking has joint control over another and, subsequently, acquires sole control.[197] Likewise, it amounts to a concentration if an undertaking has sole control over another undertaking and acquires joint control (its sole control deteriorates to joint control).[198]

276. According to the CC's decisional practice, it qualifies as a concentration if the number of the undertakings having joint control decreases.[199] In Case *Vj-40/2008 Ringier and others*, the CC held (this principle was published in Position Statement No. 23.19) that the circumstance whether a reduction in the number of the controlling undertakings may change the controlled undertaking's market conduct has no bearing on the notification duty; this circumstance has to be examined when deciding on the merger clearance. Since the failure to submit a merger application entails serious consequences, no uncertainty should be left as to whether a transaction is notifiable.[200]

277. Likewise, it qualifies as a concentration if the number of the controlling undertakings increases or one or more controlling undertaking changes (i.e., it is replaced). In this case, there is at least one undertaking that acquires joint control; hence, acquisition of joint control occurs as defined in section 23(1)(b) CA. This rule has an important role also from a substantive perspective. The entry of a new undertaking having joint control (either through the increase of the number of controlling undertakings or through the change of one of them) displays new interests that may be capable of fundamentally changing the controlled undertaking's market conduct (for instance, if there are horizontal or vertical relations between the new undertaking having joint control and the controlled undertaking).[201]

278. The above practice that regards, in the field of joint control, the decrease and increase of the number of the controlling undertakings, as well as the change (i.e., replacement) of one of the controlling undertakings as a concentration, departs from EU merger control law. Namely, the Commission's Jurisdictional Notice[202] provides that '[w]here the operation involves a reduction in the number of jointly controlling shareholders, without leading to a change from joint to sole control, the transaction will normally not lead to a notifiable concentration.'[203]

---

197. Position Statement No. 23.13, *see* Case *Vj-95/2001 KBC Bank N.V.*; Position Statement No. 23.5, *see* Case *Vj-146/1999 METRO Cash and Carry International Holding GmbH*.
198. Position Statement No. 23.2, *see* Case *Vj-26/1997 Bayernwerk AG*.
199. Position Statement No. 23.13, *see* Case *Vj-95/2001 KBC Bank N.V.*
200. Position Statement No. 23.19, *see* Case *Vj-40/2008 Ringier and others*.
201. Position Statement No. 23.22, *see* Case *Vj-124/2008 Bonitas and others*.
202. Consolidated Jurisdictional Notice under Council Regulation (EC) No. 139/2004 on the control of concentrations between undertakings. OJ [2008] C 95/1.
203. Paragraph 90.

Part I, Ch. 4, Overview of Main Notions 279–282

IV. Joint Ventures

279. It qualifies as a concentration if the undertakings establish a full-function joint venture, that is, when more independent undertakings jointly create an enterprise controlled by them that is able to perform, on a lasting basis, all the functions of an independent undertaking. Accordingly, in line with EU competition law, not all but only full-function joint-ventures qualify as a concentration. In the absence of a lasting and full-function there is no concentration and the transaction is to be assessed on the basis of the rules on restrictive agreements.

280. In its decisional practice, the HCO follows the Commission's Jurisdictional Notice when examining whether the joint-venture has full-function or not.[204] Accordingly, it takes into account the following factors: whether the joint-venture has sufficient resources to operate independently on the market, the activities the joint-venture pursues beyond the specific functions provided for the parent companies, the sales and purchase relations the joint-venture has with its parent companies, and whether it operates on a lasting basis.[205] A joint-venture may qualify as a full-function joint-venture even in case it cannot make strategic decisions independently; otherwise, an undertaking under joint control would never be regarded as having a full-function.[206]

281. In Position Statement No. 23.16, the CC established that a joint-venture has normally no full-function if it maintains business relations exclusively with its parents.[207] If the joint-venture's activities are confined to the coordination of its parents' operations (e.g., a sales arrangement or purchasing cooperation serving the parents), it does not qualify as a concentration and it is to be assessed on the basis of the provisions on restrictive agreements.

§9. JOINT VENTURES

282. A joint venture may be assessed either under the provisions on restrictive agreements or under the merger control provisions, depending on whether it is a full-function joint venture, which can perform all functions of an independent undertaking on a lasting basis, or merely a cooperative joint-venture, coordinating the parents' activities. Full-function joint ventures qualify as concentrations and are notifiable if the relevant turnover thresholds are exceeded. On the other hand, cooperative joint ventures are treated as agreements and come under the purview of the provisions on restrictive agreements.[208] Such joint ventures are not notifiable to the HCO and have to comply with the rules on restrictive agreements.

---

204. Consolidated Jurisdictional Notice under Council Regulation (EC) No. 139/2004 on the control of concentrations between undertakings. OJ [2008] C 95/1.
205. Paragraphs 91–105.
206. Paragraph 93.
207. Case *Vj-191/2006 Vöröskő and others.*
208. Sections 11-20 CA.

Chapter 5. Consequences of Violations and Enforcement Institutions

§1. Administrative Enforcement

I. The Competition Authority: The Hungarian Competition Office

283. The administrative authority responsible for enforcing competition law (both Hungarian and EU) is the Hungarian Competition Office (in Hungarian: '*Gazdasági Versenyhivatal*').

A. *The HCO's Autonomy*

284. The HCO is an autonomous central administrative body. The HCO (head, deputy heads and members of the CC) have fixed tenure for six years[209] and cannot be removed before the end of this, with the exception of certain cases of grave breaches of duty.[210]

285. The leaders' fixed tenure and the protection against dismissal is meant to guarantee the HCO's independence. In 2010, the Hungarian parliament adopted an act amending the CA, which provided that the tenure of the deputy heads of the HCO ends with that of the head of the HCO. In this case, the tenure of the HCO's head was going to expire in November 2010, while the two deputies' tenure only in 2015; so this rule would have entailed the removal of the deputy heads before the expiry of their tenures.

286. The amendment of the CA was attacked before the Constitutional Court and in Case *183/2010*[211] the Court declared it unconstitutional. The Constitutional Court emphasized that the HCO's autonomy is constitutionally protected, and one of the guaranties of this autonomy and independence is the leaders' fixed tenure. The government could not show any compelling reason justifying the removal of the deputy heads before the expiry of their tenures. Nonetheless, after the Constitutional Court's decision, the two deputy heads resigned voluntarily.

B. *Formation, Composition*

287. The HCO's structure is essentially twofold: it consists of an investigative and a *quasi*-judicial branch,[212] albeit the latter is incomparably smaller in terms of staff and has no independent budget or resources.

---

209. Sections 35(2), 37(3) and 38(1) CA.
210. Sections 38(1) and 38(5) CA.
211. For a case-note on the Constitutional Court's decision, *see* Levente Szabó, *Az Alkotmánybíróság határozata a szervezetátalakítás szabadságáról*, 2(special issue) Jogesetek Magyarázata 26 (2011).
212. Section 47 CA.

Part I, Ch. 5, Consequences of Violations 288–292

288. In the Hungarian system, investigations are conducted by the case-handlers, who are working in different bureaus. The bureaus are responsible for the investigative and analyst functions. Case-handlers are responsible for discovering the facts, collecting evidence and, at the end of the investigation, submitting the file together with the 'case-handler's report' to the CC. Case-handlers work under the direction and control of the head of the HCO. After the phase of investigation, the case-handlers submit the file accompanied with a report to the CC, which is responsible for making the final decision in the merits.

289. The CC, the HCO's adjudicatory body, has a fairly controversial status. On the one hand, it is an independent, *quasi*-judicial body, responsible for making decisions in the merits. On the other hand, it is part of the HCO both from an institutional and a budgetary point of view, and is dependent on the HCO's head from a budgetary and institutional perspective. This self-contradictory structure has been fiercely criticized in the scholarship.[213]

290. The HCO's head is appointed by the president (head of state) upon the proposal of the prime minister.[214] The head of the HCO nominates the two deputy heads (one of the deputy heads serves as the chair of the CC) to the prime minister, who – in case he agrees with the proposal – submits the nominations to the president; the deputies are appointed by the president, who charges one of them with the responsibility of heading the CC.[215] The head and the deputy heads of the HCO are appointed for six years; they can be reappointed, with the exception of the CC's chair (deputy head responsible for heading the CC), who can be reappointed only once.[216]

291. The members of the CC are appointed and dismissed by the president (head of state) upon the proposal of the HCO's head. They are appointed for a term of six years and they can be reappointed once.[217]

292. As noted above, the HCO has an idiosyncratic structure. There are essentially two models of authority organization in Europe (and globally), based on the institutional relationship between investigation and decision-making in the merits (administrative adjudication). Most competition authorities can be clearly classified as falling into one of the two categories. The first is the monolithic model, where the functions of investigation and administrative adjudication are not distinguished but fulfilled by the same entity. On the contrary, in the dualistic model, the functions of investigation and administrative adjudication are allocated to two organizations, which are independent from each other. In some monolithic models, the

---

213. See e.g., Barna Berke, *Egy korszerH versenyhatóságért: strukturális és hatékonysági szempontok (a jogharmonizáció intézményfejlesztési vonásaihoz)*, in *Válaszúton az Európai Unió: intézményi reformok és csatlakozás. Európajogi Tanulmányok 6.* 163–194 (ELTE ÁJK, Nemzetközi Magánjogi és Európai Gazdasági Jogi Tanszék – Jean Monnet Centre of Excellence 2001).
214. Section 35(2) CA.
215. Section 35(2) CA.
216. Section 35(2) CA.
217. Section 37(3) CA.

competition authority has an internal but relatively autonomous decision-making body. However, in the dualistic model the two entities are completely separated: decisions in the merits (including the imposition of fines) are rendered by the entity responsible for administrative adjudication, while the investigative entity's remit is to discover the facts, collect the evidence and submit a *quasi* 'indictment'.

293. The HCO has a hybrid structure, making the status of the CC controversial. Although the HCO is a unitary organization, the decisions in the merits are always made by the CC, which is, nonetheless, not an independent entity but it is included and, to some extent, subordinated to the HCO. Although the CA declares that the members of the CC are independent and cannot be influenced, the institutional guarantees of this freedom and independence are missing.

294. On the one hand, section 37(1) CA provides that the chair and members of the CC are independent during the decision-making, have to make their decisions on the basis of the rules of law and their internal conviction, they cannot be influenced or instructed in connection to their decision-making.

295. On the other hand, the CC's chair is the deputy head of the HCO; the CC has no independent budget, thus, it cannot hire staff on its own; the CC has no legal personality: formally, it is not the CC but the HCO that renders the decisions and if the decision is attacked before the court, the defendant in the judicial procedures is the HCO, due to the lack of legal personality, no action may be launched against the CC. Furthermore, the employer's rights over the chair and members of the CC are exercised by the head of the HCO.[218]

C. *Investigating Powers*

296. The HCO has very wide investigative powers. Case-handlers, in the frame of a dawn raid, can enter premises, search documents and electronic devices, make copies (mirror-copy) and seize documents and electronic devices.[219] The party is obliged to communicate the information necessary for deciding in the merits of the case.[220]

297. The HCO's investigation powers have only slight limits. A court warrant is needed to carry out a dawn raid;[221] the dawn raid should remain within the limits set out in the court warrant. However, this restriction (i.e., the dawn raid shall remain within the frame of the subject-matter determined by the warrant) is not easy to apply in practice, as a mere reference to this circumstance does not block the case-handler from investigating the piece of evidence covered by the objection. Case-handlers do have the right to examine a piece of evidence in order to decide whether

---

218. Section 36(1)(d) CA.
219. Section 65/A(1) CA.
220. Section 64/B(1) CA.
221. Section 65/A(3) CA.

Part I, Ch. 5, Consequences of Violations

it comes under the scope of the warrant or not. The situation is further complicated by the rule that if the case-handler seizes a piece of evidence not covered by the court warrant (i.e., the piece of evidence is not connected to the subject-matter of the case), the HCO can use the evidence, provided it acquires the court's posterior authorization.

298. EU competition law's principle, according to which the evidence obtained during a dawn raid can be used only for the purpose of the procedure in the frame of which it was collected,[222] does not prevail in Hungarian competition law. That is, if the case-handler finds a piece of evidence that is completely unrelated to the investigation's subject-matter but can be used to prove another violation, and he seizes it, the HCO will be able to use this evidence in another proceeding (provided that the court posteriorly authorizes the collection of evidence, as detailed below).

299. This principle was established by the Supreme Court in Case *Vj-27/2003*,[223] where the case-handlers conducted a dawn-raid at the premises of some construction companies in the frame of an investigation concerning an alleged bid-rigging as to certain renovation works in Budapest. On the spot, however, the case-handlers found written evidence on a much bigger bid-rigging case concerning a high-way construction project. This evidence was seized and used to institute another competition proceeding against the construction companies. The Supreme Court held that this evidence was admissible and ruled against the defendants. Afterwards, this principle was included in section 65/A(9) CA, which provides that if during the dawn raid the case-handler finds evidence that is not covered by the judicial authorization (i.e., it is not connected to the investigation's subject-matter) but may be related to a violation of Hungarian or EU law on restrictive agreements or dominant position, he can seize and copy this evidence. Nonetheless, the judicial authorization as to this evidence has to be gained subsequently; the HCO has to submit the request for this within sixty days. Failing posterior judicial authorization (i.e., if the court's authorization is not requested within the deadline or the authorization is rejected), the evidence is not admissible.

300. The HCO can collect also evidence that contains business/trade secrets and personal information, the provision of the data cannot be refused with reference to the protection of these secrets. Of course, this evidence is treated confidentially by the HCO, and access to these documents may be restricted.[224]

301. An important restriction of the HCO's investigative powers is the 'legal privilege', which applies to the communication between the external lawyer and the client. It is to be stressed that the party has to object to the seizure of the document; in the absence of such a statement, the document will not be covered by the legal privilege.[225] In the judicial practice, legal privilege was interpreted in a wide manner

---

222. Article 28(1) of Regulation 1/2003.
223. Case *Kfv. IV. 39. 399/2007/28.* (Supreme Court).
224. Section 55/B CA.
225. Section 65/C(8) CA.

and is understood, *inter alia*, to cover external lawyer's advice given prior to the initiation of the investigation.

302. The defendant has the duty of cooperation and is obliged to hand over all data and evidence requested by the HCO. The only limit to this duty is the prohibition of self-incrimination: the undertaking does not have to 'plea guilty'; however, if requested, all data and evidence proving the violation has to be submitted to the HCO.[226]

D. Adjudicating Powers (Ascertaining and Sanctioning)

303. The adjudicating powers are completely vested in the CC.

304. The HCO can terminate the competition proceeding for various procedural reasons. These occur in the form of an order. According to section 31(1) APA, the authority terminates the administrative proceeding if:[227]

– the request should have been rejected without an inquiry into the merits under section 30 APA but the authority became aware of the ground of rejection only after the opening of the procedure;
– the asset serving as the matter's subject-matter got destroyed or became damaged to an extent that the procedure became groundless;
– the procedure was launched upon request and the party revoked its request, except the procedure can be opened also ex officio and the authority continues the procedure ex officio or more than one applicant took part in the procedure and not all of them revoked its request;
– as a consequence of the party's death or the termination of the legal person, the procedure became groundless and procedural legal succession did not occur;
– the circumstance giving rise to the continuance of the proceeding no longer persists;
– the party in the procedure launched upon its request, in case the representative is rejected, fails to appoint a person that is capable of accomplishing the representation or does not act in person, except the procedure can be launched also ex officio and the authority continues the procedure ex officio or more than one applicant takes part in the procedure and they act in person or their representative was not rejected by the authority;
– due to the amendment of the law, the matter's adjudication no longer comes under administrative authority competence;
– a fee or a service fee has to be paid for the authority's procedure and the party does not pay it in spite of the authority's call within the term set for this purpose and does not receive immunity from the costs;

---

226. Section 64/B(1) CA.
227. According to s. 44 CA, s. 31(1)(j) APA does not apply to matters governed by the CA.

Part I, Ch. 5, Consequences of Violations

- in an ex officio proceeding, the facts could not be clarified to the extent necessary for adopting a decision and no result can be expected from the continuation of the proceeding; and
- the authority recognizes during the ex officio proceeding that it had no jurisdiction or competence already at the time the procedure was opened and the case cannot be transferred.

The CC can adopt the following decisions in the merits of the case:

- it can establish that the conduct is unlawful or not unlawful;[228]
- it can establish pursuant to Article 16/A CA[229] that the benefit of the application of the block exemption does not apply to the agreement;[230]
- it can order that the situation violating the CA shall be eliminated[231] and can prohibit the continuation of the infringing conduct;[232] where it finds that there is an infringement of the law it may impose obligations including in particular the obligation to conclude a contract where there is an unjustified refusal to create or maintain business relations appropriate for the type of the transaction;[233]
- it can order the performance of the commitment undertaken on the basis of section 75 CA;[234]
- it can order the publication of a rectifying declaration in connection to the illegal declaration;[235]
- in case of a merger notification or an ex officio investigation of a merger launched because it was implemented in breach of the prohibition of implementation, it can authorize or prohibit the concentration, if necessary, with the prescription of a preliminary or posterior condition or obligation;[236] in case the concentration was implemented and the CC prohibits the concentration, it adopts the measures necessary for the termination of the concentration, as specified in section 31 CA;[237]
- it can, on the basis of section 25, permit the prolongation of the one-year transitory period or reject the application;[238]

---

228. Sections 76(1)(e) and 76(1)(j) CA.
229. Article 16/A CA provides as follows. The group exemption from the prohibition on the restriction of competition does not apply to the agreement where, by the cumulative effect of those agreements and similar other agreements on the relevant market, the requirements provided by Art. 17 are not satisfied. The Hungarian Competition Authority may establish in the course of its proceedings that, taking into account the foregoing provision, the benefit of the group exemption shall not apply to such an agreement for the future. In such cases, no fine may be imposed.
230. Section 76(1)(d) CA.
231. Section 76(1)(f) CA.
232. Section 76(1)(f) CA.
233. Section 76(1)(h) CA.
234. Section 76(1)(c) CA.
235. Section 76(1)(i) CA.
236. Section 76(1)(a)-(b) CA.
237. Section 76(2) CA.
238. According to s. 25 CA, the temporary acquisition of control (for a period not longer than one year) of certain organizations (insurance companies, credit institutions, financial holding companies, holding companies with mixed operation, investment companies, trustee organizations) does not entail a notification duty, if the purpose of the acquisition of control is to prepare the resale of the enterprise, and the undertaking acquiring control does not exercise its controlling rights or it does only to the

– it can impose a fine; the amount of the fine shall not exceed 10% of the net turnover achieved in the business year preceding the one in which the decision establishing the violation is adopted by the undertaking or by the group of undertakings identified in the decision .[239]

305. It is to be noted that notwithstanding the above statutory authorization, according to its decisional practice, the CC, in line with the CJEU's judgment in *Tele2 Polska*,[240] does not establish the conduct's illegality in cases where EU competition law is applied but terminates the procedure on procedural grounds on the basis of section 31(1)(e) APA: the circumstance justifying the continuation of the procedure does not persist any more.[241] Accordingly, section 76(1)(j) CA is not applied in EU competition law cases.

306. In *Tele2 Polska*,[242] the CJEU held that:

'Article 5 of (…) Regulation [1/2003] must be interpreted as precluding a national competition authority, in the case where, in order to apply Article 102 TFEU, it examines whether the conditions for applying that article are satisfied and where, following that examination, it forms the view that there has been no abuse, from being able to take a decision stating that there has been no breach of that article';[243] 'a national competition authority cannot take a decision stating that there has been no breach of Article 102 TFEU. According to the second paragraph of Article 5 of (…) Regulation [1/2003], such an authority may, however, decide, in cases where, on the basis of the information in its possession, the conditions for prohibiting a practice under Article 102 TFEU are not met, that there are no grounds for action on its part'.[244]

307. The reason of this restriction of competence is that a negative decision (establishing that the undertaking's conduct was lawful) 'would risk undermining the uniform application of Articles 101 TFEU and 102 TFEU (…), since such a decision might prevent the Commission from finding subsequently that the practice in question amounts to a breach of those provisions of European Union law'.[245] The CJEU established: '[i]t is thus apparent from the wording, the scheme of the Regulation and the objective which it pursues that the Commission alone is empowered

---

extent inevitably necessary. The HCO, upon the request of the enterprise acquiring control submitted before the end of the one-year-long transitory period, can prolong the transitory period on one occasion by, at most, one year, if the enterprise proves that the sale, for a reason it is not responsible for, was not possible within one year.

239. Section 78 CA.
240. Paragraphs 27–28 and 32.
241. Case *Vj-2/2010*, paras 488 and 499(b).
242. Paragraphs 27–28 and 32.
243. Paragraph 30.
244. Paragraph 32.
245. Paragraph 28.

to make a finding that there has been no breach of Article 102 TFEU, even if that article is applied in a procedure undertaken by a national competition authority'.[246]

308. As noted above, if the competition proceeding is launched because the concentration was not notified as required by the law, the CC can approve the concentration, if it comes to the conclusion that the concentration could have been cleared.[247] However, if the CC establishes that the notifiable concentration implemented without merger permission could not have been authorized, or the concentration was implemented despite the CC's interdictions or it was implemented without the fulfilment of the condition established in the clearing decision, the CC, for the sake of eliminating the detrimental effects of the concentration and of restoring the conditions of competition existing before the concentration, prescribes the termination of the concentration and sets a proper deadline for accomplishing this; in particular, it may order that the merged undertakings (or parts of undertakings), assets and shares be severed or sold, the joint control be terminated and it may establish also other obligations necessary for this purpose.[248]

309. The CC can also adopt interim measures, provided such measures are necessary to restore or maintain competition on the relevant market. However, this power is rarely used.[249]

E. Other Institutional Tasks (Consultancy to Parliament/Government)

310. The HCO's overall tasks are threefold: competition supervision (enforcement procedures – as detailed above), competition advocacy and competition culture. The first encompasses the conduction of investigations and competition proceedings. The second activity consists of the representation of the interest and value of market competition before the various law-making and administrative bodies and of making legislative proposals that promote market competition. The third activity comprises the popularization of market competition, promotion of scholarship in the field of competition law and policy and of increasing the undertakings' and consumers' competition law awareness.

II. Government Direct Enforcement Activities

311. As noted above, the HCO is an autonomous central administrative authority and, as such, it is not subordinated to the government. Although the president of the republic, upon the proposal of the prime minister, can relieve the head and the deputy heads of their offices, this can occur only on the basis of specific grounds enumerated

---

246. Paragraph 29.
247. Section 77(1)(b) CA.
248. Section 31 CA.
249. Section 72/A CA.

in section 38(5) CA.[250] The Constitutional Court established in Case *183/2010*[251] that the head's and the deputies' tenure is constitutionally protected; in principle, no new grounds of dismissal can be introduced in respect of the incumbent leaders.

312. Antitrust law is applied exclusively by the HCO; the government has no direct enforcement activities or remits, with the exception of agricultural products and merger control.

In respect of agricultural products, the ministry of agriculture is authorized to grant individual exemption to certain agreements. Section 18/A of Act CXXVIII of 2012 on inter-professional organizations and on certain questions of the regulation of the agricultural market, which entered into force on 28 November 2012, provides that in respect of agricultural produces, the violation of the prohibition embedded in section 11 CA cannot be established, if the distortion, restriction or prevention of competition accruing from the agreement as defined in section 11 CA does not exceed the extent necessary for achieving the economically justified, equitable income and the operation on the market is not excluded from gaining this income, furthermore, Article 101 TFEU has not been applied.[252] The decision on whether the agreement meets the foregoing conditions comes under the competence of the minister of agriculture.[253] When investigating the infringement of section 11 CA in respect of agricultural produces, the HCO has to request a position statement from the minister of agriculture and is bound by that statement. The minister has sixty days to issue the position statement, and during this time the HCO's competition proceeding has to be suspended.[254]

313. In respect of merger control, section 24/A CA authorizes the government to exempt a concentration from the notification duty, if this is warranted by the public interest: the government – if this is justified by the public interest, especially the preservation of the workplaces for the sake of the security of supply – may proclaim a concentration to have a national strategic significance; such concentrations, contrary to section 24 CA, do not have to be notified to the HCO.

314. In the domain of unfair commercial practices against consumers, the HCO has parallel competences with the National Consumer Protection Authority and the Hungarian National Bank.[255]

---

250. Section 38(5) CA.
251. For a case-note on the Constitutional Court's decision *see* Levente Szabó, *Az Alkotmánybíróság határozata a szervezetátalakítás szabadságáról*, 2(special issue) Jogesetek Magyarázata 26 (2011).
252. 18/A(1) of Act CXXVIII of 2012 on inter-professional organizations and on certain questions of the regulation of the agricultural market.
253. 18/A(2) of Act CXXVIII of 2012 on inter-professional organizations and on certain questions of the regulation of the agricultural market.
254. 18/A(3) of Act CXXVIII of 2012 on inter-professional organizations and on certain questions of the regulation of the agricultural market.
255. Section 10 of Act XLVII of 2008 on the prohibition of unfair commercial practices against consumers.

Part I, Ch. 5, Consequences of Violations   315–320

III. Other Administrative Agencies Applying Antitrust Rules

315. The HCO has exclusive competence in the field of antitrust law (restrictive agreements, abuse of dominant position and merger control) over the entire territory of Hungary, and therefore it is the only administrative authority in Hungary that deals with this field of law.

316. However, it is to be noted that sectoral regulation is often based on competition law principles and, hence, sectoral regulatory authorities often carry out competition law analysis when applying sectoral competition rules. For instance, the Hungarian Energy and Public Utility Regulatory Authority, when applying the rules on significant market power in the electricity and natural gas industries, has to cooperate with the HCO and take into account the HCO's professional position (and to give its reasons if it departs from the HCO's professional position).[256]

IV. Administrative Fines

317. In the application of the CA, two types of fines may be imposed: fine in the merits and procedural fine. An undertaking ('whistle-blower') may obtain full or partial immunity from the fine in the merits if it reveals a cartel before the HCO that has been unknown to the authority or, failing this, supplies evidence of added value (leniency policy).

A. *Fine in the Merits*

318. The fine in the merits may be imposed against anyone who violates the provisions of a rule of law that comes under the HCO's remit, including the CA, the UCP Act and the competition rules of the TFEU.

319. Section 78(1) differentiates between four cases where the CC may, upon its discretion, impose a fine in the merits and section 78(2) establishes a case where the CC has to apply a fine.

320. The CC may impose a fine against the person:

– who commits an illegal act coming under the HCO's competence;
– who implements the concentration prohibited in the CC's decision in spite of the prohibition;
– who does not perform its obligation prescribed in the decision authorizing the concentration;

---

256. Section 112 of Act LXXXVI of 2007 on electric energy and s. 61 of Act XL of 2008 on natural gas.

– who fails to request the HCO's permission for a concentration as defined in section 24 and the concentration is implemented, even if the CC, subsequently, authorizes it in its decision.

321. The CC has to impose a fine in case an undertaking does not fulfil its commitments under section 75, save the commitment decision is withdrawn and the competition procedure is re-started.[257] That is, if the CC terminates the competition proceeding due to the undertaking's commitments and, subsequently, the undertaking fails to perform its commitments, the CC has two options. It may withdraw the commitment decision and re-start the competition investigation. If it does not withdraw the commitment decision, it has to impose a fine for the non-fulfilment of the commitments.

322. The fine is imposed by the CC and (in line with EU competition law) it may range up to 10% of the annual turnover of the undertaking or (where the undertaking is part of a group of undertakings and the group is identified in the decision) the group of undertakings the perpetrator is part of realized in the previous business (calendar) year (i.e., the calendar year preceding the date of the decision establishing the violation). Accordingly, the base of the calculation of the fine is the net turnover of the group and not that of the undertaking; however, this rule applies only if the group of undertakings is named in the CC's decision.[258]

323. In case of associations of undertakings (i.e., if the fine is imposed on an association of undertakings), the maximum fine is 10% of the net turnover realized by the member undertakings in the preceding business (calendar) year.[259]

324. The term 'net' turnover, in line with EU competition law, covers all income with the deduction of sales taxes (VAT and other taxes directly related to sales, like excise tax).

325. Special rules apply in case the HCO's permission for a concentration is not requested and the concentration is implemented (despite the prohibition to implement before clearance), even if the CC, subsequently, authorizes it in its decision. In such matters, the fine is calculated on a daily basis.

The relevant period's starting point is the earliest moment from the following: the publication of the public call for offer creating the concentration, the conclusion of the contract or the acquisition of the right of control. When calculating the fine, the period referred to in section 25 has to be disregarded: as noted above, according to section 25 CA, the temporary acquisition of control of certain organizations does not entail a notification duty, if the purpose of the acquisition of control is to prepare the resale of the enterprise, and the undertaking acquiring control does not exercise its controlling rights or it does only to the extent inevitably necessary.

---

257. Section 78(1a) CA.
258. Section 78(1b) CA.
259. Section 78(1b) CA.

Part I, Ch. 5, Consequences of Violations

326. The daily fine may range from HUF 50,000 to HUF 200,000, and it is covered by the 10% cap described above: the final amount of the fine cannot exceed 10% of the net turnover realized by the undertaking or group of undertakings in the preceding business (calendar) year.

327. Section 78(2) CA contains detailed rules on ascertaining the net turnover of the preceding business year. If available, this has to be calculated on the basis of the annual report or simplified annual report of the preceding business year. If the undertaking's time of operation in the given year was less than one year, the data has to be extrapolated to one year (i.e., if the enterprise was operational only for six months, the relevant net turnover will be the double of this). If there is no authentic data on the undertaking's (or group's) net turnover in the preceding year, the net turnover realized in the last business year is to be used that has been authentically closed. In case of a newly founded undertaking having no report, the first year's business plan has to be taken into account; failing this, the undertaking, upon the call of the case-handler or the CC, has to calculate and submit, in accordance with the rules on the preparation of the interim balance, its net turnover on the day of the start of the procedure.

328. When determining the amount of the fine, according to section 78(3) CA, the CC has to take into account all the circumstances of the case, in particular the gravity of the violation, the duration of the unlawful situation, the benefits gained through the infringement, the market positions of the parties violating the law, the imputability (culpability) of the conduct, the cooperation by the undertaking assisting the procedure and the repeated commission and frequency of the unlawful conduct (recidivism). The gravity of the violation is to be defined, in particular, on the basis of how dangerous the conduct was to competition in the market and on the basis of the circle and weight of the impairment to the interests of the final trading partners.[260]

329. Section 78(4) CA sets out special considerations as to matters where the fine is imposed because the undertaking failed to perform its obligation prescribed in the decision authorizing the concentration or to fulfil its commitments endorsed in a commitment decision under section 75 (except the commitment decision is withdrawn, since in the latter case no fine can be imposed but the competition procedure is restarted).[261] In such cases, the CC has to take into account all the circumstances of the case, in particular the gravity of the breach of the commitment, the characteristics of the market, economic relations concerned by the commitment, the existing competitive conditions, as well as the public interest serving as the basis of the commitment decision, the imputability (culpability) of the conduct and the fulfilment of the commitment until the decision-making. The gravity of the breach of the commitment has to established, in particular, on the basis of how dangerous the conduct was to the competition in the market and on the basis of the circle and weight of the impairment to the interests of the final trading partners.

---

260. Section 78(3) CA.
261. Section 78(1a) CA.

330. The HCO's policy on setting the fines in the merits is summarized in Notice 1/2012 on setting the amount of the fine in case of conducts violating the prohibitions included in sections 11 and 21 of Act No. LVII of 1996 on the prohibition of unfair market practice and restriction of competition, as well as Articles 101 and 102 of the Treaty on the Functioning of the European Union. This Notice entered into force on 25 January 2012 (it applies to procedures where the CC's preliminary position had not been sent to the parties before this date[262]) and stepped in place of Notice 1/2009 on the repeal of Notice 2/2003 on the method of setting fines in antitrust cases as amended by Notice 2/2005, which repealed, on 18 May 2009, Notice 2/2003 on the method of setting of fines in antitrust cases (amended by Notice 2/2005).

331. Notice No 1/2012 establishes the following scheme for the calculation of the fine in the merits.

332. The fine is determined in two steps: the CC establishes the base-amount, which is, subsequently, corrected on the basis of further factors.[263]

333. The starting point of the calculation of the base-amount is the relevant turnover, that is, the turnover realized by the infringing undertaking in the relevant market. The relevant turnover is the turnover of the entire period of the violation; however, if the violation lasted for less than twelve months, the turnover realized in the year of the violation has to be taken into account.[264]

334. The base-amount is the product of the relevant turnover and the percentile ratio established on the basis of the gravity of the violation and the undertaking's attitude as to the infringement. In the worst case, the base-amount is equal to 10% of the relevant turnover.[265] In this system, the gravity of the violation represents 60 points (6%), while the undertaking's attitude 40 points (4%).[266]

335. Within the gravity of the infringement, the danger to competition and the violation's market impact have equal weight (30-30 points from the 60 points are allocated to the gravity of the infringement).[267]

336. As to the violation's effects on the market, the CC takes into account the undertaking's market power (determined on the basis of its market share and other relevant circumstances), as well as the conduct's actual or likely effect.[268]

337. In respect of the undertaking's attitude as to the infringement, the CC takes four factors into consideration (the first two may increase, while the last two may

---

262. Paragraph 48 of Notice 1/2012.
263. Paragraph 9.
264. Paragraph 16.
265. Paragraph 15.
266. Paragraph 14.
267. Paragraph 19.
268. Paragraphs 24–25.

Part I, Ch. 5, Consequences of Violations 338–341

decrease the percentile ration with, at most, 40 points): the degree of imputability (culpability), the undertaking's role in the infringement, active remedy, cooperation during the procedure, external factors.

The base-amount has to be corrected with the following circumstances:

– repetition of the infringement (recidivism);
– the advantage acquired due to the violation;
– deterrent effect;
– the statutory cap on the fine (10% of the net turnover);
– leniency policy; and
– payment difficulties.[269]

338. Section 78(5) CA establishes the subsidiary liability of the members of the economic unit (group of undertakings) the perpetrator is part of, while section 78(6) CA establishes a similar rule as to those members of the association of undertakings that took part in the adoption of the incriminated decision.

339. Section 78(5) CA provides that if the undertaking having committed the violation directly does not pay the fine and the enforcement measures for the collection of the fine are unsuccessful, the CC establishes in a separate order that the members of the group of undertakings have joint and several liability for paying the fine (or the part that could not be collected), provided, these members were 'named' in the administrative decision. This order can be appealed.[270] This provision establishes the strict subsidiary liability of group members for the fine imposed on the perpetrator.

340. In Case *Vj-147/2007 Railway Construction Companies*,[271] the Supreme Court held that in the administrative procedure the undertakings with subsidiary liability have to appear as parties so as to ensure they can exercise their right of defence and right of appeal. The CC has to identify the concerned (parent) undertaking in its decision; a mere identification of the group does not suffice. Furthermore, the identification has to occur in the decision's operative part.[272]

341. Section 78(6) CA deals with the scenario when the association of undertakings does not pay the fine (the association does not pay the fine voluntarily and the enforcement for the collection of the fine is unsuccessful) and provides that the CC may establish in a separate order that the member undertakings that participated in the adoption of the incriminated decision and were 'named' as such in the administrative decision have joint and several liability for paying the fine. This order can be appealed.[273]

---

269. Paragraph 32.
270. Section 78(7) CA.
271. Case *Kfv.III.37.690/2013/9* (Supreme Court).
272. *See* the Constitutional Court's decision in Case *353/B/2009. AB határozat*.
273. Section 78(7) CA.

342. As noted above, in Case *Vj-199/2005/246 Egg cartel*,[274] the Supreme Court held in the context of section 78(6) CA that the members of a group of undertakings have to be 'named' in the operative part of the decision; otherwise, section 78(6) CA cannot be applied and, thus, the member undertakings allegedly having participated in the adoption of the decision cannot be held subsidiarily liable for the fine imposed on the association.

343. For a long time, it was uncertain how the term 'named' has to be interpreted in section 78(5) CA and whether the Supreme Court's interpretation on section 78(6) CA (in Case *Vj-199/2005/246 Egg cartel*[275]) can be applied to section 78(5) CA by analogy. Namely, there is a remarkable difference between the two provisions (section 78(5) CA and section 78(6) CA) as to the nature of the subsidiary liability. Group members' liability under section 78(5) CA is strict: this subsidiary liability is automatic and unconditional, that is, it comes into existence irrespective of the undertaking's conduct and it rests merely on the undertaking's membership. On the contrary, the member of an association has no strict liability: it is liable only if it did take part in the decision-making, that is, if with its own conduct it made itself involved in the mischief. These differences may warrant a differential interpretation of the term 'named' in section 78(5) CA and section 78(6) CA.[276]

344. However, in Case *Vj-147/2007 Railway Construction Companies*,[277] the Supreme Court established that these two provisions have to be interpreted in the same way.

B. Leniency

345. In line with EU competition law, Hungarian competition law confers full or partial immunity from fines on cartelist enterprises ('whistle-blowers') that reveal a cartel before the HCO or contribute to the evidence the authority already has (leniency policy). Sections 78/A-79 CA contain the statutory rules on leniency. Prior to 1 June 2009, the HCO's leniency policy had no detailed statutory rules and was included in Notice 3/2003 on the application of the leniency policy facilitating the discovery of cartels as amended by Notice 1/2006 and Notice 2/2009. Leniency applications submitted as from 1 June 2009 are governed by the statutory rules on leniency.[278]

346. As a matter of practice, it is to be noted that contrary to EU practice where leniency policy is the heavy cavalry of anti-cartel investigations (in the last decade

---

274. Case *Kfv.III.37.557/2009/18*.
275. Case *Kfv.III.37.557/2009/18*.
276. *See* Csongor István Nagy, *III. Rész: Antitröszt jog*, in *Magyar versenyjog* 171-172 (Kinga Pázmándi ed., HVG-Orac 2012).
277. Case *Kfv.III.37.690/2013/9* (Supreme Court).
278. Sections 8 and 17(4) of Act XIV of 2009.

Part I, Ch. 5, Consequences of Violations 347–350

cartel investigations usually have been launched as a result of a leniency application), in Hungary the annual number of leniency applications is fairly low.

347. By way of example, between 2002 and 2008, the Commission sent out fifty-two statements of objections concerning price cartels, and forty-six of these were based on evidence obtained on the basis of a leniency application.[279]

348. In contrast to this, according to the HCO's annual reports, leniency was not applied in cases decided in 2006;[280] in 2007, there was a single case where the leniency policy was applied;[281] the decisions rendered in 2008 did not apply the leniency policy.[282] In 2009, there was a single case involving a leniency application,[283] 2010 saw a (relative) boom: three leniency applications were submitted this year. The HCO's annual report of 2011 makes mention of no leniency application, although 14 cartel proceedings were launched this year.

349. The failure of the leniency policy in Hungary has cultural reasons. Furthermore, the unsuccess of the leniency policy may also be explained with the circumstance that Hungary is a small country, that is, a small geographical market, and this may impact the career of the managers engaging in whistleblowing.

350. It is to be noted that the HCO interprets the conditions of leniency very generously. Although, as noted below, Hungarian leniency policy applies only to horizontal agreements, in Case *Vj-81/2006/74. Olympus* the CC granted full immunity from the fine in respect of a vertical agreement. Kortex Kft. and Olympus Kft. concluded a cooperation agreement for the purpose of submitting an offer to a call. The parties stipulated mutual exclusivity: in respect of the call, Kortex Kft. agreed to purchase the medical equipment (endoscopy products) exclusively from Olympus Kft., and the latter, in turn, agreed to supply these products only to Kortex Kft.[284] The CC granted Olympus Kft. full immunity from the fine, notwithstanding the fact that Hungarian leniency policy applies solely to horizontal hard-core agreements. The CC established that is had to be taken into consideration that the HCO admitted the leniency application, it would have gone counter to the principle of legal certainty, if it had departed from this to the applicant's detriment.[285] The CC established that the agreement's categorization was not obvious (albeit it did not specify why it could have qualified as a horizontal agreement) and (due to the agreement's secrecy and actual consequences) the leniency application's acceptance was in line with the purposes of the leniency policy. Nonetheless, it is to be noted that

---

279. European Parliament, Parliamentary questions: *Joint answer given by Ms Kroes on behalf of the Commission to Written questions: E-0890/09, E-0891/09, E-0892/09*, 2 Apr. 2009; Alan Riley, *The Modernisation of EU Anti-Cartel Enforcement: Will the Commission Grasp the Opportunity?* CEPS Special Report, January 2010. 5.
280. HCO's Annual Report of 2006, 51.
281. HCO's Annual Report of 2007, 65.
282. HCO's Annual Report of 2008, 64.
283. HCO's Annual Report of 2009, 86.
284. Paragraph 13.
285. Paragraph 94.

the CC made it express: this decision does not imply that it would be warranted to apply the leniency policy to vertical agreements.[286]

1. Substantive Issues

351. Leniency is available in case of horizontal agreements and concerted practices that, directly or indirectly, aim at fixing the purchase or sales prices, dividing the market (including collusions on tenders) or establishing production or sales quotas and violate Article 101 TFEU or section 11 CA.[287] The leniency applicant may be granted full immunity, if providing, directly or indirectly, determinant evidence, or partial immunity, if providing evidence that has an added value in comparison to the evidence already available to the HCO. It is to be noted that in the application of the provisions on leniency, the term 'undertaking' also covers associations of undertakings, the decisions of which come under the purview of the rules on restrictive agreements.

352. The following four general conditions apply to all leniency applications (irrespective of whether it is for full or partial immunity from the fine):

– disclosure of the violation (agreement, concerted practice, as well as participation in these): the admission of the infringement of the law and full data disclosure;[288]
– the leniency applicant has to terminate its participation in the violation immediately after the submission of the leniency application, except the participation of an indispensable extent and nature to which the HCO obliged it in an order in the interest of the success of the dawn raid;[289]
– good faith, complete and continuous cooperation with the HCO until the end of the competition proceeding.[290]
– secrecy: the confidential treatment of the leniency application and its content.[291]

353. Full immunity from the fine is available to the undertaking that is first to provide determinant evidence concerning the cartel: the undertaking may supply the evidence directly or may assist the HCO to find it (e.g., through a dawn raid). An undertaking is eligible for full immunity from the competition fine:

– if it helps the HCO to find the evidence proving the violation: it supplies evidence that enables the HCO to obtain a court warrant to conduct a dawn raid, provided at the time the leniency application is submitted the HCO does not have sufficient information to obtain a court warrant;

---

286. Paragraph 95.
287. Section 78/A(1) CA.
288. Section 78/A(1) CA.
289. Section 78/A(7)(a) CA.
290. Section 78/A(7)(b) CA.
291. Section 78/A(7)(c) CA.

Part I, Ch. 5, Consequences of Violations

– if it supplies the evidence proving the violation, provided at the time the leniency application is submitted the HCO does not have sufficient evidence to prove the violation and no undertaking fulfils the requirements of the preceding point;[292]
– as a negative condition: no undertaking can be granted immunity from the fine that coerced another undertaking or other undertakings to participate in the cartel.[293]

354. Section 78/A(8) CA provides that an undertaking that acted in order to coerce another undertaking to take part in the violation cannot be granted full immunity from the fine. The language of this provision clearly refers to the exclusion of full immunity and makes no mention of partial immunity, suggesting that enterprises that coerce others to take part in the cartel may still be eligible for partial immunity (reduction in fine). This interpretation is reinforced by sections 78/C(2) and 78/C(4) CA; these provide that the CC has to make a decision (order) on the leniency application and thereafter the CC cannot depart from this, with some exceptions. As to full immunity, the CC may depart from the order if it proves that the leniency applicant coerced another undertaking to take part in the cartel; however, in case of partial immunity the order cannot be departed from with reference to this circumstance. Accordingly, the requirement that the leniency applicant did not coerce others to participate in the violation seems not to be applicable to applications for partial immunity; although an undertaking that coerced others to take part in the violation cannot receive full immunity from the fine, even such an undertaking can be granted a fine-reduction; coercion excludes only the possibility of full immunity.

355. As noted above, the CA's rules on leniency are applicable as from 1 June 2009; applications submitted until 31 May 2009 were governed by the HCO's Notice on Leniency Policy (which was repealed as from 1 June 2009). This Notice, contrary to the CA's provisions currently in force, provided that the requirement that the undertaking did not take steps to coerce other undertakings to take part in the cartel was of general application; according to paragraph 15 of the HCO's Notice on Leniency Policy, the HCO would release the undertaking, fully or partially, from the fine only if the enterprise did not pursue any activity coercing other undertakings to participate in the violation. In other words, the HCO considered the above requirement as applicable both to full and partial immunity. This approach was not in line with EU leniency policy. According to paragraph 13 of the Commission's Leniency Notice, '[a]n undertaking which took steps to coerce other undertakings to join the cartel or to remain in it is not eligible for immunity from fines. [However,] [i]t may still qualify for a reduction of fines if it fulfils the relevant requirements and meets all the conditions therefor.' This approach was overruled by the CA's 2009 Amendment: currently, an enterprise that coerced others to join or to operate the cartel does not lose the hope to any leniency whatever.

---

292. Section 78/A(2) CA.
293. Section 78/A(8) CA.

356. No strict time-limit applies to the submission of the application for full immunity. While immunity under the first point (helping the HCO to find the evidence) cannot be granted once the HCO has already conducted the down raid, immunity under the second point (supplying evidence proving the violation) remains available, provided the HCO has not collected sufficient evidence during the procedure. Section 78/A(4) contains specific provisions as to leniency applications submitted after the launch of the procedure. If the leniency application is submitted after the moment the preliminary position or the case-handler's report is sent out or the access to the file is opened for any of the parties, the fine can be reduced only if the undertaking conveys clear evidence substantively affecting the adjudication of the infringement as to a fact or circumstance that was unknown for the HCO.[294]

357. Partial immunity from the competition fine (reduction of the fine) is available to the undertaking if full immunity cannot be granted (the undertaking does not fulfil the above conditions) and supplies evidence that represents a significant added value relative to the evidence the HCO has at the time the leniency application is submitted.[295] Partial immunity may be granted to more than one undertaking, if the evidence supplied by the subsequent whistle-blower has added value, by way of example, through strengthening the proof of the violation or revealing that the cartel had a broader purview.

358. On the basis of an application submitted after the CC's preliminary position (or the case-handler's report, if section 73 CA[296] is applied) is served or, if this occurs earlier, before the file is opened for access by the parties, the fine can be reduced only if the applicant provides clear evidence as to a fact or circumstance that has been unknown for the HCO.[297] Section 78/A (5) establishes the scale of fine reduction: the first undertaking is entitled to a 30%–50%, the second to a 20%–30% and the third and later undertakings to an up to 20% reduction.

359. In certain cases, the undertaking may be concerned that the provision of added value evidence would entail a higher fine, which would not only offset but even exceed the reduction of fine the leniency application entails. This is the case if on the basis of the evidence provided the imposition of a higher fine were warranted; for instance, the added value evidence may reveal that the leniency applicant played a major role in the cartel, was fully aware of the consequences of the collusion or the anti-competitive impact was enormous. In this case, the evidence, through revealing aggravating circumstances, may increase the fine more than it decreases due to the partial immunity from the fine. Section 78/A(6) CA addresses this concern and provides

---

294. Section 78/A(3) CA.
295. Before 1 Jul. 2014, s. 78/A(3) CA embedded a strict time-limit and provided that the application for partial immunity has to be submitted before the CC's preliminary position is served or, if this occurs earlier, before the file is opened for access by the parties.
296. The case-handler's report is not served automatically on the parties; however, the CC may decide to send out the case-handler's report to the parties before preparing its preliminary position; in this case, the CC also calls the parties to comment on the report within the deadline set by the CC.
297. Section 78/A(4) CA.

that if the undertaking provides evidence concerning a fact that is unknown to the HCO and has direct relevance in respect to the circumstances that are to be taken into consideration when setting the fine, the CC disregards this aggravating evidence when determining the fine against the undertaking that provided this evidence. Obviously, this provision has relevance only if the undertaking is not entitled to full immunity from the fine and is granted only partial immunity; in case of full immunity no fine is imposed on the undertaking that provided the evidence.

360. The joint submission of leniency applications of undertakings independent from each other (i.e., those not belonging to the same group of undertakings) is excluded: it is not acceptable if more than one undertaking submits a joint application or an undertaking submits an application on behalf of other undertakings.[298] Section 78/A(9) CA provides that an undertaking can submit, without the need of a mandate, a leniency application in representation of a controlled undertaking. Accordingly, undertakings forming part of the same group can submit a joint leniency application or an undertaking can submit a leniency application on behalf of another group member; furthermore, controlling undertakings can submit leniency applications on behalf of controlled undertakings without the need for a specific mandate.

2. Procedural Issues

361. The CA also contains the concept of a 'leniency marker'. The HCO has to grant immunity from the fine, provided the substantive law requirements of this are met, in case of an incomplete leniency application for full immunity, where the applicant cannot convey all the evidence prescribed by the law but undertakes to complete the application within the deadline set by the HCO, provided it does convey this. Such a 'non-final application for immunity' has to set out the reasons why the evidence cannot be handed over forthwith and the applicant's express commitment to complete the application with the necessary evidence. It is to be noted that the statutory language suggests that the marker is not available in case of applications for partial immunity (reduction in fine); it is available solely in respect of applications for full immunity. Furthermore, contrary to the rules effective before 1 July 2014, where it came under the HCO's discretion whether it accepted the 'non-final application' (as the CA provided that the HCO 'might' regard the application as submitted but it did not have to), currently, the statutory language is categorical.[299]

362. In the EU, it may be uncertain for the undertaking which competition authority (including the European Commission) will institute the proceeding at the end of the day. This may cause complications as to leniency applications; for instance, the competition proceeding may be started by the Commission, even in case the undertaking submitted the leniency application to the HCO and there is no guarantee that the leniency rights obtained in Hungary will be respected also in the Commission's procedure.

---

298. Section 78/A(9) CA.
299. Section 78/B(3) CA.

363. The CA addresses the foregoing problem through the 'marker system', providing that if the European Commission is particularly well placed to conduct the proceeding, the enterprise may submit, simultaneously and with the same content, a provisional application ('non-final preliminary application') to the HCO (both for immunity from and reduction of the fine), if it considers that the HCO may be well placed to proceed (in accordance with the Notice on Cooperation within the Network of Competition Authorities). If the HCO institutes the competition procedure, it shall call the undertaking to submit the required evidence; if the undertaking submits this evidence, when examining whether the undertaking is eligible for full immunity, the leniency application shall be regarded as having been submitted on the day the provisional application was made. The 'non-final preliminary application' can be submitted also in English, French or German language.[300]

364. The leniency application has to be adjudicated in the sequence of submission.[301] Section 78/B(7) provides that an application for full immunity may be withdrawn until a decision is made on it and, in case of rejection, within eight days after the rejecting order was served on the undertaking; apart from these, the leniency application cannot be withdrawn. Accordingly, applications for fine reduction cannot be withdrawn, while applications for immunity can be withdrawn under the foregoing circumstances.

365. If the leniency application does not fulfil the requirements of full immunity, the undertaking does not withdraw it and the application may be susceptible of meeting the conditions of partial immunity, the CC has to, ex officio, assess the application also as an application for partial immunity.[302]

The CC's decisions on full and partial immunity are prepared by the case-handler, who examines and comments on the application and reveals before the CC the information the HCO has as regards the violation.[303]

366. If the application for immunity meets the requirement of determinant evidence, the CC has to establish this in an order. This order, with four exceptions, estops the CC from subsequently imposing a fine.[304] First, the undertaking does not terminate its participation in the violation immediately. Second, it does not cooperate, in good faith, completely and continuously with the HCO until the end of the competition proceeding. Third, the undertaking does not treat the leniency application and its content confidentially. Fourth, in case of a leniency application for full immunity, the initial order can be departed from if it is proved that the undertaking took steps to coerce another undertaking to take part in the violation.[305] The first, the second

---

300. Section 78/B(4) CA.
301. Section 78/C(1) CA.
302. Section 78/C(3) CA.
303. Section 78/C(1) CA.
304. Section 78/C(2) CA.
305. Section 78/B(5) CA.

Part I, Ch. 5, Consequences of Violations   367–370

and the third requirements relate to acts done after the leniency application is submitted; hence, these cannot be examined at the time a decision on the application is made. Although the fourth requirement relates to circumstances that occurred before the application is submitted, normally, the CC can establish whether this condition is met only after conducting the competition investigation. Since the HCO, when receiving the leniency application and before conducting the competition investigation, has no information on whether this negative condition is met, the CA provides that notwithstanding the initial order granting full immunity, the CC may impose a fine on the undertaking, if it acted in order to coerce another undertaking to take part in the cartel. As noted above, if this is the case, the CC is expected to assess the application under the rules on partial immunity; namely, partial immunity may be granted also to undertakings that coerced others to take part in the cartel.

367. If the statutory requirements are not met, the CC rejects the application.[306]

368. If the application for immunity meets the requirement of significant added value, the CC has to establish this in an order. The CC, with three exceptions, cannot depart from this order. These are the same as the first three exceptions mentioned above in respect of full immunity: the undertaking does not terminate its participation in the violation immediately after the submission of the leniency application, it does not cooperate in good faith, completely and continuously or it does not treat the leniency application and its content confidentially.[307]

C. *Settlements*

369. According to section 79 CA, the CC deduces the fine to be imposed on the basis of the provisions of the Act by 10%, if the undertaking made a settlement declaration in accordance with section 73/A CA. This is a novel instrument inserted by the 2014 amendment of the CA and therefore does not have any case law.

370. In restrictive agreement or abuse of dominance matters (i.e., in a wider scope than settlements before the European Commission), the CC may call the party to indicate in writing whether it wants to take part in a negotiation to reach a settlement, if on the basis of the case-handler's report, taking into account the discovered facts and the underlying evidence, it considers this to be expedient from the perspective of the procedure's fast and successful conclusion.[308]

---

306. Section 78/C(2) CA.
307. Section 78/C(4) CA.
308. Section 73/A(1) CA.

371. If the party, in response to the above call, indicates in writing, within the deadline set by the CC (which cannot be longer than fifteen days), that it is ready to attempt to reach a settlement, the CC hears the party and on the hearing it informs the party about the violation it may establish, the conduct it may condemn and the evidence it may base its decision on, as well as about the aspects it may take into account when setting the fine and the likely maximum and minimum amount of the fine. If the party and the CC reach a common position within a time not endangering the procedure's fast and successful conclusion, the CC calls the party to submit its settlement declaration within the deadline set by the CC. The deadline cannot be longer than fifteen days and it is strict (the party cannot exonerate itself for missing the deadline).[309]

372. The settlement declaration has to contain, in accordance with the above-mentioned common position,

– the party's clear declaration that it admits its participation in the illegal conduct;
– the factual and brief description of the conduct, its legal characterization, purpose, method of implementation, duration and the mode and extent of the party's involvement;
– the maximum fine the party considers to be acceptable;
– the party's declaration that the CC informed it about the provisions of section 73/A(2) CA appropriately (see preceding paragraph) and gave it a chance to advance its position;
– the party's declaration that in case the content of the preliminary position and the decision are in line with the party's declaration, it will not initiate further steps, in particular it will not request access to the file and not request a hearing;
– the party's declaration that, in advance, it waives its right to appeal against the decision (which is an important deviation from the settlement proceedings before the European Commission, where such waiver is not required).[310]

The party, within fifteen days, has to make a clear statement in respect of the preliminary position on whether the preliminary position's statement is in line with the settlement declaration or it withdraws the settlement declaration.[311]

373. The settlement declaration can be withdrawn until the end of the deadline of appeal against the decision and solely in case the content of the CC's preliminary position and subsequently its decision departs from the settlement declaration, including the case if the amount of the fine imposed exceeds the maximum fine indicated by the party as acceptable. In such case, the party's clear declaration, included in the settlement declaration, that it admits its participation in the illegal conduct cannot be used as evidence.[312]

---

309. Section 73/A(2) CA.
310. Section 73/A(3) CA.
311. Section 73/A(4) CA.
312. Section 73/A(5) CA.

Part I, Ch. 5, Consequences of Violations 374–380

374. The party entering into settlement negotiations has to keep this fact and all information it learned during this secret until the end of the competition proceeding.[313]

375. The settlement declaration and, until the access to the file is opened, the fact that such a declaration was submitted qualifies as information to which access is limited. The settlement declaration can be learned only by the other parties after access to the file is opened,[314] provided this is necessary for exercising the right of defence; third parties cannot access the settlement declaration. In case the settlement declaration is withdrawn, the declaration and its copies have to be returned to the undertaking.[315]

D. Procedural Fine

376. A procedural fine can be imposed by both the case-handlers and the CC.

377. According to section 61(1) CA, a procedural fine can be imposed against the person whose act or conduct aims at protracting the procedure or frustrating the discovery of the real facts or has such an effect. It is to be stressed that a procedural fine can be imposed in case of both intention and effect. That is, if the conduct's purpose is illegitimate, the imposition of a fine is warranted, even if in effect it neither protracts the procedure, nor frustrates the discovery of the real facts. Likewise, a fine can be imposed if the conduct results in any of these illegitimate consequences unintentionally.

Furthermore, a procedural fine can be imposed on the party if it breaches the restriction of control as established in section 29/A CA.[316]

378. The minimum amount of the procedural fine is HUF 200,000 as to undertakings and HUF 50,000 as to natural persons not qualifying as undertakings. In case of undertakings, the maximum amount is 1% of the net turnover realized in the preceding business year; in case of natural persons not qualifying as undertakings, it is HUF 500,000.[317]

379. A daily procedural fine is established for cases where someone fails to meet a deadline set for the performance of a procedural duty. The daily procedural fine has to be calculated on the basis of the period between the end of the deadline set for the performance of the duty and the performance of the duty.

380. In case of undertakings, the daily procedural fine may range up to 1% of the per-day net turnover realized in the preceding business year (i.e., the daily average of the net turnover realized in the preceding business year); in case of natural persons

---

313. Section 73/A(6) CA.
314. *See* Section 55(5) CA.
315. Section 73/A(7) CA.
316. Section 61(2) CA.
317. Section 61(3) CA.

not qualifying as undertakings, the maximum of the daily procedural fine is HUF 50,000.[318]

381. The case-handler and the CC may amend or revoke the order imposing the procedural fine even in the absence of a legal error, provided this occurs in favour of the person on whom the fine was imposed.[319]

V. Administrative Injunctions and Other Restrictive Orders

382. As noted above, the CC can issue administrative injunctions and adopt other restrictive orders.

383. The CC can order that the situation violating the CA shall be eliminated[320] and can prohibit the continuation of the infringing conduct;[321] where it finds that there is an infringement of the law it may impose obligations including in particular the obligation to conclude a contract where there is an unjustified refusal to create or maintain business relations appropriate for the type of the transaction.[322]

384. The CC can order the performance of the commitment undertaken on the basis of section 75 CA.[323]

It can order the publication of a rectifying declaration in connection to the illegal declaration.[324]

385. In case of a merger notification or an ex officio investigation of a merger launched because it was implemented in breach of the prohibition of implementation, the CC can authorize or prohibit the concentration, if necessary, with the prescription of a preliminary or posterior condition or obligation;[325] in case the concentration was implemented and the CC prohibits the concentration, it adopts the measures necessary for the termination of the concentration, as specified in section 31 CA.[326] According to section 31 CA, if it is established during the competition proceedings that the notifiable concentration implemented without a permission could not have been cleared, the CC, in its decision, prescribes the dissolution of the merged undertakings or assets (or shares of business) or the termination of the joint control within a particular deadline, or may establish any other obligation for reinstating efficient competition.

---

318. Section 61(4) CA.
319. Section 61(5) CA.
320. Section 76(1)(f) CA.
321. Section 76(1)(f) CA.
322. Section 76(1)(h) CA.
323. Section 76(1)(c) CA.
324. Section 76(1)(i) CA.
325. Section 76(1)(a)-(b) CA.
326. Section 76(2) CA.

Part I, Ch. 5, Consequences of Violations   386–389

VI. Commitment Decisions

386. In EU law, under Article 9 of Regulation 1/2003, the Commission may accept commitments from undertakings that address the competition concerns identified by the Commission. Section 75 CA[327] contains a similar provision, which was inserted in the CA in 2005.[328] Nonetheless, it is noteworthy that the original text of section 75 already embedded a similar possibility, entitled the 'suspension of the proceeding'. According to the original provision, the proceeding could be suspended, if the conduct at stake endangered the freedom and fairness of competition only to a minor extent and the defendant assumed that it would refrain from the pursuance of the conduct and take the appropriate measures to prevent the emergence of damages, provided there was such a peril.

387. The currently effective section 75(1) CA provides that if the party, in respect of the conduct investigated in the competition supervision proceedings started ex officio, offers commitments to bring his conduct, in a specified manner, in conformity with the applicable provisions of the law and the effective safeguarding of public interest can be ensured in this manner, the CC may, in a decision, make the performance of these commitments binding, without establishing the occurrence or lack of the violation of the law.[329]

388. Section 75/A provides for the possibility of market testing as to commitments. The CC, before adopting the decision endorsing the commitments, if it deems this necessary, contemporaneously with the dispatch of the preliminary position to the party, through publishing the commitments (in the version that contains no information access to which is limited), can invite stakeholders to comment on the draft commitments.[330]

389. The CC has developed a fairly unique practice on the basis of section 75 CA, often using this regulatory tool as a *quasi*-surrogate of private enforcement: the CC has accepted numerous commitments that aimed at providing a civil remedy or a similar restitutive effect.[331] It pertains to the Hungarian decisional practice that commitments often remedy the detrimental consequences of competition violations from a civil law perspective and, as far as technically possible, provide compensation for the victims (occasionally even in the form of 'fluid recovery' or 'cy

---

327. Act LVII of 1996 on the Prohibition of Unfair and Restrictive Market Practice.
328. Section 75 was inserted by Act LXVIII of 2005.
329. The presentation and analysis of the Hungarian practice of commitment decisions is based on the author's following publications: Csongor István Nagy, *Kötelezettségvállalások a GVH gyakorlatában*,19(10) Gazdaság és Jog 3 (2011); Csongor István Nagy, *Commitments as Surrogates of Civil Redress in Competition Law: The Hungarian Perspective*, 33(11) Eur. Comp. Law Rev. 531 (2012).
330. Section 75(6) CA.
331. On commitment decisions *see* Bálint Bassola, Ákos Kékuti & Zoltán Marosi, *Versenyjogi vádalku? – A kötelezettségvállalás intézménye kritikus szemmel*, 58(12) Magyar Jog 722 (2011).

pres',[332] if the individual harms cannot be identified properly). By accepting such commitments, the HCO tends to 'generate' *quasi* private enforcement.

390. It is to be noted that the HCO's remit embraces also certain consumer protection cases (unfair commercial practices)[333] and most commitment decisions have been rendered in consumer matters. Nonetheless, until 28 September 2012, the HCO's policy towards commitments had been, in principle, uniform and had not treated antitrust and consumer protection matters differently. The HCO adopted a notice that addresses specifically commitments in matters involving unfair commercial practices.[334] Nevertheless, although the Notice is applicable solely to unfair commercial practices, there is no indication that its principles would not be applicable *mutatis mutandis* in antitrust matters.

391. Due to the idiosyncrasy of the Hungarian policy on commitments, the CC's decisional practice merits a detailed presentation. This unique decisional practice is analysed in the following steps. First, the actual and potential aims of commitment procedures are examined. Second, those matters (violations) are identified where there is no place for commitments (these are the cases where the CC outright refuses to accept or even to consider commitments). Third, it is examined what the defendant may proffer in the frame of a commitment procedure: what are the engagements that are usually accepted in the CC's decisional practice. Fourth, it is briefly analysed whether due to the commitment order legally enforceable civils rights accrue to the individual victims.

---

332. 'Fluid recovery' is used in US class action matters where the provision of individual recovery for all class members is impossible or unfeasible, e.g., class members cannot be identified. In such cases, the court may order that the recovery awarded shall be devoted to the 'next best use'. *See* e.g., *State of California v. Levi Strauss & Co.*, 41 Cal.3d 460 (1986); *Six Mexican Workers v. Arizona Citrus Growers*, 904 F.2d 1301 (9th Cir. 1990); J.C. Alexander, *An Introduction to Class Action Procedure in the United States*, Paper for Conference 'Debates over group litigation in comparative perspective.' Geneva, 21–22 Jul. 2000, 16, *available at* http://law.duke.edu/grouplit/papers/classactionalexander.pdf. As to 'cy pres' *see* Albert A. Foer, *14 Cy pres as a Remedy in Private Antitrust Litigation*, in *Private Enforcement of Antitrust Law in the United States* 349–364 (Albert A. Foer & Randy M. Stutz eds., Edward Elgar 2012) ('The normal remedies in a private antitrust case are a combination of injunctions and treble damages that are paid to the victim or victims of the anticompetitive activity. When an aggregate amount of damages is established, the primary objective is to distribute the damages to those who were injured. In antitrust class action litigation, however, it is often impossible or impracticable to compensate all victims. Administrative concerns may work against payments to individual plaintiffs, as in the case of an extremely large class where the fund is not sufficient to justify the transaction costs of distribution to individual claimants. Consequently, in some cases, there is money left over in the form of unclaimed funds. In such cases, courts sometimes employ the doctrine of "cy pres" to put the unclaimed funds to "the next best use," which may include awarding funds to public interest organizations or charities for purposes related to the case.').
333. This is based on the Hungarian legislation (Act XLVII of 2008) implementing the Unfair Commercial Practices Directive (Directive 2005/29/EC [2005] OJ L 149/22.). The HCO has 'the power to proceed against infringements of the prohibition of unfair commercial practices where the commercial practice is capable of materially affecting competition'. s. 10(3) UCP Act.
334. Notice 3/2012 on commitments in proceedings instituted regarding assumed violations of the prohibition of unfair commercial practices against consumers. This was replaced by Notice 6/2014 on commitments in proceedings instituted regarding assumed violations of the prohibition of unfair commercial practices against consumers.

Part I, Ch. 5, Consequences of Violations

A. *The Purposes of Commitment Procedures*

392. The notion of commitment decisions is not in compliance with the concept of public administration based on the principle of legality, which would imply that the authority has to investigate each and every perceived violation unconditionally and it does not have the possibility not to investigate small cases or violations the chasing of which it does not prioritize. On the other hand, the principle of opportunity refers to the authority's possibility to pick and choose from the cases.

393. Section 75 CA raises interesting questions in the context of the principle of legality: if a practice is unlawful, why is the competition authority not proceeding and imposing a fine; on the other hand, if there is no illegality, why is it justified to assume commitments in order to get rid of the competition procedure?

394. Commitment procedures may have different purposes. Unfortunately, the decisional and judicial practice has not spelled out these; similarly, section 75 CA and its explanatory memorandum are also silent in this regard. The scholarship lists the following potential purposes.

395. The first potential purpose of commitment decisions is procedural economy. If the procedure is put to an end due to commitments, the competition authority does not have to carry the case through. Accordingly, it may save resources, which otherwise would be exhausted to fully and comprehensively reveal the factual situation, to spell out the legal reasoning expansively and to render a formal decision. These assignments can be avoided through the acceptance of commitments. Consequently, the resources liberated here may be devoted to other, possibly more aggravated mischiefs.

396. The second potential aim is tackling the competition authority's factual and legal risks, i.e., risks attached to the judicial review of the decision's fact pattern, the competition procedure and the legal conclusions. The competition authority may perceive certain hazards related to the proof of the facts and their legal evaluation, and it may be concerned that the court may find some points of the decision unfounded, reversing or quashing it. Since in competition practice, legal norms often enable a very wide margin of appreciation, the legal risks attached to judicial review cannot be fully excluded. Likewise, it is easy to find cases where the competition authority's decision wrecked on the 'technicalities' of procedural law. The same holds true for the establishing of the fact pattern. Accordingly, the competition authority may not be able to fully exclude the factual and legal risks, and in certain cases may use commitment decisions to tackle this.

397. Third, the uncertainties related to the interpretation of competition law on the side of the undertaking may also justify the acceptance of commitments. Competition rules are impregnated by economics and secure a wide margin of appreciation to the competition authority; this entails a lower level of legal certainty. The purpose of prevention (deterrence) warrants that if the violation is not crystal-clear and the interpretation of the legal norm was uncertain, a more relaxed sanction is to be imposed. This is especially the case if the competition authority deviates from its prior practice and introduces new principles.

398. Fourth, commitments may also facilitate remedies that, notwithstanding the provisions of the law, would otherwise not materialize in practice due to technical difficulties. For instance, normally, the wrongdoer has to compensate the victims for the loss they sustained due to the violation of competition law. Nevertheless, as a matter of practice, numerous (and perhaps most) competition violations do not end up with compensation, especially in those matters where the violation harms 'large numbers of people in small amounts'.[335] Thus, although these claims legally do exist, they are rarely satisfied in practice, and '[r]ights which cannot be enforced in practice are worthless'.[336] The added value of the commitment procedure could be that it may make legally existing but practically unenforceable rights a reality.

399. Fifth, commitments may also enable remedies that could not be prescribed by the competition authority; either because they are not required by the law or because the competition authority has no competence to prescribe them.

B. Cases Where There Is No Place for Commitments

400. There are certain matters, where the acceptance of commitments is excluded due to the violation's nature. Deliberate mischiefs and aggravated violations should not call for mercy. The possibility of commitments does not encompass infringements, the pursuit of which lies at the heart of competition law (hard-core violations) but centres around the application of uncertain legal norms and 'petty offences'.

401. In the CC's decisional practice, commitments cannot be accepted in respect of clear violations. This proposition was confirmed in Case *Vj-118/2007/21 Unicredit*[337] and in Case *Vj-137/2008/33 Allianz*. If it is obvious that the conduct at stake falls foul of competition law, the CC will not accept commitments but it will carry the case through and impose an appropriate penalty. It is submitted that once it is established that the conduct clearly violates the law, the size and the weight of the detrimental consequences should be irrelevant: it would deteriorate the authority of competition law if clear, bad faith and malicious infringements would be left without an adequate penalty.[338]

402. Accordingly, hard-core violations cannot count on mercy: these mischiefs infringe the principles and values of competition law to such an extent that the acceptance of commitments is out of question. In Case *Vj-18/2008 MIF*, where the CC condemned

---

335. *State of California v. Levi Strauss & Co.*, 41 Cal.3d 460, 472 (1986).
336. Towards a Coherent European Approach to Collective Redress. SEC(2011)173 final. 2.
337. The CC held that the posterior remedy did not ensure the effective safeguarding of public interest, because the conduct the defendant wanted to remedy violated a clear and obvious legal requirement, which was set out in the CC's decisional practice and confirmed by the courts.
338. Csongor István Nagy, *Kötelezettségvállalások a GVH gyakorlatában*, 19(10) Gazdaság és Jog 3, 4 (2011).

Part I, Ch. 5, Consequences of Violations 403–406

Hungarian banks for fixing the domestic multilateral interchange fee and treating, in this regard, the two card companies alike, the CC made it clear that the 'restrictive conduct was of such a nature that it is not to be penalized with prospective future commitments but with the declaration of illegality and with an appropriate sanction'.[339]

403. It is an interesting practical question whether commitment decisions should have precedential value: that is, may the HCO regard a particular conduct as clearly violating the law simply because beforehand it accepted commitments as regards the same conduct. In Case *Vj-137/2008/33 Allianz*, the HCO suggested that this is the case; the message of the commitment decision is that the conduct is contrary to the law. This approach goes counter to the express rule of section 75 of the HCA that commitment decisions cannot establish the illegality of the conduct. This firm rule would be ignored if commitment decisions were used as *quasi* declarations of illegality. On the other hand, the circumstances that the HCO instituted a proceeding and the defendant submitted commitments suggest that the conduct at stake does raise competition law concerns.

404. In Case *Vj-18/2008 MIF*, the HCO announced that in matters involving restrictive agreements all participants are required to submit commitments;[340] no commitment order can be rendered, if one of the undertakings refuses to assume the engagements. It is to be noted, however, that this case involved a horizontal agreement and not a vertical arrangement; it is doubtful whether this proposition would be equally applicable to vertical relations, for instance, if the producer inserts different restrictive clauses into its distribution agreements and subsequently commits itself to amend these agreements and to refrain from stipulating similar clauses. In such cases, unilateral commitments may be sufficient for putting the procedure to an end.

405. Finally, it is to be noted that it is generally a mitigating circumstance from the perspective of the fine if the undertaking offers commitments, even if they are not accepted.[341]

C. *What Can Be Offered?*

406. The first group of offerings embraces restitutive commitments, i.e., commitments to restore the initial status in broader sense. The restoration of the initial status is to be grasped in its everyday (and not legal) meaning. The clearest case of restitution is refunding. This occurred in Case *Vj-10/2009 Megasztár*[342] and in Case *Vj-16/2008 K&H Bank*. In Case *Vj-41/2006/60 OTP*, the competition procedure was

---

339. Paragraph 228.
340. Paragraph 229.
341. Case *Vj-137/2008/33 Allianz*, Case *Vj-70/2009 Update*, para. 62, Case *Vj-18/2008 MIF*, para. 223.
342. *See* para. 20.

instituted because the defendant (a bank) abused its dominant position by increasing the fees of pre-redemption. The bank refunded the difference to those customers who redeemed the full debt or part of it under the fees of pre-redemption, the legality of which was questionable under competition law.

407. Practically, in certain cases the initial status is restored and the detriment is, in essence, lifted, if the consumer is granted a right of unilateral cancellation or termination. This happened in Case *Vj-118/2007/20 Unicredit*. In this case, it was alleged that the bank committed an unfair commercial practice when not disclosing certain important contractual terms, and as a result of the commitment decision the consumer was granted the chance to quit the contract.

408. Examples may be found for cases where the CC, through a commitment order, obligated the undertaking to do what it promised to do. In these matters, the undertaking made certain allegations concerning the product's characteristics, which subsequently turned out to be false; during the procedure, the enterprise entered into an engagement to 'keep its word'. In Case *Vj-135/2007 T-Kábel Kft.*, the CC perceived that the cable-television operator declared that the channels in the undertaking's portfolio were available in digital picture and voice quality, while the set-top-boxes used by the firm could not be connected to digital television devices. After the institution of the procedure, the T-Kábel undertook to make the purchase of such set-top-boxes available that were compatible with digital television devices. A similar fact pattern emerged in Case *Vj-63/2010 Digi Kft.* and in Case *Vj-7-37/2011 Invitel*, which also resulted in a commitment order. In Case *Vj-118/2007/20 UniCredit*, the enterprise, among others, accepted to compensate those customers who broke up their fixed deposits.

409. In numerous cases, the undertaking entered into an engagement to conduct an informational or an educational campaign. The difference between these two is that while educational campaigns relate to the promotion of the general economic or financial knowledge and awareness of consumers, informational campaigns relate to the products or services of a particular enterprise.

410. As far as civil law consequences are concerned, it could be argued that the undertaking is obliged to provide compensation for the damages it caused, notwithstanding the fact that, in terms of practice, it would probably not do that voluntarily. Here, the undertaking does not promise more than it has to do anyway. Nevertheless, educational and informational campaigns are, even if they increase consumer welfare, obligations beyond legal duties.

411. The defendant undertook to accomplish an educational campaign in Case *Vj-189/2007 Raiffeisen* and in Case *Vj-118/2007/20 Unicredit*. In Case *Vj-189/2007 Raiffeisen*, the enterprise's commitment was that it would conduct an educational campaign concerning residential loan and other credit products in order to increase the consumers' knowledge.

Part I, Ch. 5, Consequences of Violations

412. An informational campaign was undertaken in Case *Vj-148/2006/49 Tesco*. Here, the firm failed to inform the consumers that the warranty over the product entered into force only if the product was registered at a professional shop, and this registration was done in exchange for an extra fee. The firm undertook general information obligations that went beyond the products concerned.[343] Likewise, commitments related to the informational practice are to be found in Case *Vj-19/2009 OTP*, where the Hungarian bank changed its informational practice concerning investment funds.

413. An interesting question concerning the practice of commitment decisions is whether the restoration of the initial status and comprehensive civil law redress are the pre-conditions of accepting commitments. In some matters, the HCO suggested that failing this the enterprise cannot bring its conduct in conformity with the law, as required by section 75 of the HCA. And indeed, if interpreting section 75 literally, the conclusion may be reasonably drawn that the illegal plight ends only if the detrimental consequences are lifted. One of the conditions of accepting the proffered commitments is that the 'party offers commitments to bring his conduct, in a specified manner, in conformity with the provisions of this Act or of Article 101 or 102 of the TFEU'. The mere fact that the undertaking stops violating the law certainly does not imply that it would bring its conduct in conformity with the law, at least not retrospectively. According to this interpretation, the undertaking is required to bring also its past conduct in conformity with the law. It calls for compensation under civil law, if consumers suffer a detriment; this 'conformity' may be reached only if remedying the violation also from the perspective of civil law.

414. Nonetheless, such a strict and inflexible approach would be very counter-productive in matters where civil law redress cannot be provided simply because the injured persons cannot be identified. Insisting on civil law redress would exclude the use of commitments in such cases; in a number of matters, it is impossible or unfeasible for the undertaking to compensate the victims. Fortunately, the practice of the HCO seems to avoid this trap. In Case *Vj-19/2009 OTP*, it was needless to provide for a civil remedy because the bank compensated its complaining customers on a voluntary basis. Nevertheless, in Case *Vj-148/2006/49 Tesco* and in Case *Vj-189/2007 Raiffeisen*, there was no voluntary compensation and the HCO did not treat this as the pre-condition of accepting commitments.

D. The Legal Consequences of Not Performing the Commitments

415. Before 1 July 2014, if the undertaking failed to execute the commitment order (at that time commitments were endorsed in an order and not in a decision), the CC could impose a fine,[344] which could range up to 10% of the undertaking's net turnover in the preceding business year, and could launch a procedure for the enforcement of the order. Both tools were used in Case *Vj-157/2007/58 'N&P KEGYELET 2006'*.

---

343. Paragraph 11.
344. Section 76(4)(a) CA.

416. The currently effective provisions of the CA follow a 'fork in the road' approach: if the undertaking fails to do what it promised (commitments), the CC can either impose a fine for the breach of the commitments or withdraw the commitment decision and re-start the competition procedure against the undertaking (what may, of course, result in the imposition of a fine).[345]

417. It is an interesting question whether the undertaking's legal obligation (commitment) to compensate implies that the injured persons have a legally enforceable right to get compensated on the basis of the commitment order. Section 6:2(3) HCC provides that a legally enforceable obligation may emerge also from an administrative decision (and from a rule of law or a court decision), if the decision provides so and defines the obligor, the obligee and the service (i.e., the behaviour to be performed in the fulfilment of the duties).

418. On the basis of this provision, it could be argued that the commitment decision confers legally enforceable rights on the victims of the competition violation, and hence, the injured persons may sue if the undertaking does not execute the commitment. Unfortunately, there is no judicial practice in this regard.

VII. Interim Measures

419. Interim measures are proposed by the case-handlers and adopted by the CC. This procedural tool is seldom used in practice.

420. In the 'case-handler's report' the case-handler, if necessary, may propose the adoption of interim measures.[346] If justified, the case-handler may submit a proposal, in the form of a separate report, to adopt interim measures even before the completion of the investigation.[347]

421. Interestingly, the language of the CA suggests that the CC can adopt interim measures only if this is proposed by the case-handler ('[t]he CC, on the basis of the case-handler's report … '). Before 1 July 2014, the CA provided that the CC can adopt interim measures 'after receiving the case-handler's report'. However, the CC may interpret this provision in a way that it is not a pre-condition that the case-handler, in his report, proposes the adoption of interim measures and the CC can adopt interim measures also in case the case-handler failed to propose this.

422. On the basis of the case-handler's report, the CC can adopt interim measures, in the form of an order, in three cases.

---

345. Section 75(6) CA, s. 78(1a) CA.
346. Section 71(2)(c) CA.
347. Section 71(3)(c) CA.

Part I, Ch. 5, Consequences of Violations

423. First, the CC can forbid the carrying on of the likely unlawful conduct and enjoin that the likely unlawful situation be ceased, if this is urgently needed for the protection of the stakeholders' legal or economic interests or due to the danger to the coming into existence, subsistence or development of market competition.[348]

424. Second, in ex officio proceedings, if the concentration, which is probably not authorizable on the basis of section 30 CA, was implemented contrary to the prohibition of implementation embedded in section 29 or if the concentration was implemented in breach of the HCO's decision prohibiting the merger or without the fulfilment of the condition established in the authorization, for the sake of mitigating the concentration's detrimental effects on competition and of ensuring the applicability of the measures of section 31 CA, the CC can adopt, to the necessary extent, measures restricting the undertaking's control.[349]

425. Third, the CC can revoke the permission of section 29/A(1) CA on the basis of section 29/A(3) CA or can decide to amend the control-restricting prescription adopted in the permission, if it is likely that the concentration resulted in the significant lessening of competition in the relevant market.[350]

426. The order establishing interim measures can be appealed separately. The CC can withdraw or amend the interim measures order ex officio even in the absence of the breach of the law, if the change of the circumstances underlying the adoption of the interim measures warrants this.[351] The interim measures order can be declared enforceable notwithstanding an application for the suspension of the enforcement, if the delay of the enforcement caused irreparable loss.[352]

§2. CIVIL ENFORCEMENT

427. In private actions, the plaintiff's claim (*petitum*) can aim at three pleas: declaration, recovery and modification of the legal status. The latter is, nevertheless, not relevant from the point of view of competition law's private enforcement, as it encompasses situations where the decision of the court constitutes or terminates rights and obligations (e.g., divorce, filiation). The plaintiff can petition a declaratory judgment if the declaration is necessary for protecting his rights against the defendant and the plaintiff cannot claim recovery.[353] In case of peril of damages, the imperilled person can claim that the court enjoins the endangering person from the endangering conduct and oblige him to take the measures that are necessary for

---

348. Section 72/A(1)(a) CA.
349. Section 72/A(1)(b) CA.
350. Section 72/A(1)(c) CA.
351. Section 72/A(3) CA.
352. Section 72/A(4) CA.
353. Section 123 CCP.

avoiding the damages and to give security, if necessary.[354] Courts can also adopt interim measures.[355]

I. Competent Civil Courts

428. Hungary has a four-tiered court system. Local courts ('*járásbíróság*') and labour and administrative courts are first instance courts, while county courts ('*törvényszék*') act both as first instance and appellate courts, hearing appeals against the judgments of the local courts and the labour and administrative courts. Local courts have general jurisdiction: they have the power to hear all cases, except the matter is vested in another court's competence. The court system's third tier consists of the courts of appeals ('*ítélőtábla*'), which have solely appellate jurisdiction. The system is headed by the Supreme Court ('*Kúria*').

429. Monetary claims come under the county court's competence if the claim's value exceeds HUF 30,000,000, with the exception of actions related to matrimonial property if it is consolidated with a marital action or it is instituted during a marital action.[356]

II. Sanctions

A. *Nullity*

430. Similarly to EU competition law (Article 101(2) TFEU), agreements violating the prohibition on restrictive agreements enshrined in section 11 of the CA are automatically void. Section 11(3) CA provides that the legal consequences established by the CA for the violation of the general prohibition on restrictive agreements have to be applied jointly with the consequences the Civil Code establishes for illegal contracts. Since agreements going counter to the general prohibition on restrictive agreements embedded section 11 CA, provided they do not benefit from an individual or a block exemption, infringe a legal rule, they qualify as illegal agreements; according to section 6:95 HCC, illegal contracts (i.e., contract violating the law) are automatically invalid.[357]

---

354. Section 341 CC.
355. Section 156 CPA.
356. Section 23(1)(a) CCP.
357. Péter Miskolczi-Bodnár, *A versenytörvény magyarázata* 172–173 (KJK-Kerszöv 2002); Csongor István Nagy, *Kartelljogi Kézikönyv. A közösségi és a magyar kartelljog kézikönyve* 720 (HVG-Orac 2006). For detailed analyses on the nullity of restrictive agreements *see* Lénárd Darázs, *A kartellek semmissége* (Complex 2009); Lénárd Darázs, *A semmisség mint a versenyjogi jogsértések (kartellek és gazdasági erőfölénnyel való visszaélés) esetén alkalmazható polgári jogi jogkövetkezmény*, in Versenyjogi jogsértések – magánjogi jogkövetkezmények 119 (Kisfaludi András ed., ELTE Eötvös Kiadó 2012).

Part I, Ch. 5, Consequences of Violations

431. It is an important question of interpretation whether follow-on or fruit contracts, i.e., contracts concluded by the cartelist firms with their clients following the conclusion of the cartel, are also covered by the sanction of nullity. The Budapest Court of Appeals established in Case *14.Gf.40.137/2010/5 Nemzeti Infrastruktúra Fejlesztő Zrt. v. Strabag Zrt*[358] that such contracts are not automatically void; and the sanction of nullity extends only to contracts that infringe section 11 CA directly.[359]

432. In this case, the plaintiff (NIF) published a call for tender for construction services, which was won by the defendant (Strabag). The parties concluded a works contract. Afterwards, the CC established that the defendant (Strabag) participated in a bid-rigging cartel and imposed a fine. The CC's decision was finally and conclusively affirmed by the courts.

433. The plaintiff sued the defendant for damages before the Budapest Court. Its statement of claim was initially based on delictual liability but afterwards the plaintiff changed the claim's legal base: in the first place, it requested the Budapest Court to establish that the price clause of the works contract was illegal due to the defendant's violation of the competition rules, while retaining delictual liability as a secondary legal base.

434. Under Hungarian law, the court may adopt an interim judgment as to the legal base of the plaintiff's claim. The interim judgment can be appealed.

435. The Budapest Court rendered an interim judgment establishing that the legal base of the plaintiff's claim is well-founded. Albeit that the plaintiff requested the court to establish the partial invalidity of the works contract, the Court finally came to the conclusion that the entire contract is invalid.

436. The defendant attacked the interim judgment before the Budapest Court of Appeals, arguing, among others, that the nullity sanction addressed to agreements infringing competition law covers only restrictive agreements (cartels) but not those contracts that were concluded following to and in accordance with the restrictive agreement (follow-on agreements). Although the latter are the 'fruits' of the cartel, which determines their content, the prohibition of the restriction of competition does not extend to these.

437. The Budapest Court of Appeals distinguished between two agreements. First, the defendant concluded a cartel with its competitors, which resulted in presumably higher prices (i.e., in the absence of the bid-rigging the contract price would have been probably lower). Second, the plaintiff concluded a works contract with the defendant as the winner of the tender.

---

358. Number of the Administrative Case: *Vj-27/2003*.
359. This approach is advocated also in the scholarship. *See* Csongor István Nagy, *III. Rész: Antitröszt jog*, in *Magyar versenyjog* 310 (Kinga Pázmándi ed., HVG-Orac 2012).

438. The Court of Appeals held that while the cartel agreement is invalid, the follow-on contract is not. The Court advanced that although it is true that as a consequence of the bid-rigging the plaintiff could not get the service under the best conditions available, this circumstance, in itself, does not warrant the nullity of the works contract. The basis of nullity is the violation of the competition rules, and it is only the cartel agreement that falls foul of the legal prohibition; the works contract does not violate the prohibition on restrictive agreements, even if the contract price is the 'fruit' of the bid-rigging.

439. Accordingly, the Budapest Court of Appeals quashed the Budapest Court's interim judgment and remanded the case and ordered the Budapest Court to continue the proceeding regarding the plaintiff's secondary claim (claim for damages on the basis of delictual liability).

440. The order of the Budapest Court of Appeals clarified a pivotal question of competition law's private enforcement and its interpretation seems to be well-found both from a conceptual and a policy perspective. The relevant question to be examined was whether the works contract concluded by the parties qualified as a prohibited agreement. Conceptually, it could have been hardly argued that the prohibition of restrictive agreements covers all contracts, the economic content of which happens to be influenced by the restriction of competition. Furthermore, such an interpretation would have been unfortunate also from a practical perspective, due to the unforeseeable consequences of declaring all follow-on contracts automatically void.

441. A related question of interpretation is whether the violation of the rules on abuse of dominant position may entail nullity, i.e., whether contracts concluded with a dominant undertaking may qualify as invalid if the abuse of dominant position materialized in the contract; for instance, if a loyalty rebate or excessive prices are included in the contract. It is submitted that such contracts would not qualify as automatically invalid, since it is not the contract itself but the dominant undertaking's conduct that is legally prohibited. The victim of the violation may claim damages under delictual liability (non-contractual liability).

B. Damages

442. Under Hungarian law, the injured party may claim damages if he was the victim of a competition violation. Although the judicial practice is not unequivocal in this regard, it is submitted that, in principal, damages can be claimed under delictual liability and not contractual liability. That is, if the victim concludes a contract with one of the cartelist undertakings and has to pay an inflated price, the price difference between the contract price and the would-be price (the price that would have prevailed in the absence of the cartel) may be claimed under delictual liability and not under contractual liability. Namely, under Hungarian law damages under contractual liability can be claimed only for the breach of the contract, while claims in

Part I, Ch. 5, Consequences of Violations　　　　　　　　　　　　　　**443–446**

overcharge matters are based on the violation of the law. However, due to the CJEU's ruling in *Courage*, certain claims may be based on contractual liability.[360]

443. Under Hungarian law, the elements of delictual liability are the following: illegal conduct, occurrence of damages, causal link between the illegal conduct and the damages, and fault (culpability).[361] The illegality of the conduct is, however, presumed if the conduct causes damages.[362] In other words, there is a general presumption that a conduct causing damages is illegal, except a special legal provision authorizes the alleged tortfeasor to act in a certain way. The burden of proof as to the pre-conditions of delictual liability rests on the plaintiff with the exception of fault: if a conduct causes damages, it is to be presumed that the defendant was in fault; however, he may prove the contrary (i.e., his conduct was not culpable).

444. The requirement of foreseeability applies to the ascertaining of the causality: no causal link can be established as to a loss the tortfeasor did not foresee, nor ought to have foreseen.[363]

445. Hungarian law essentially recognizes the passing-on defence,[364] since it rests on the principle of full compensation. The injured party may claim recovery exclusively for the loss he suffered, whilst the damages awarded to the plaintiff cannot exceed the amount of the loss.[365] The person liable for damages has to compensate the injured person for the entire loss he suffered. Hungarian law differentiates between three types of damages: depreciation in the property of the injured person (positive damages, *damnum emergens*), loss of profit (consequential damages, *lucrum cessans*) and costs devoted to the reduction or elimination of the pecuniary or non-pecuniary detriment.[366] The HCC, specifically, addresses the issue of benefits emerging from the tort: the advantages accruing to the injured party due to the wrong are to be deducted from the amount of damages he or she suffered, unless this is unjustified taking into account the circumstances of the case.[367]

446. The loss the injured party suffers can be defined only through comparing the actual situation with the situation that would have emerged in the absence of the

---

360. On the application of the *Courage* doctrine under Hungarian law *see* Csongor István Nagy, *A kartellkár egy speciális esete: a vétlen szerződő fél kártérítési igénye*, in *Versenyjogi jogsértések esetén érvényesíthető magánjogi igények* (HVG-Orac 2009), 125–143.
361. Section 6:519 CC.
362. Section 6:518 CC.
363. Section 6:521 CC.
364. Tamás Éless & Ágnes Németh, *Study on the Conditions of Claims for Damages in Case of Infringement of EC Competition Rules. National Report: Hungary* 10 (Ashurst Report 2004).
365. *See* Gyula Eörsi, *A polgári jogi kártérítési felelősség kézikönyve* 99–101 (1966); The Hungarian Supreme Court's Civil Council Opinion ('PK') No. 48 – in the context of the tortfeasor's duty to pay allowance to the victim of an accident – stresses that the tortfeasor has to recover only the damages caused by the accident, but he is not obliged to bring the victim into a status that is more favourable for him than his status if the accident had not occurred. The compensation in the form of allowance may not trigger unjustified enrichment or gain in excess of the loss suffered.
366. Section 6:522(1)-(2) CC.
367. Section 6:522(3) CC.

wrong (counter-factual). This is reinforced by the rule that the advantages accruing to the injured party due to the wrong, in principle, have to be deducted from the amount of damages he or she suffered. Therefore, it is essential to determine the situation that would have emerged in the absence of the tort, and this is the point where the passing-on defence becomes relevant. Accordingly, the costs passed on appear to decrease the amount of compensation the injured party is entitled to. Unfortunately, there is no judicial practice in this regard. However, courts may take into account the amount of the costs passed on only if the passing-on is a direct or automatic consequence of the competition infringement. On the other hand, if the passing-on of the costs is not a general market phenomenon, but it is due to the specific circumstances of the case, (the most important of them being the efforts of the injured party), the advantage might be regarded as not having been caused by the infringement, and thus not resulting from the tortious act; or the court may conclude that it would be unjustified to take it into account. Accordingly, it is not merely the individual transactions of the injured party that are to be taken into account, but the increase of the (output) market price should also be considered.

447. Therefore, in passing-on cases the amount of loss suffered by the undertaking consists not only of the increase to the input price, but also encompasses some quantitative reduction in terms of turnover. If the demand on the output market is not perfectly inflexible, the increase of the output price certainly leads to a reduction in the demand.

448. Since Hungarian law recognizes the passing-on defence, the damages can be defined as the difference between the would-be and the actual profit. However, technically, the calculation should take the various advantages and disadvantages as a basis: increase of the input price (-), increase of the output price (+) and reduction of the turnover (-).

C. Hungarian Competition Law's 10% Rule

449. The CA contains an idiosyncratic rule addressing specifically cartel damages, providing that it is to be presumed that (horizontal) cartels result in a 10% price increase.[368] This calculation is to be applied in civil proceedings instituted after the rule's entry into force, which was 1 June 2009.[369] Accordingly, the 10% presumption also covers infringements that occurred prior to that date, provided the civil action is instituted after this date.

---

368. On Hungarian law's 10% rule *see* Csongor István Nagy, *Kártérítési felelősség kartelljogsértések esetén: gondolatok a Tpvt. új szabályai kapcsán*, 56(9) Magyar Jog 513–520 (2009); Csongor István Nagy, *Schadensersatzklagen im Falle kartellrechtlicher Rechtsverletzungen in Ungarn: neue Schadensersatzvorschriften des ungarischen Kartellgesetzes*, 60(9) Wirtschaft und Wettbewerb 902 (2010); Csongor István Nagy, *New Hungarian Rules on Damages in Competition Matters*, 32(2) Eur. Comp. Law Rev. 63 (2011).
369. Section 17(7) of the Amendment.

Part I, Ch. 5, Consequences of Violations 450–454

450. Section 88/C CA provides as follows:

> [i]n the course of civil proceedings for any claim conducted against a party to a restrictive agreement between competitors aimed at directly or indirectly fixing selling prices, sharing markets or setting production or sales quotas that infringes Article 11 of this Act or Article 101 TFEU, when proving the extent of the influence that the infringement exercised on the price applied by the infringer, it shall be presumed, unless the opposite is proved, that the infringement influenced the price to an extent of ten per cent.

451. Accordingly, in any civil action against a member of a horizontal price-fixing, market-sharing or quota agreement cartel[370] falling foul of section 11 CA or Article 101 TFEU, it is to be presumed, albeit in a rebuttable manner, that the infringement raised the price by 10%.

452. In respect of the 10% rule's scope, it should be emphasized that the presumption of a price increase is far from being a remedy for all of the troubles of competition law's private enforcement. Although it applies to the most harmful matters, its scope of application is fairly restricted. First, the above presumption governs only horizontal hard-core infringements, i.e., horizontal price, market sharing and output cartels, and it does not apply to any other cartel law violation. Furthermore, it contains no provision concerning damages caused by abuses of dominant position. What is more, its scope of application does not cover all horizontal hardcore cartels: contrary to the horizontal fixing of the selling price, it deliberately ignores buyer cartels (purchase price-fixing).[371] Second, even in the event of the cases covered, it applies merely to overcharge matters, while disregarding disputes / situations where the loss is not or not entirely triggered by price increase; for instance, where a potential competitor suffers damages because its market entry is prevented.

453. According to the practice of the CC, the concept of horizontal hardcore agreements embraces only 'naked' agreements, the purpose of which is to directly fix prices, share markets or limit output. Nevertheless, in case an agreement generates such a result only indirectly, it certainly does not qualify as a hardcore cartel.[372]

454. The above presumption has a rather modest relevance regarding the calculation of damages. The new rule establishes a presumed price increase and not a presumed amount of loss; the distinction between the two is of utmost importance in Hungarian law, since the latter, as noted above, encompasses a passing-on defence. The explanatory

---

370. Agreements directly or indirectly fixing selling prices, sharing markets, determining production or selling quotas.
371. The Amendment's explanatory report asserts that the technical circumstances related to evidence justify the prescription of the presumption only on the side of the seller (service provider); hence, the new rules do not cover buyer cartels.
372. *See* Case *Vj-195/2001 REÁL Hungária et al.*, para. 26.

memorandum of the Amendment inserting the 10% rule[373] admits to this shortcoming.[374] In case of a sale to a final consumer, e.g., public procurement, the price increase may usually equal the amount of damages. Nonetheless, if the purchaser uses the product only as input, the situation may be completely different, since the input cartel may consequentially entail a price increase on the output market.

D. Special Rules on Whistle-Blowers in Actions for Damages

455. Section 88/D CA tries to tackle the problems that arise from the inevitable clash between private enforcement and leniency policy. Namely, the competition authority is not empowered to award immunity from civil law consequences. Thus, the encouragement of private enforcement and actions for damages may counter the proper functioning of leniency policy. Section 88/D CA tries to mitigate this tension and to reconcile leniency policy with actions for damages.

456. Leniency policy clashes with private antitrust enforcement at two points. First, even though the whistle-blower may enjoy immunity from fines under competition law, through its cooperation it owns up to the wrong and practically acknowledges its tort liability. What is more problematic is the fact that in the case of cartels there are multiple tortfeasors, and individual cartel members have joint and several liability. Second, the whistle-blower may get into a situation that is even worse than the plight of the rest of the cartel. As no fine is imposed on the former at the end of the competition authority's administrative procedure, the whistle-blower normally does not challenge the CC's decision before the court. Therefore, the decision would become final and conclusive against him, thus the illegality of its conduct becoming finally settled. This situation is very disadvantageous to the whistle-blower, since the court procedure initiated by the rest of the cartel may last for years and it is a reasonable decision for the injured party to single out the whistle-blower from the cartel members with joint and several liability and to sue him instantly after the completion of the administrative procedure.

457. Section 88/D CA contains solutions for both of the above-mentioned problems; it provides that the injured party first has to seek recovery from the cartelists that have not been awarded immunity from fines. He can only demand compensation from the whistle-blower if he could not recover the whole amount of damages from the rest of the cartel. The person who was granted immunity from fines on the basis of leniency is entitled to refuse to pay compensation for the damages caused by his conduct infringing section 11 CA or Article 101 TFEU, until the claim is collectable from any other wrongdoer liable for the same violation. These rules do not

---

373. The explanatory report is a government document attached to bills submitted to the Parliament, which explains the policy considerations underlying the bill and provides laconic comments on the text's individual sections.
374. Amendment's explanatory report, remarks on s. 14.

Part I, Ch. 5, Consequences of Violations 458–460

prevent the plaintiff from suing the wrongdoers jointly. Nonetheless, the lawsuit against the person qualifying for immunity from fines has to await the final and conclusive decision on the competition authority's condemnation, provided it is challenged in due course before the court. The lawsuit against the whistle-blower is to be stayed until the administrative procedure against the entire cartel ends.

458. Any person to which immunity from fine was granted under Article 78/A CA may refuse to pay damages for the harm caused by his conduct infringing Article 11 CA or Article 101 TFEU until the claim can be recovered from any other person responsible for causing harm by the same infringement. This rule is without prejudice to the possibility of bringing a joint action against the persons causing the harm. Lawsuits initiated to enforce claims against persons responsible for harm-causing to which immunity from fine was granted shall be stayed until the date on which the judgment made in the administrative lawsuit initiated upon request for a review of the decision of the HCO establishing an infringement becomes legally binding.

459. The following two features of section 88/D CA deserve attention. First, the new rule does not embrace both subsets of leniency (immunity from fines *and* reduction of the fine) but it is applicable exclusively to the whistle-blowing that results in a (full) immunity from fines. The undertaking qualifying for a penalty reduction is not granted any protection from civil law claims. This is partially explained by the fact that in this case, the illegality of the conduct has probably already been established. At the same time, nevertheless, the evidence submitted by the undertaking in order to qualify for a fine reduction has to represent significant added value in relation to the evidence already in the possession of the competition authority. Thereby, the evidence leading to penalty reduction may make the whistle-blower worse off from the perspective of civil law liability. The CA contains no protection in this regard.

460. Second, the liability of the undertaking that qualifies for immunity from fines becomes subsidiary in relation to the liability of the rest of the cartel. In this regard, it is to be stressed that the draft of section 88/D CA initially contained a different rule, which broke only with the joint and several liability of the whistle-blower, stating that the latter is liable only to the extent of its fault.[375] According to the Hungarian Civil Code, in case of concurrent tortfeasors, in the absence of proof to the contrary, it is to be presumed that the extent of the wrongdoers' fault is equal.[376] 'Liability according to the extent of the fault' is practically also part of the final version, although only implicitly. As the undertaking qualifying for immunity has subsidiary liability, the injured person will demand recovery from the rest of the cartel, who do have joint and several liability (joint tortfeasors). At the same time, the tortfeasors' liability, (including the successful immunity applicant), among

---

375. Ministry of Justice Doc No IRM/CKFO/437/2008.
376. Section 344(1)-(2) CC.

themselves, is determined according to the extent of their respective fault (contribution between tortfeasors).[377]

461. In terms of consequences, there is a real difference between the initial draft of section 88/D CA and the version finally adopted (and currently in force). If the tort claim cannot be collected from the rest of the cartel, the whistle-blower may be obliged to pay beyond the extent of its fault.

E. Stand-Alone Actions

462. Until 1 May 2004, stand-alone actions were not possible at all: on the basis of the then-effective provisions of the CA, the Supreme Court held that the HCO had exclusive competence to rule on the issue whether a particular behaviour violated the CA or not.[378] In case of stand-alone actions, the court was obliged to stay or end the procedure since section 152(1) CCP was applied, which provides that if the adjudication of the case depends on a decision on a prejudicial question, the court has to stay the procedure until the prejudicial question is decided. If the corresponding procedure for deciding the prejudicial question has not been started, the court determines a deadline within which the plaintiff has to institute the procedure. If the case concerned exclusively issues that came under the competence of the HCO, the court had to terminate the civil procedure due to lack of competence. Accordingly, if the case raised only competition law issues, the judicial procedure was terminated. Actions for damages raise both competition law (i.e., whether the action violates competition law) and civil law (i.e., whether damages can be claimed) questions; hence, courts ought to have stayed the procedure.

463. The above system was changed first regarding EU competition law as from 1 May 2004; namely, Article 6 of Regulation 1/2003 authorizes (and obliges) national courts to apply EU competition law, providing that 'national courts shall have the power to apply Articles 101 and 102 of the Treaty'. Section 91/H(1) CA confirms that Regulation 1/2003 has precedence over the provisions of the CA. Since it was unreasonable to maintain a bifurcated system for EU and Hungarian competition law, in 2005 a new section 88/A was introduced into the CA, which virtually empowers courts to adjudicate stand-alone claims, providing that '[t]he power of the Hungarian Competition Authority (...) to safeguard (...) the public interest shall not prevent civil law claims arising out of the infringement of the provisions

---

377. Both the wording and the policy considerations of the new s. 88/D suggest that it governs solely the relationship between the cartelists and the victims, while not touching upon the issue of contribution among tortfeasors. *See* Gábor Fejes & Zoltán Marosi, *Hungary*, in The International Comparative Legal Guide to: Competition Litigation 2013. 103 (5th ed., 2012); Csongor István Nagy, *Kártérítési felelősség kartelljogsértések esetén: gondolatok a Tpvt. új szabályai kapcsán*, 56(9) Magyar Jog 513–520 (2009). *Contra* Ch. Bán, *Az engedékenységi politika és a magánjogi igények kapcsolata*, in *Versenyjogi jogsértések – magánjogi jogkövetkezmények* 69 (Kisfaludi András ed., ELTE Eötvös Kiadó 2012).
378. Case *Pf. IV. 24 909/2000/1* (Supreme Court).

Part I, Ch. 5, Consequences of Violations 464–467

(...) [on unfair manipulation of business decisions, restrictive agreements and abuse of dominant position], from being enforced directly in court.'

F. Access to Evidence

464. Access to evidence is a crucial question in actions for damages. In stand-alone actions, the collection of evidence raises acute problems, since the civil claim is not antedated by an administrative investigation. The concept of pre-trial discovery is unknown to Hungarian civil procedure. Although there are some mechanisms that can be used for similar purposes, these are only very far substitutes of a pre-trial discovery.

465. By way of example, if certain documents are necessary, the person in possession of these documents can be summoned by the court as a witness; namely, the obligations of the witness, besides appearing before the court and testifying, also embrace the duty to produce the documents in his possession.[379] If the party does not know the witness, the court can oblige the opposing party to provide information on the name and the address of the witness, if it is substantiated that the opposing party knows or should know the witness. The court can oblige any of the parties to produce a deed in his possession, if the party is obliged to hand over or produce the deed according to the rules of civil law, especially if the deed was issued for the interest of the other party, it certifies a legal relationship relating to him or relates to a negotiation connected to such a legal relationship.[380] Section 8(2) CCP prohibits acts in bad faith; section 8(3) CCP provides that the court has to fine the party that makes false factual declarations or conceals important facts.

466. In follow-on actions, the plaintiff is in a better situation in terms of access to evidence. Before 1 July 2014, third parties had virtually no access to the administrative file. Although the CC's decision was published and disclosed important information that could be used in the civil proceeding, private parties had no access to the administrative file; accordingly, the only available document was the text of the decision.

467. Access to the administrative files was restricted to the parties of the procedure; even in this case, access was restricted to documents that had not been declared confidential by the HCO and that did not qualify as internal documents. Nevertheless, the victims of the competition law violation were not considered to be the parties of the administrative procedure. In restrictive agreement and dominant position cases, the undertaking against whom the administrative procedure was started qualified as a party. Accordingly, in these cases the victims of the infringement were not parties of the administrative procedure and, hence, had no access to the files of the case.[381] Nevertheless, in the course of the judicial procedure, the court could call the HCO to transmit all evidence that was at its disposal and was relevant for adjudicating

---

379. *See* s. 174(1) CCP.
380. *See* s. 190(2) CCP.
381. Section 52 and 55(1) CA.

the case at stake (and this is what actually happened in such follow-on cases). Furthermore, the language of the CA suggested that access to the file was restricted in terms of time even in respect of the parties. Section 55(1) CA provided that the party could access the file (make copies, take notes) during the procedure, after the completion of the investigation, from the date set by the CC. That is, this suggested that the parties could access the file only during the competition procedure but not after its termination.

468. The above provision, when applied to EU competition law cases, raised serious concerns in the context of the CJEU's ruling in *Donau Chemie*,[382] since it appeared to categorically exclude access to the file for third parties. In *Donau Chemie*, the CJEU held that the rule of Austrian law that made access to the competition matter's file subject to the assent of all parties to the competition proceeding is incompatible with EU law and with the principle of effectiveness:

> European Union law, in particular the principle of effectiveness, precludes a provision of national law under which access to documents forming part of the file relating to national proceedings concerning the application of Article 101 TFEU, including access to documents made available under a leniency programme, by third parties who are not party to those proceedings with a view to bringing an action for damages against participants in an agreement or concerted practice is made subject solely to the consent of all the parties to those proceedings, without leaving any possibility for the national courts of weighing up the interests involved.[383]

469. As from 1 July 2014, third parties can access the administrative file (as the CA puts this: the documents that came into existence during the procedure). Third parties, in principle, can access the file after the final completion of the procedure; before that, they can access it only in case access to the document is necessary for exercising a right or fulfilling an obligation based on a rule of law.[384] Furthermore, the HCO can reject the third party's access to the file, if access to the document would endanger the HCO's lawful mode of operation, the requirement that it does its duties without undue external influence or the effective pursuance of conducts violating Articles 101 and 102 TFEU and their national equivalents (sections 11 and 21 CA), in particular the leniency policy.[385] Accordingly, it is up to the HCO, whether it grants access to leniency documents for third parties; interestingly, the structure of the statutory provisions would suggest that the rejection of access should be the exception and not the rule.

470. Access to certain data is limited (e.g., business and private secrets).[386]

---

382. Case C-536/11.
383. Operative part.
384. Section 55(3) CA.
385. Section 55(4) CA.
386. Section 55/A CA.

Part I, Ch. 5, Consequences of Violations

471. The request to have access to the file is adjudicated in an order; if access is rejected, the applicant can appeal the order.[387]

G. Burden of Proof

472. In general, the plaintiff bears the burden of proof. In principle, the facts that are necessary for adjudicating the case are to be proved by the party that is interested in the court's accepting them as true.[388]

473. According to Hungarian delictual (tort) law, the plaintiff has to prove the occurrence of the conduct, its illegality, the occurrence and amount of the damages, and the causal link between the conduct in question and the damages suffered.[389] Section 88/B(7) CA slightly departs from the foregoing principle as to the question of illegality (i.e., whether the conduct violated competition law). It provides that in judicial actions:

> the burden of proving the facts evidencing an infringement of the provisions (...) [on unfair manipulation of business decisions, restrictive agreements and abuse of dominant position] shall rest on the party alleging the infringement; the burden of proving that the conditions for claiming the benefit of the application of a group exemption (...) or the conditions (...) [of an individual exemption] are fulfilled, shall rest on the party alleging this.

474. It is to be noted that the plaintiff's duty to prove the existence of an infringement is limited to stand-alone actions, since section 88/B(6) CA, contrary to the general principle,[390] provides that the final decisions of the HCO are binding on courts concerning the issue whether competition law was violated.

475. The legal test of delictual (tort) liability also embraces the requirement of fault. Furthermore, the requirement of foreseeability applies to causality: the causal link with the loss cannot be established if the wrongdoer did not foresee, nor ought to have foreseen it.[391] As to the questions of fault, the burden of proof rests on the wrongdoer. Although there is no specific rule on this, it is submitted that the burden of proof as to foreseeability[392] and as to passing-on[393] should rest on the defendant, since it is the defendant's interest to have these rules applied.

476. It is to be noted that under the old Civil Code (which was replaced by the new Civil Code as from 15 March 2014), the burden of proof concerning the passing-on defence was unsettled. One position was that the question of whether the

---

387. Section 55/B CA.
388. Section 164(1) CCP.
389. Section 6:519 CC.
390. Section 4(1) CCP.
391. Section 6:521 CC.
392. Section 6:521 CC.
393. Section 6:522(3) CC.

costs were passed on was part of the 'amount of damages' element, and, hence, it was the plaintiff who bore the burden of proof. The person liable for damages had to restore the injured person to the initial status. Therefore, the situation was to be determined that would have emerged in the absence of the tort, and this was the point at which the passing-on defence was relevant. The latter was connected to the definition of damage: if the injured person passed some of the costs caused by the wrongdoing onto his customers, the costs passed on were obviously not part of the loss the injured person suffered. Another position could be that the passing-on argument was the defence of the defendant and as it was the latter who raised the issue in the procedure it was him who bore the burden of proof in this regard. Unfortunately, there was no judicial practice in this regard.

H. Interim Measures

477. The court, upon request, can order with an interim measure the performance of the claim (counter-claim) and of what is requested in the application for interim measure, if this is necessary for obviating a direct danger of damages or for preserving the situation that gave rise to the legal dispute, as well as if the applicant's legal protection of particular appreciation makes this necessary, and the detriments entailed by the interim measure do not exceed the advantages that can be achieved. The applicant has to present a prima facie case, i.e., the applicant has to prove that the facts the application is based on are likely to have occurred.[394]

478. The court can make the adoption of the interim measure dependent on the provision of a security.[395]

479. The application for interim measures cannot be submitted before the statement of claims is submitted. The court has to decide on the application as soon as possible and can do this before the first hearing.[396]

480. Before making a decision, the court has to hear the parties and enable them to submit a written declaration concerning the application. The hearing of the parties can be skipped only in case of extreme urgency and in case the party fails to meet a deadline or does not attend the court in the time ordered by the court.[397]

481. When adjudicating the application for interim measures, the court can take evidence only if it cannot assess the application without this.[398]

---

394. Section 156(1) CCP.
395. Section 156(1) CCP.
396. Section 156(2)-(3) CCP.
397. Section 156(4) CCP.
398. Section 156(5) CCP.

482. The court adjudicates the application for interim measures in an order, which is appealable. The court can amend the order upon request and on its own motion in the event the plaintiff reduces his claim.[399]

483. The deadline set for performance starts on the day after the order was served in writing.[400]

484. The order becomes immediately enforceable (i.e., it becomes enforceable once adopted and remains enforceable even if appealed) and remains in force until the court overrules it upon the request of one of the parties and after hearing the opposing party or quashes it in its judgment. Namely, once the court adopts final measures in its judgment, the interim measures become needless. If the court of first instance does not quash its interim measures in the judgment or order terminating the procedure, the interim measures expire once the judgment or order terminating the procedure becomes final and conclusive (res judicata).[401]

§3. CRIMINAL ENFORCEMENT

485. Under Hungarian law, with the exception of restrictive agreements concluded in public procurement and concession proceedings, the violation of competition rules does not qualify as a criminal act. Accordingly, apart from the foregoing exceptions, the natural persons who contribute to the violation (i.e., the direct 'perpetrators' of the violation of competition law) face no personal liability, and all legal sanctions (administrative fine, damages and exclusion from public tenders) apply only to the undertaking but not to its directors, decision-makers or representatives.

486. Hungarian law provides for criminal sanctions to be imposed on legal persons in case an employee commits a criminal act. Accordingly, in case a restrictive agreement or concerted practice is concluded or occurs in a public procurement and concession proceeding, not only the direct perpetrator but also the company may face criminal sanctions.

487. It is to be noted that the criminal enforcement of competition law is highly under-developed: since the introduction of the criminal prohibition in 2005 (this rule applies as from 1 September 2005), according to the available information, no one has ever been convicted under this provision.

488. In 2008, the Hungarian parliament adopted an amendment to the CA, which, among others, envisaged introducing an occupational ban for the executives of cartelist companies. However, the Constitutional Court quashed these provisions, finding them unconstitutional.

---

399. Section 156(6) CCP.
400. Section 156(7) CCP.
401. Section 156(8) CCP.

I. Criminal Sanctions in Case of Restrictive Agreements in Public Procurement and Concession Proceedings

489. The criminal prohibition of restrictive agreements in public tenders and concession procedures was introduced in 2005 (effective as from 1 September 2005). The provision was included in section 296/B of the old Criminal Code, entitled 'Agreement in restraint of competition in public procurement and concession procedures'. In 2012, the Hungarian parliament adopted a new Criminal Code (Act C of 2012), which reiterated the same statutory language in section 420.

490. The person who, so as to manipulate the result of a public procurement procedure or of an open or closed tender published in respect to an activity that can be pursued only on the basis of a concession, concludes an agreement or engages in concerted practice concerning the fixing of the prices, fees, other contractual conditions or the division of the market and thereby restricts competition, may be liable to imprisonment for a term between one and five years. The same punishment applies if someone, so as to manipulate the result of a public procurement procedure or that of an open or closed tender published in respect to an activity that can be pursued only on the basis of a concession, takes part in the adoption of a decision of an association of undertakings that restricts competition.[402]

491. The punishment is milder if the above is committed in respect of a public procurement value not exceeding HUF 50 million. In this case, the perpetrator is liable to imprisonment for a term not exceeding two years.[403]

492. Section 420 of the Criminal Code reconciles the criminal punishment with the operation of the leniency policy, giving the perpetrator the same (full or partial) immunity from criminal liability as his enterprise receives from competition law liability.

493. First, the perpetrator cannot be punished if he reports the above acts to the authority and reveals the circumstances of the commission before the criminal authority gains knowledge. This option is independent of the operation of the leniency rules under competition law: it is available also in cases the undertaking connected to the perpetrator submits no leniency application.[404]

494. Second, the perpetrator is not punishable if the undertaking submits a successful leniency application for full immunity from the competition fine: the undertaking's executives, members, supervisory board members, employees and their agents (who had this status at the time the act was committed) cannot be punished if the undertaking, before the institution of the HCO's competition proceeding, submits a successful leniency application entailing full immunity from the fine and reveals the circumstances of the commission. It is to be noted that according to the CA, an undertaking may

---

402. Section 420(1)-(2) of the Criminal Code.
403. Sections 420(3) and 459(6) of the Criminal Code.
404. Section 420(4) Criminal Code.

Part I, Ch. 5, Consequences of Violations 495–498

be granted full immunity from the fine also in case the application is submitted after the institution of the competition proceeding (albeit it is certainly more difficult for the undertaking to comply with the requirements imposed against full immunity). On the other hand, immunity from criminal liability is available only if the undertaking submitted the leniency application before the institution of the competition procedure; that is, if the leniency application is submitted after the start of the proceeding, the undertaking may but the perpetrator may not automatically benefit from a full immunity from the punishment.[405]

495. Third, the punishment can be reduced with no restrictions and in case it is particularly equitable the perpetrator may be exempted from it, if the undertaking submits a leniency application for full or partial immunity: the punishment of the undertaking's executives, members, supervisory board members, employees and their agents (who had this status at the time the act was committed) can be reduced or put aside if the undertaking submits a successful leniency application to the HCO that entails full or partial immunity from the fine and reveals the circumstances of the commission.[406]

496. It is to be noted that under this provision it is irrelevant when the application for full immunity was submitted, that is, whether before or after the institution of the competition proceeding; however, as in the event the submission predates the institution of the proceeding, the perpetrator is automatically entitled to full immunity, this provision in fact applies only to cases where the application for full immunity is submitted after the procedure's institution and where an application for partial immunity is submitted.

497. Accordingly, it is to be noted that the restriction in terms of time, included in point two above, does not completely deprive the perpetrator of the perspective of a full immunity, albeit if the leniency application for full immunity is submitted after the procedure's institution, it comes under the court's discretion whether it grants this benefit: if it is equitable, the court may still decide to grant full immunity; failing this, the perpetrator is automatically entitled to a reduction in the criminal punishment. Furthermore, it is to be noted as well that the perpetrator may be granted full immunity from criminal liability (if the court finds that this is equitable) even in case the undertaking submitted merely an application for partial immunity. In sum, in cases where the application for full immunity is submitted after the institution of the competition proceeding and where an application for partial immunity is submitted, the perpetrator may be granted full immunity on an equitable basis and, in any case, he is automatically entitled to a partial immunity.

498. As to the practical application of the above criminal prohibition, it is to be noted that no one has been convicted under section 296/B of the old Criminal Code and under section 420 of the Criminal Code since this provision's (or its predecessor's) entry into force on 1 September 2005. This is probably due to the differences between

---

405. Section 420(5) Criminal Code.
406. Section 420(6) Criminal Code.

the standards of proof in administrative and criminal matters. Although the CC has condemned cartels concluded in public procurement in numerous matters, the evidence sufficient for an administrative fine may not be sufficient for establishing criminal liability. While the threshold of proof is pretty low in cartel cases, in criminal matters the 'beyond reasonable doubt' standard applies.

II. Criminal Sanctions on Undertakings

499. Under Hungarian law, there are no specific criminal sanctions on undertakings for the breach of the competition rules. However, legal persons have criminal liability in certain cases, where a natural person connected to the legal person commits a criminal act. Since, as noted above, restrictive agreements in public procurement and concession proceedings amount to a criminal act, an undertaking runs the risk of facing derivative criminal liability if a person connected to it gets involved in a restrictive agreement.

500. Act CIV of 2001 on the criminal law measures applicable to legal persons establishes certain measures, which can – under certain circumstance – be applied to legal persons if there is a certain link between the wrongdoer and the legal person, and the former committed a criminal act. The link between the wrongdoer and the legal person is defined as follows:

– the commission of the criminal act aimed at or entailed a benefit to the legal person or the criminal act was committed with the use of the legal person and the criminal act was committed by the legal person's executive, the legal person's member or employee authorized to represent the legal person, the legal person's officer, general manager (*'cégvezető'*), the member of the supervisory board or the agent of these in the legal person's field of operation;[407]
– the criminal act was committed by the legal person's member or employee (i.e., member or employee having no right of representation; members and employees having a right of representation are covered by the preceding point), and the commission of the criminal act could have been prevented if the legal person's executive, general manager or the supervisory board had fulfilled its controlling or supervisory duties;[408]
– apart from the above cases, the measures set out in the Act can be applied also if the commission of the criminal act conferred a benefit on the legal person or the criminal act was committed with the use of the legal person, and the legal person's executive, member or employee who was authorized to represent the company, as well as its officer, general manager or a member of the supervisory board was aware of the commission of the criminal act.[409]

---

407. Section 2(1)(a) of Act CIV of 2001.
408. Section 2(1)(b) of Act CIV of 2001.
409. Section 2(2) of Act CIV of 2001.

Part I, Ch. 5, Consequences of Violations　　　　　　　　　　　　　　**501–503**

III. Occupational Ban[410]

501. In 2008, the Hungarian parliament enacted a statute amending the CA, which envisaged establishing, among others, a personal punishment for the executive officers of cartelist enterprises (occupational ban for two years).[411] Nevertheless, this provision raised constitutional concerns on the part of the head of state (president), former chief justice of the Constitutional Court, who – instead of promulgation – sent the amendment to the Constitutional Court in the frame of a preliminary constitutional control. The Constitutional Court held that the challenged provisions of the amendment fell foul of the Constitution; hence, the text reverted to the Parliament, which re-enacted it in March 2009; in order to avoid any further delay and complication, the rules on occupational ban were not revised but deleted. This time the amendment was promulgated without further ado. There has been no legislative initiative to introduce an occupational ban since the Constitutional Court's judgment, albeit probably the initial provisions could have been made constitutional with relatively slight corrections (see below).

502. The provisions concerned were destined to introduce a special punishment for the executives of cartelist enterprises (companies and cooperatives): they would have been enjoined from working as an executive officer for two years ('occupational ban') if the enterprise was caught in participating in a horizontal hard-core cartel.[412] As noted above, in Hungary cartels are generally not pursued by criminal law, with the exception of cartels relating to concession procedures and public procurement.[413] There has been no endeavour to utterly criminalize Hungarian antitrust; instead, the introduction of the above special deterrence was favoured.

503. Besides the personal sanction, the above amendment also introduced a very odd procedure, and intrinsically this was the source of constitutional concerns. The new provisions provided that once an enterprise is finally and conclusively condemned for a horizontal hard-core cartel, all its executive officers are caught in the net of the new regime, i.e., the enterprise's participation in the hard-core cartel was rebuttably presumed to be attributable to all its executive officers, which were to be identified in an HCO order, issued after the final and conclusive closure of the proceedings. Afterwards, an executive officer had only two ways of escape: first, he could prove that he was not the enterprise's executive officer during the period in question; second, he could try to prove that he did not take part directly in the decision-making that led to the participation in the violation, or even if having taken part in the decision-making, he did object to it. Direct involvement could be falsified by simply proving that the operation concerned by the violation was not part of his fields of responsibility, except the evidence at disposal confirmed that he did actually take part in the decision-making.

---

410. This section is based on the author's following article: Csongor István Nagy, *The Constitutional Court Condemned Hungarian Statute Imposing 'Occupational Ban' on Executives of Cartelist Companies*, 30(8) Eur. Comp. Law Rev. (2009).
411. Bill No T-5657.
412. Only horizontal price-fixing and market sharing agreements were covered by the provisions in question.
413. Section 420 of the Criminal Code.

504. Nonetheless, the executive officers were not only hit by the 'presumption of guilt', bearing the burden of proof in this regard; they also encountered fairly restrictive evidentiary rules, diminishing their arsenal of defence. The above presumption could indeed be challenged before courts, but the pattern of procedure applicable was highly summary. The executive officer's appeal was to be adjudicated in the frame of a non-contentious procedure ('*nemperes eljárás*'),[414] which is an *ex parte* summary procedure lacking several elements of an ordinary trial, where normally no parole evidence can be introduced: the statute governing these proceedings provides that except otherwise provided by a special piece of legislation only documentary evidence can be submitted to the court. Accordingly, no full-blown trial was afforded to the challenge of the 'presumption of guilt'.

505. The Constitutional Court analysed the new provisions on the basis of the right to a fair trial and the presumption of innocence and found them unconstitutional. It concluded that the nature of the sanction imposed, being based on personal responsibility and having a *quasi*-criminal character, demanded a full-blown judicial review. It is the enterprise that is the addressee of the administrative proceedings in the frame of which the HCO applies competition law and these proceedings do not concern the issue of the executive officers' *actus reus* (personal responsibility). While the new provisions were based on the proposition that the executive officers were inevitably responsible for the breach of competition law, they did not afford discretionary powers to the HCO as regards the application of the sanction or the period of the ban. The entire issue of personal liability was left to the court procedure, which was, nevertheless, an *ex parte*, summary proceeding. The merits of the case could be examined only in the phase before the court, while the rules of evidence were fairly restricted here: the procedure was non-contentious, there was no adversary trial (solely a simple, *ex parte* court hearing), and only documentary evidence was admissible. Accordingly, the executive officers were deprived of the right to challenge the merits of the case, whilst their personal involvement was not clarified in the administrative proceedings against the enterprise concerned.

506. In respect to the aftermath of the Constitutional Court's judgment, it is to be noted that the HCO and the Hungarian parliament has not re-tried to introduce an occupational ban against the executive officers of cartelist enterprises, although such an approach would not be irreconcilable with Hungarian law (since participation in hard-core cartels relating to concession proceedings and public procurement does qualify as a crime under Hungarian criminal law) and the Constitutional Court seems to have suggested that the endeavour to punish cartelists personally and the reversing of the burden of proof under the above circumstances are, in principle, in conformity with the Hungarian Constitution and, hence, acceptable.

---

414. Non-contentious civil procedures resemble the German '*freiwillige Gerichtsbarkeit*', nevertheless, in Hungary not all matters covered by this regime get to court *freiwillig* (voluntarily). Non-contentious procedures also embrace, for instance, bankruptcy proceedings.

IV. Role of Prosecutors and Competent Criminal Courts

507. As noted above, cartels concerning public tenders and concession procedures are prohibited by criminal law. Hungarian criminal procedure consists of three phases: investigations phase, normally carried out by the police, public prosecutor's phase and judicial phase. The operations of the police are supervised and controlled by the public prosecutor. The investigation (or parts of it) can be executed also by the public prosecutor. The prosecutor is in charge of submitting the indictment to the court. Cartels concerning public tenders and concession procedures come under the competence of local courts; the judgments of the local court can be appealed to county courts, while county court judgments can be attacked before the Courts of Appeals.[415] The judgment of the Court of Appeals can be attacked with a plea for supervision, which is an extraordinary appeal coming under the competence of the Supreme Court.[416]

§4. EXCLUSION FROM PUBLIC TENDERS AS A SANCTION (DEBARMENT)

508. Cartelist enterprises can be excluded from public tenders. Section 57(1)(b) of the Act on Public Procurement specifically provides for the possibility to exclude from public tenders those undertakings that engaged in bid-rigging (as to public or private tenders). This is a facultative basis of exclusion; it is up to the tenderer whether it includes this exclusion into the call. However, the Public Procurement Council interprets section 57(1)(a) of the Act on Public Procurement, which contains a more general ground of exclusion, in a way that it may be used to exclude those cartelists from public tenders that are not covered by section 57(1)(b) of the Act on Public Procurement, provided the violation is established in a court judgment.

509. According to section 57(1)(b) of the Act on Public Procurement,

> The contracting authority may stipulate in the notice launching the procedure that the following economic operators are excluded from participating in the procedure as a tenderer, a candidate, a subcontractor, and may not contribute to the certification of suitability (...) who have violated the law under Article 11 of CA, or according to Article 101 of the Treaty on the Functioning of the European Union, and this fact has been stipulated in the final and enforceable decision of the Hungarian Competition Office – delivered within the previous five years —, or in the event of the court review of the decision of the Hungarian Competition Office, by a final judgment of the court, and have been issued a pecuniary penalty; or if the establishment of such violation of the law by the tenderer has been ascertained by a final decision and a pecuniary penalty of another competition office or court within the previous five years.[417]

---

415. Section 13 of the Criminal Code.
416. Section 416 of the Criminal Code.
417. Translation of the Public Procurement Authority, available at http://kozbeszerzes.hu/data/documents/2014/07/16/PPA_2014_07_16.pdf.

510. Accordingly, the contracting authority can (but is not obliged to) stipulate in the tender notice that an enterprise cannot be a tenderer, an offerer for participation, a subcontractor or an economic entity participating in the certification of eligibility, if in a final and enforceable HCO decision not older than five years or in case of the HCO decision's judicial review in a final and enforceable (res judicata) judgment not older than five years it was established that in the frame of a tender it committed an offence under section 11 CA or Article 101 TFEU and a fine was imposed; the same rules apply to tenderers if the decision or judgment was rendered by another competition authority or court.[418]

511. It is to be noted that the foregoing provision refers to 'tenders' in general, which may be either public or private.

512. Furthermore, it is to be highlighted that the above rule applies only if the commission of the mischief was established and a fine was imposed. Accordingly, if the leniency applicant is awarded full immunity from the fine, it cannot be excluded from public tenders on the basis of the above: although the HCO's final decision will establish the undertaking's involvement in the violation, it will impose no fine. On the other hand, leniency applicants receiving partial immunity are not excluded from the purview of the above provision, since they are imposed a fine, even if a reduced one.

513. As noted above, section 57(1)(a) of the Act on Public Procurement contains a more general ground of exclusion.

> 1. The contracting authority may stipulate in the notice launching the procedure that the following economic operators are excluded from participating in the procedure as a tenderer, a candidate, a subcontractor, and may not contribute to the certification of suitability:
>
> (a) who have violated the law concerning their business activities or professional conduct and this fact has been stipulated in a final judgment delivered within the previous five years.

514. In Case *D.224/11/2012.*, the Public Procurement Council held that section 57(1)(a) of the Act on Public Procurement can be used by the contracting authority to exclude from the public tender undertakings that committed a serious violation not referred to in section 57(1)(b) of the Act on Public Procurement. In this case, an insurance company was excluded from a public tender because it was condemned for entering into restrictive agreements with repair shops and insurance brokers; relationships that certainly do not qualify as horizontal but rather as vertical. With this, the Public Procurement Council, unfortunately, disregarded fundamental principles of statutory interpretation, like *lex specialis derogat legi generali* and legislative intent (the purpose of section 57(1)(b) of the Act on Public Procurement was to address violations of competition law under a specific heading); the approach that section 57(1)(a) of the

---

418. Section 57(1)(b) of the Act on Public Procurement.

Part I, Ch. 5, Consequences of Violations

Act on Public Procurement covers all violations of competition law, including the ones not covered by section 57(1)(b), deprives the latter of all functions and reason. Furthermore, this construction of the statute may entail controversial situations and anomalies. First, section 57(1)(a) of the Act on Public Procurement, as constructed by the Public Procurement Council, may be applied to all competition law violations, that is, abuse of dominant position and merger control infringements (e.g., unlawful implementation of an authorizable concentration). Second, section 57(1)(a) of the Act on Public Procurement applies only if the violation was established in a final court judgment, while section 57(1)(b) applies also in case this occurs in a CC decision, provided, of course, it is not attacked before the court. This implies that if an enterprise condemned by the CC does not attack the administrative decision, section 57(1)(a) of the Act on Public Procurement would not apply; if it committed a violation not covered by section 57(1)(b) (e.g., any cartel apart from bid-rigging), it can avoid debarment simply by not attacking the administrative decision; or the other way around: with the exercise of its constitutional right of appeal, it automatically undergoes the risk of a severe public procurement sanction. Finally, it is to be noted that section 57(1)(a) of the Act on Public Procurement applies also to cases where no fine is imposed but the court merely establishes the illegality of the conduct. In some cases, the CC may establish the illegality of the conduct without imposing a fine. Such cases might be covered by section 57(1)(a) of the Act on Public Procurement if attacked before the court and that latter affirms the illegality of the conduct; however, it is to be noted that the Public Procurement Council's decision suggests that section 57(1)(a) applies only to serious infringements. Furthermore, it is noteworthy that while section 57(1)(b) does not apply in case of a successful leniency application for immunity from the fine, section 57(1)(a) contains no such restriction (as it applies also in case no fine was imposed). So, at least theoretically, section 57(1)(a) could lift the protection section 57(1)(b) affords to such whistle-blowers. However, as a matter of practice, it is unlikely that such scenarios would emerge in practice, since section 57(1)(a) applies only in case the illegality is established in a court judgment; and successful leniency applicant rarely attack administrative decisions granting them full immunity.

Part II. Application of the Prohibitions

Chapter 1. Restrictive Agreements

§1. HORIZONTAL AGREEMENTS

I. Cartels

515. Cartels, i.e., horizontal hardcore agreements, qualify as restrictions by object and are, as such, outright condemned, without an effects-analysis. Although, at theoretically, even horizontal hardcore agreements can benefit from an individual exemption under section 17, in practice, they have no realistic chance to escape condemnation.

A. Price-Fixing

516. Horizontal price-fixing agreements are considered anti-competitive by object.[419] They are prohibited irrespective of the parties' market share.

B. Market/Client Allocation

517. Horizontal market-sharing agreements are anti-competitive by object.[420] They are prohibited irrespective of the parties' market share.

518. Market sharing encompasses both territorial division and customer-allocation agreements.

519. In Case *Vj-28/2003 Baucont and others*,[421] the CC characterized 'mirror contracts' between undertakings participating in the same tender as anti-competitive by object: here, the enterprises agreed that the winner will hire the unsuccessful bidders as sub-contractors.[422]

---

419. Case *Vj-64/2000 Délhús and others*; Case *Vj-92/2003 Mentők és Betegszállítók Országos Egyesülete*.
420. Case *Vj-74/2004 Construm és Royal Bau*, para. 89.
421. *See* Case *Vj-154/2002 Baucont, Klíma-Vill. és Középületépítő*.
422. Paragraphs 81 and 83.

520. In Case *Vj-74/2004 Construm and Royal Bau*, the CC established that it qualifies as market-sharing if two bidders of a public tender agree on which of them will submit the better offer.[423]

521. In Case *Vj-162/2004 SAP Hungary*, some enterprises cooperated in order to win jointly on public tenders: they agreed to submit offers in parallel, jointly influenced the drafting of the calls and conducted anti-competitive negotiations.[424]

522. In the context of section 13 CA, embedding the *de minimis* rule, the CC held that taking into account that this occurred in connection with a public tender, it qualified as horizontal market-sharing and excluded competition between team members and restricted the possibilities of outsider undertakings.[425]

C. *Production/Innovation Limitation*

523. Production/innovation limitation agreements qualify as anti-competitive by object. They are prohibited irrespective of the parties' market share.

D. *Group Boycott*

524. There is no specific practice on group boycotts in Hungarian competition law. Taking into account that the status of such practices is not clear under EU competition law[426] either and they may have various targets, it is likely that the CC would take a differentiated approach as to them.

E. *Collusion on Other Objects*

525. The list of horizontal hardcore agreements is not exhaustive and the CC may regard any type of agreement as anti-competition by object on a case-by-case basis, provided it meets the general test of anti-competitive object. This approach of the CC was endorsed by the CJEU in *Allianz*,[427] where it held that:

---

423. Paragraph 89.
424. Paragraph 1. In this case, the agreements had two layers. The undertakings concerned concluded a cooperation framework agreement (teaming agreement). However, the CC established that the competition investigation addressed not solely the teaming agreement, in particular the issue whether this arrangement qualifies as a common research and development entailing a new product. It was not the teaming agreement the decision pronounced illegal but the cooperation between the defendants based on the teaming, aiming at jointly winning on the public tenders published by the universities, that violated s. 11 CA. para 367.
425. Paragraph 435.
426. Richard Whish, *Competition Law* 535–538 (OUP 2009).
427. Case C-32/11 *Allianz, Generali and others v GVH*, not published yet.

Part II, Ch. 1, Restrictive Agreements 526–527

[i]n order to determine whether an agreement involves a restriction of competition 'by object', regard must be had to the content of its provisions, its objectives and the economic and legal context of which it forms a part. When determining that context, it is also appropriate to take into consideration the nature of the goods or services affected, as well as the real conditions of the functioning and structure of the market or markets in question.

526. According to the CJEU, an agreement:

can be considered to be a restriction of competition 'by object' within the meaning of that provision, where, following a concrete and individual examination of the wording and aim of those agreements and of the economic and legal context of which they form a part, it is apparent that they are, by their very nature, injurious to the proper functioning of normal competition on one of the two markets concerned.[428]

This approach, if used intensively, is expected to make the application of the law extremely unpredictable.[429]

II. Information Exchange Practices

527. The treatment of information exchange practices under Hungarian competition law is complex. According to the judicial practice, albeit the exchange of pricing information may warrant a more stringent treatment, the HCO has to prove that the exchange of information was capable of having a negative impact on competition in the market. This may suggest an effects-based approach as to information-sharing, with the exception of the exchange of pricing data. It is to be noted that the exchange of certain data, in particular commercially sensitive data, information on future conduct, could qualify as an implied cartel (e.g., price-fixing)[430] or lead to the establishing of a concerted practice.[431] Accordingly, although the exchange of information can be condemned only if it is susceptible of restricting competition, the exchange of commercially sensitive information may come under one of the per se categories (e.g., agreement or concerted practice to fix the price). Therewith, the difference between Hungarian and EU competition law practice as to information-sharing is slight and mainly notional. Under EU competition law, the exchange of certain data may qualify as a restriction by object, while the rest of information-exchanges can be condemned only if having

---

428. Paragraph 51.
429. Csongor István Nagy, *The Distinction between Anti-competitive Object and Effect after Allianz: The End of Coherence in Competition Analysis?*, 36(4) World Comp. Law and Eco. Rev. 4 (2013).
430. For cases where information-exchange was connected to a hardcore agreement (price-fixing, market-division), *see* Case *Vj-56/2004/190*, paras 134–135, Case *Vj-199/2005/246*, Case *Vj-20/2005/47*, paras 115–118.
431. For cases where the exchange of information was connected to a concerted practice concerning prices, *see* Case *Vj-130/2006/239*, paras 408–409, Case *Vj-34/2003/73*, para. 40, Case *Vj-83/2005/100*, Case *Vj-138/2002*, Case *Vj-57/2007/432*.

a restrictive effect.[432] Under Hungarian competition law, although the HCO can condemn the exchange of information only if it demonstrates that is capable of having a restrictive effect on competition (potential effect), the exchange of commercially sensitive information may serve as a basis for establishing an anti-competitive agreement, e.g., an agreement or concerted practice to fix the price. Furthermore, the approach spelled out in the Commission's Horizontal Guidelines (which, in historical sense, introduced a somewhat novel approach in EU competition law as to information exchange, providing that the exchange of commercially sensitive data is an independent category of agreements restrictive by object), may have a spillover effect on how the HCO and Hungarian courts grasp the treatment of information exchange agreements.

528. Hungarian courts dealt with the issue of horizontal information-exchange extensively in Case *Cement cartel*[433] and adopted a rather lenient approach as to information exchange between competitors. Here, the Hungarian Association of the Cement Industry collected from producers, on a monthly basis, data on quantity concerning production, sales and storage. However, no data was collected in respect of the prices and the territorial division of the sales.[434]

529. The HCO found that the information-exchange was illegal; however, the Budapest Court reversed the decision and quashed the finding of illegality on the basis of the specific set of facts.[435] The Budapest Court of Appeals[436] and the Supreme Court[437] affirmed this judgment.

530. Nevertheless, the HCO's decision is still instructive as to the main aspect to be taken into account when assessing information exchange arrangements between competitors. The HCO's decision enumerated the following factors that have to be taken into consideration when assessing the anti-competitive effects of the exchange of information: the characteristics of the data (what they relate to), how detailed they are, the age of the data, the frequency of the information-flow, the structure of the market (primarily the number of market operators).[438]

531. The HCO's decision was not clear as to whether it regarded the information-sharing anti-competitive by object or by effect; however, the Budapest Court's judgment suggests that in case of information-exchange the effects (including potential effects) have to be examined.[439] The Court held that the exchange is illegal only if the information is capable of influencing the market in an illegal way or distorting it. This phrasing suggests that an analysis into the potential effects cannot be saved.

---

432. Guidelines on Horizontal Cooperation Agreements, paras 72 and 75.
433. Case *Vj-73/2001*.
434. Paragraph 17.
435. Case *3.K.33417/2006/20* (Budapest Court).
436. Case *2.Kf.27.578/2008/12* (Budapest Court of Appeals).
437. Case *Kfv.III.37.514/2009/11* (Supreme Court).
438. *See* HCO's Position Statement No. 11.16. (Case *Vj-73/2001*.).
439. *See* para. 46.

Part II, Ch. 1, Restrictive Agreements

532. The Court established that the HCO failed to prove that the information had or might have had any impact. Since the database contained no prices, the HCO could not base its position on unproved speculation. The flow of information, in itself, does not imply the breach of competition law. The language of the judgment suggests that the exchange of pricing data may warrant a different treatment.

533. The exchange of information has to be assessed through the prism of the competition-problem such arrangements may raise. According to the HCO's decision, competition law expects undertaking to render their market decisions independently; the exchange of information, in case it makes possible the prediction of the future prices of competitors, switches off an element of uncertainty in the market and, thus, may restrict competition.[440] This suggests that the exchange of information may raise competitive concerns only in case of certain market structures, in particular oligopolistic markets.[441] In this case, the CC came to the conclusion that the market was fairly concentrated and had an oligopolistic structure.[442]

534. The Budapest Court held that the exchange of information is not unlawful, if the undertakings could obtain the information from other sources; it also established that, in this regard, the burden of proof rests on the HCO.

III. Cooperation Agreements

535. Cooperation agreements, provided they do not qualify as hardcore, have to be assessed on the basis of their effects; accordingly, in such cases an effects-analysis is to be conducted. However, the government adopted block-exemption regulations in respect of research and development agreements (Hungarian R&D BER) and specialization agreements (Hungarian Specialisation BER), which are essentially in line with their EU counterparts.

A. Research and Development

536. The Hungarian R&D BER covers not only research and development collaborations in narrower sense but also the joint exploitation of the results.[443] The R&D activity may be carried out by the parties jointly or may be contracted out (outsourcing).[444] The R&D agreement may cover both R&D and exploitation or only one of them; however, the block exemption covers only those joint exploitation collaborations that are related to an earlier research and development cooperation between the same parties. Accordingly, the block exemption covers the following arrangements: joint R&D and the joint exploitation of the results, joint exploitation of the results of an

---

440. Paragraph 45.
441. Paragraphs 52 and 56.
442. Paragraph 53.
443. Section 1(10) of Gov. Reg. 206/2011.
444. Section 1(5) of Gov. Reg. 206/2011.

earlier R&D, joint R&D without joint exploitation, outsourced (paid) R&D and the joint exploitation of the results, joint exploitation of the results of an earlier outsourced (paid) R&D, outsourced (paid) R&D without joint exploitation.[445] The block exemption extends to the transfer or licensing of intellectual property connected to the R&D agreement.[446]

537. The Hungarian R&D BER, for the application of the block exemption, sets out both substantive conditions (related to the agreements' content) and market share conditions.

538. For instance, in principle, all participating undertakings have to have access to the results of the R&D,[447] albeit the restriction of access is acceptable under certain circumstances.[448]

539. Furthermore, the block exemption does not apply if the R&D agreement contains a hardcore restraint.[449] In case of a black-listed restraint, the block exemption's benefit is lost only as regards the incriminated contractual clause.[450]

540. Hungarian R&D BER establishes different market share caps as to agreements between non-competitors and competitors. In case of non-competitors, the block exemption covers the entire period of the R&D, as well as the first seven years of the joint exploitation (as from the time the products or technologies were first put into circulation).[451] In case of competitors (if two or more of the participating undertakings are competitors), the block exemption applies during the foregoing period only if the parties' joint market share, on the relevant product and technology markets, does not exceed 25% at the time of the R&D agreements conclusion.[452] After the end of the above period, the block exemption applies if the parties' market share is less than 25%.[453]

B. Specialization

541. Specialization agreements are covered by the safe harbour of the Hungarian Specialisation BER, which is in line with its EU counterpart. The Hungarian Specialisation BER defines specialization agreements as agreements between competitors where one of the undertakings specializes in the production of a commodity or the undertakings produce the commodity jointly.

---

445. Section 1(11) of Gov. Reg. 206/2011.
446. Section 2(2) of Gov. Reg. 206/2011.
447. Section 3(1) of Gov. Reg. 206/2011.
448. Section 3(2)-(4) of Gov. Reg. 206/2011.
449. Section 6 of Gov. Reg. 206/2011.
450. Section 7 of Gov. Reg. 206/2011.
451. Section 4(1) of Gov. Reg. 206/2011.
452. Section 4(2) of Gov. Reg. 206/2011.
453. Section 4(3) of Gov. Reg. 206/2011.

542. The Hungarian Specialisation BER distinguishes between unilateral and reciprocal specialization agreements and joint production agreements.[454] In case of a unilateral specialization agreement, one of the undertakings agrees to stop, fully or partially, producing a certain commodity and to acquire it from the other undertaking, which, in turn, agrees to produce and supply these goods.[455] A reciprocal specialization agreement is an agreement concluded by undertakings active in the same relevant market where at least two undertakings mutually agree to stop, fully or partially, producing certain commodities that are different from each other and to purchase these commodities from another contracting undertaking, which agrees to produce and supply them.[456] In case of a joint production, the undertakings participating in the agreement agree to produce certain commodities jointly.[457]

543. The block exemption applies if the joint market share of the contracting undertakings does not exceed 20% in any of the relevant markets affected by the agreement[458] and the agreement contains no hardcore restrictions, such as the fixing of the prices in respect of the sales to undertakings not being part of the agreement, the restriction of production or marketing, the division of the market or of customers. However, the restriction does not qualify as hardcore, if it is ancillary to the specialization agreement or the joint distribution, such as the determination of the prices charged against direct purchasers in frame of joint distribution, dispositions on the products' agreed quantity in the frame of unilateral or reciprocal specialization agreements, the determination of the capacity and production quantity in the frame of a joint production agreement, determination of sales targets in case of joint distribution.[459]

544. The block exemption also covers certain restrictions ancillary to the specialization agreement: dispositions on the transfer or licensing of intellectual property rights,[460] connected exclusive purchasing and supply obligations, the distribution of the goods produced in the frame of the specialization agreement;[461] the term 'joint distribution' covers not only the case when the parties appoint a third (non-competing) undertaking to distribute the goods but also the case when this is accomplished through a common working group, organization or enterprise.

C. *Joint Production, Joint Purchasing and Joint Selling*

545. Joint production, purchasing and selling (commercialization), in principle, do not qualify as restrictions by object and, accordingly, have to be assessed on the basis of their impact on the market (effects-analysis).

---

454. Section 1(15) of Gov. Reg. 202/2011.
455. Section 1(2) of Gov. Reg. 202/2011.
456. Section 1(10) of Gov. Reg. 202/2011.
457. Section 1(11) of Gov. Reg. 202/2011.
458. Section 3 of Gov. Reg. 202/2011.
459. Section 6 of Gov. Reg. 202/2011.
460. Section 2(2) of Gov. Reg. 202/2011.
461. Section 2(3) of Gov. Reg. 202/2011.

546. Although such arrangements normally involve some collusion on prices, the latter is inevitable and ancillary to the joint production, joint purchasing and joint selling does not qualify as price-fixing, since they do not aim directly at fixing or influencing the prices charged by the enterprises.[462]

§2. VERTICAL AGREEMENTS

547. As a general rule on vertical restraints, it is to be noted that under Hungarian competition law the *de minimis* rule fully applies to vertical agreements (only horizontal hardcore agreements are excluded from this benefit), that is, all vertical restraints can benefit from the safe harbour of agreements of minor importance; contrary to EU competition law, where vertical hardcore agreements (e.g., resale price-fixing, absolute territorial protection) are excluded from the benefit of *de minimis*.[463] Accordingly, those vertical restraints that are regarded anti-competitive by object are condemned only if the market share exceeds 10%.

548. It is to be highlighted that under EU competition law the market share cap for vertical agreements is 15% (while the market share cap for horizontal agreements is 10%).[464] The figure used by Hungarian competition law equally applies to both horizontal and vertical restraints, and as to vertical restraints, it is lower than in EU law (10% instead of 15%).

I. Distribution

549. In respect of the treatment of restrictions included in distribution agreements, Hungarian competition law, essentially, follows the pattern of EU competition law, with the difference of the approach of the Hungarian *de minimis* rule. The Hungarian Vertical BER is, largely, a transplantation of the VBER, its EU counterpart. Furthermore, vertical restraints treated as restrictions by object under EU competition law,[465] face a similar treatment in Hungarian competition law.

A. Resale Price Maintenance

550. Under 10% market share all vertical restraints, including resale price-fixing, benefit from the safe harbour of agreements of minor importance. If both the supplier's and the reseller's market share is lower than 30%,[466] the fixing of maximum prices and recommended prices are block-exempted; however, both resale

---

462. *See* Case *Vj-195/2001 REÁL Hungária and TEMPO Szupermarket*, para. 22; Case *Vj-176/2003 METRO, SPAR and PRAKTIKER*, para. 26.
463. De Minimis Notice, paras 13–14.
464. De Minimis Notice, para. 8.
465. Guidance on restrictions of competition 'by object' for the purpose of defining which agreements may benefit from the De Minimis Notice. SWD(2014) 198 final, C(2014) 4136 final, 13–17.
466. Section 3 of Gov. Reg. 205/2011.

Part II, Ch. 1, Restrictive Agreements

price-fixing and the fixing of the minimum resale price qualify as hardcore under the Hungarian Vertical BER and, hence, agreements containing such restrictions are excluded from the benefit of the block exemption.[467] The supplier's market share has to be calculated on the relevant market where he sells the relevant products, while the buyer's market share has to be calculated on the relevant market where he purchases the relevant products.[468]

551. The fixing of maximum prices and recommended prices are considered to be 'effect' type agreements; hence, if either the supplier's or the reseller's market share exceeds 30%, they are to be assessed on the basis of their effects.

552. The fixing of a minimum or a concrete resale price qualifies as a restriction by object; thus, if the market share is higher than 10%, it automatically infringes the general prohibition on restrictive agreements (section 11 CA) and is not covered by a block-exemption; although theoretically such arrangements might benefit from an individual exemption (section 17 CA), it is highly unlikely that they could meet the corresponding requirements.

553. In Case *Vj-171/2002/15 MOL*, the CC held that the fixing of the resale price or of a minimum resale price is, according to competition law practice, evidently anti-competitive.[469] This decisional practice has not changed; in Case *Vj-7/2008/178 Castrol Hungária*, the CC confirmed that it is anti-competitive by object and violates section 11 CA if the enterprise fixes the minimum or concrete final or consumer price; namely, in this case the trader, due to the restraints on pricing policy, is restricted in using the most important tool of competition.[470]

554. It is to be noted that in Case *Vj-164/2006 Büki Ásványvíz* the CC considered a vertical price-fixing scheme not to infringe section 11 CA. Here, the producer fixed no generally applicable resale price but agreed with the distributors individually. The decision's reasoning suggests that resale price-fixing does not violate competition rules automatically and without exception. The CC held that although it regards horizontal price-fixing as the most serious restriction of competition, this case centred around vertical price-fixing, which required a more complex analysis, due to the potential efficiency arguments. The CC found that in this matter it was probable that the enterprise's conduct did not aim at switching-off price competition and had no such effects, either. First, only a few of the contracts contained resale price-fixing clauses. Second, the supplier established no uniform resale price of general application; the resale price was determined on an individual basis, taking into account the market circumstances and there were huge differences between the individual prices (the lowest price was HUF 260, while the highest was HUF 850). The CC found that the enterprise did not intend to influence the uniform market price. It happened that within the same settlement one of the traders had a fixed price, while the rest did not. The CC noted

---

467. Section 7(a) of Gov. Reg. 205/2011.
468. Section 3 of Gov. Reg. 205/2011.
469. Paragraph 52. *See* Case *Vj-47/2004 Magyar Könyvkiadók és Könyvterjesztők Egyesülése*, para. 101.
470. Paragraph 47.

that although selective resale price-fixing may fall foul of competition law, as, for instance, it may be susceptible of driving rivals out of the market, no anti-competitive consequences were proved in the proceeding.[471] It is to be noted that in this case the CC examined the arrangement of resale price-fixing under the general prohibition on restrictive agreements (section 11 CA) and not under the individual exemption (section 17 CA) and came to the conclusion that it did not violate the law.

555. The decision in Case *Vj-164/2006 Büki Ásványvíz* clearly suggests a more lenient approach towards resale price-fixing, as the CC in fact regarded this arrangement as not being anti-competitive by object and considered that an effects-analysis would be warranted. However, this trend was not followed subsequently, and in Case *Vj-7/2008/178 Castrol Hungária*, as noted above, the CC reiterated the old rule that resale price-fixing per se violates the general prohibition on restrictive agreements (i.e., section 11 CA).

556. Although the chance that resale price-fixing or the fixing of the minimum resale price could meet the conditions of individual exemption is miniscule, in the history of Hungarian competition law, there has been a single case where such an arrangement was granted an individual exemption.

557. In Case *Vj-150/1995 Kontavill Kontakta*, the CC granted an individual exemption to such a restriction. The decision was rendered under the old CA and was rather exceptional; hence, its precedential value is questionable. The case concerned agreements for the resale of electricity spare parts. The CC established that economic competition is not an aim but merely a tool to facilitate efficient economic activities serving the public interest and the interests of consumers. In this context, the CC regarded price competition between market operators as desirable only if price competition does not force market operators to deteriorate the conditions of marketing (or the product's quality) to such an extent that is harmful to consumers. In case of luxury products, technically complex and widely diversified commodities, and in case of merchandise where a huge inventory is needed, the producer is interested in the distributor's selling its products under appropriate conditions and proper standards. The CC argued that resale price-fixing can serve the interests of consumers, provided it is in accordance with the costs necessary for complying with the required standards, as resale price-fixing, in terms of financing, enables the distributor to provide high level marketing services. The HCO concluded that the agreement in fact enabled wholesalers not to cut relevant expenses (emerging from maintaining a full range of products, the conditions of serving the customers, storage, advertisements and related services), what would deteriorate the quality of the service to the detriment of consumers.

---

471. Paragraph 75.

B. Exclusive Distributorship (Territorial Protection)

558. Under 10% market share, all vertical restraints, including territorial and customer exclusivities, benefit from the safe harbour of agreements of minor importance.

559. If both the supplier's and the reseller's market share is lower than 30%,[472] relative territorial protection (prohibition of active sales) are block exempted; however, absolute territorial protection (prohibition of both active and passive sales) qualifies as hardcore under the Hungarian Vertical BER and, hence, agreements containing such restrictions are excluded from the benefit of the block exemption.[473] The supplier's market share has to be calculated on the relevant market where he sells the relevant products, while the buyer's market share has to be calculated on the relevant market where he purchases the relevant products.[474]

560. As to territorial exclusivity, Hungarian Vertical BER, in line with its EU counterpart, adopts the following pattern: it pronounces all territorial restriction to be hardcore and establishes exceptions to this, which, however, turn the general rule upside down.

561. First, active sales in respect of territories reserved for the supplier or another distributor can be restricted. Accordingly, the Hungarian Vertical BER contains no general exemption for the restriction of active sales: the requirement of 'reservation' applies – the territory as to which the sales are restricted has to be reserved for the supplier or another buyer; in the absence of this, not even active promotion can be restricted.[475]

562. The requirement of reservation may entail difficulties when introducing a new product, since in such cases the producer may want to restrict sales as to a geographic area, where it has not appointed a distributor. Albeit in this case it could be effectively argued that this new territory is reserved for the supplier, who will distribute the products directly or through a future trader, the Commission's Vertical Guidelines contain a special provision covering such scenarios, which provides guidance also in respect of Hungarian competition law:

> In the case of genuine testing of a new product in a limited territory or with a limited customer group and in the case of a staggered introduction of a new product, the distributors appointed to sell the new product on the test market or to participate in the first round(s) of the staggered introduction may be restricted in their active selling outside the test market or the market(s) where

---

472. Section 3 of Gov. Reg. 205/2011.
473. Section 7(b) of Gov. Reg. 205/2011.
474. Section 3 of Gov. Reg. 205/2011.
475. Vertical Guidelines, para. 51.

the product is first introduced without falling within the scope of Article 101(1) for the period necessary for the testing or introduction of the product[476]

563. The Commission's Vertical Guidelines make it clear: sole distributorship (semi-exclusivity), where the supplier grants exclusivity to a trader with the proviso that he reserves for itself the possibility of direct sales into this geographical area, meet the above conditions.[477] This rule is presumably valid also in Hungarian competition law.

564. Finally, it has to be stressed that since a geographical area or a customer group has to be reserved for another buyer or the supplier, this requirement is not met if it is reserved for a another licensee.

565. As for the second exception, the supplier can sever the wholesale and retail level: the agreement can restrict the buyer operating as a wholesaler in selling to final users.

566. As the third exception, in a selective distribution system the producer can exclude the sales to non-authorized distributors (i.e., traders that are not part of the system).

567. As the fourth exception, the regulation establishes a restraint concerning the sale of component elements.

568. Relative territorial protection is considered to be an 'effect' type restriction; hence, if either the supplier's or the reseller's market share exceeds 30%, it is to be assessed on the basis of its effects.

569. Absolute territorial protection qualifies as a restriction by object; thus, if the market share is higher than 10%, it automatically infringes the general prohibition on restrictive agreements (section 11 CA) and is not covered by a block exemption; although theoretically such arrangements might benefit from an individual exemption (section 17 CA), it is highly unlikely that they could meet the corresponding requirements.

570. In Case *Vj-156/2004 Unilever and others*, the CC held, referring to EU competition law, that the exclusion of passive sales (absolute territorial protection) is, in fact, per se anti-competitive: it violates the general prohibition on restrictive agreements automatically and cannot benefit from an individual exemption.[478] The adoption of the *Consten and Grundig* doctrine in Hungarian competition law is criticized in the scholarship; in EU competition law, the most important argument behind the harsh treatment of absolute territorial protection is the purpose of market integration (single market imperative[479]), while this purpose is not part of Hungarian national competition

---

476. Paragraph 62.
477. Paragraph 51.
478. Paragraph 88, paras 93–94.
479. Richard Whish & D. Bailey, *Competition Law* 51 (OUP 2012).

Part II, Ch. 1, Restrictive Agreements

law.[480] Furthermore, under EU competition law, absolute territorial protection falls out of the scope of the *de minimis* rule, as it is regarded as hardcore. On the contrary, under Hungarian competition law absolute territorial protection is covered by the safe harbour of agreements of minor importance: if the market share is less than 10%, vertical absolute territorial protection is lawful.[481]

C. Exclusive Dealing (Non-compete)

571. Under 10% market share all vertical restraints, including (vertical) non-compete clauses, benefit from the safe harbour of agreements of minor importance.

572. If both the supplier's and the reseller's market share is lower than 30%,[482] both in-term and post-term non-compete clauses are block exempted under certain conditions. The supplier's market share has to be calculated on the relevant market where he sells the relevant products, while the buyer's market share has to be calculated on the relevant market where he purchases the relevant products.[483]

573. Under the Hungarian Vertical BER, the term 'non-compete' covers not only express non-compete clauses, where the trader agrees not to produce, purchase, sell or market competing products, but also quantity forcing, where the trader agrees to buy a particular part (more than 80%) of its purchases from the supplier.[484]

574. In-term non-compete clauses are acceptable if stipulated for a period shorter than five years. Non-compete obligations for an indefinite period or a period longer than five years, including restrictions that are renewable tacitly or through indicative behaviour, are black-listed, that is, the contractual clause loses the benefit of the block exemption, while the rest of the agreement remains covered by it.[485] An exception applies to the case where the trader sells the goods from the supplier's premises or land.[486]

575. Contrary to in-term non-compete clauses, post-term non-compete is, in principle, excluded from the block exemption irrespective of duration. However, the Hungarian Vertical BER (similarly to its EU counterpart) contains an exception: for a period of one year after the termination of the contract, under certain conditions, post-term non-compete obligations are acceptable, if this is inevitable to protect the

---

480. Csongor István Nagy, *Kartelljogi Kézikönyv. A közösségi és a magyar kartelljog kézikönyve* 241 (Budapest: HVG-Orac, 2006); Csongor István Nagy, *EU and US Competition Law: Divided in Unity?* 163–164 (Ashgate Publishing, 2013).
481. Section 13(2) CA.
482. Section 3 of Gov. Reg. 205/2011.
483. Section 3 of Gov. Reg. 205/2011.
484. Section 1(10) of Gov. Reg. 205/2011.
485. Section 8(1)(a) and s. 8(2) of Gov. Reg. 205/2011.
486. Section 8(3) of Gov. Reg. 205/2011.

know-how given by the supplier to the buyer.[487] Of course, this rule does not impair the possibility to adopt dispositions even for an indefinite period of time so as to preserve the know-how (for instance, in the form of secrecy clauses as to business secrets).[488]

576. Non-compete restrictions are considered to be 'effect' type agreements, hence, if they are not covered by the above safe harbours (e.g., either the supplier's or the reseller's market share exceeds 30%, the in-term non-compete is for a period longer than five years and the market share is higher than 10%), they are to be assessed on the basis of their effects.

D. *Selective Distribution*

577. Under 10% market share all vertical restraints, including selective distribution arrangements, benefit from the safe harbour of agreements of minor importance.

578. If both the supplier's and the reseller's market share is lower than 30%,[489] selective distribution may benefit from a block exemption; however, the Hungarian Vertical BER, as to selective distribution, pronounces two restraints to be hardcore and one restraint to be black-listed. The supplier's market share has to be calculated on the relevant market where he sells the relevant products, while the buyer's market share has to be calculated on the relevant market where he purchases the relevant products.[490]

579. In case of selective distribution, the following restraints qualify as hardcore: the restriction of sales to end-users (either active, or passive) and the restriction of cross-supplies between distributors within a selective distribution system. Accordingly, selective distribution cannot be combined with territorial protection, since the block exemption regulation regards both the restriction of cross-supplies between selected distributors and the restriction on selling to end-users as hardcore.

580. The Hungarian Vertical BER blacklists any direct or indirect obligation that prohibits the members of a selective distribution system from selling the brands of particular competing suppliers.[491]

---

487. Section 8(1)(b) of Gov. Reg. 205/2011.
488. Section 8(4) of Gov. Reg. 205/2011.
489. Section 3 of Gov. Reg. 205/2011.
490. Section 3 of Gov. Reg. 205/2011.
491. Section 8(1)(c) of Gov. Reg. 205/2011.

E. Franchising

581. Franchising agreements are, in general, treated in the same way as distribution agreements. Though the HCO has developed no decisional practice as regards franchising agreements, the peculiar features of these systems may be taken into account in the frame of the competition analysis.

II. Technology Licensing

582. Technology transfer agreement are regulated by the Hungarian Technology Transfer BER, which is in line with (since then repealed) Regulation 240/96 on the application of Article 85 (3) of the Treaty to certain categories of technology transfer agreements.[492] Accordingly, it does not follow the currently effective TTBER.

---

492. OJ [1996] L 31/2.

Chapter 2. Dominant Undertakings' Prohibited Practices

§1. EXPLOITATIVE PRACTICES

I. Excessive/Unfair Pricing

583. Although the prohibition of excessive pricing is not the most successful field of Hungarian competition law, contrary to EU competition law where the prohibition of excessive pricing seems to be very controversial,[493] the HCO's law-enforcement has produced numerous judicially affirmed decisions. Excessive pricing cases were especially common in the '90s; during this period, the repercussions of the state-monopolies created and maintained in the socialist era were still palpable: there were a lot of dominated markets in Hungary, and excessive pricing cases were quite frequent.

584. According to the CC's decisional practice, the price charged by the dominant undertaking has to be compared to the hypothetical competitive price; if the price charged is higher than the latter, it is considered to be excessive.[494] The hypothetical competitive price is sometimes designated as 'calculated' or 'ideal' competitive price.[495] All these terms express the core feature of the reference price used in excessive pricing cases: in these cases, there is normally a single price in the market, the one charged by the dominant undertaking[496] and, hence, the calculation of the would-be competitive price is speculative.

585. There are two methods of defining the hypothetical competitive price. First, the analysis may proceed from the dominant undertaking's costs; second, the market price may be compared to the price in another market or to past prices in the same market.

586. The two methods can be used only jointly. By way of example, prices cannot be considered to be excessive simply because they are higher than the prices prevailing in another geographical region; likewise, the calculation of the dominant undertaking's margin (the cost-price ratio) is, in itself, insufficient for comprehensively judging the prices charged, since business risks vary from market to market.

587. This proposition is underpinned by the Supreme Court's judgment in Case *Vj-152/2000/51 MOL*,[497] where it held: if prices can be assessed on the basis of two

---

493. On the EU competition practice on excessive prices *see* Liyang Hou, *Excessive Prices within EU Competition Law* 7(1) Eur. Comp. J. 47 (2011).
494. On excessive pricing *see* András Bodócsi, *Az árak megítélése a versenytörvény alapján* (10) Versenyfelügyeleti Értesítő (1998); András Bodócsi, *Az árak versenyhatósági ellenőrzésének kérdőjelei'*, 5(2) Versenytükör 29–34 (2009); Csongor István Nagy, *Túlzottan magas árak megítélése a magyar versenyjogban* (4) Collega 38–47 (2002).
495. Cf. Case *Vj-73/1991*.
496. Case *Vj-17/1998*.
497. Case *Kf.II.39.048/2002/13*.

Part II, Ch. 2, Dominant Undertakings' Prohibited Practices   588–590

analytical methods (so as to ascertain whether they are excessive or not), the HCO has to use both of them; a decision can be made only if the prices are examined on the basis of both methods and the results of the two analyses have to be taken into consideration jointly; the use of one of the methods does not preclude the other and does not exclude the possibility to establish the violation. Accordingly, an adequate and well-founded decision can be reached only if the two methods are combined.

588. According to the CC's decisional practice, the dominant undertaking cannot be condemned for excessive pricing if the difference between the hypothetical competitive price and the price actually charged is insignificant.[498] Since the determination of the hypothetical competitive price is speculative and contains uncertainties, the price can be regarded as excessive only if it is clearly higher than the calculated competitive price. The burden of proof in respect of the violation rests on the competition authority; hence, in case of uncertainty, the price has to be regarded as lawful. The more accurately the hypothetical competitive price can be ascertained, the smaller the tolerable difference is; and *vice versa*, the more speculative the calculated competitive price is, the bigger the tolerable difference is.

589. It is to be noted that although the above two-prong test based on the cost-price ration (reasonable margin) and the comparison with the price prevailing in another, comparable and competitive market (benchmarking) is the principle governing excessive pricing cases in general, the CC established a special test applicable specifically to collective rights management societies. In Case *VJ-97/2004 FilmJus*, the CC held that the customary methods of inquiry applied to ascertain whether the prices charged are excessive cannot be used as to royalties. The notions used by these methods (e.g., economically justified costs, profit commensurate with investment) cannot be interpreted in case of royalties. Since the CC could not find any other calculation method, it came to the conclusion that in case of royalties not the amount of the royalty but the method (process) of its determination has to be examined. According to the CC, in this regard, it is determinative whether and how the establisher of the royalty takes into account the interests of the adverse parties.

A. *Calculation of the Necessary Costs and the Reasonable Profit*

590. In the CC's decisional practice, the price is excessive if it is higher than the undertaking's economically justified costs and the profit necessary for its operation.[499]

---

498. Case *Vj-91/1997*. *Cf.* Case *Vj-12/2000* (It does not amount to an abuse, if the calculated fee differs from the actually charged fees only slightly.)
499. Case *Vj-6/1999*; Cf. Case *Vj-18/1998*; Case *Vj-115/2000*.

591. In the decisional practice, it is also examined whether the costs are justified: the dominant undertaking cannot count in those expenditures that were not necessary or were not incurred in a cost-effective manner.[500]

592. In case of multi-product undertakings, the ascertainment of the costs raises serious anomalies: how shall the common or general costs be apportioned among the various products and services. In Case *Vj-27/2005 Antenna Hungária*, the CC did not consider the prices to be excessive, taking into account the minuscule difference between the economic value and the price; it established that when assessing the price it cannot be disregarded that there is no legally endorsed principle on apportionment as to indirect costs (i.e., costs that cannot be directly allocated to a given service).

593. The second component of the price (reasonable profit) is completely indefinable. The reasonable margin may depend on the circumstances, the risks the undertaking runs, and can be assessed only on a case-by-case basis.[501] It is not possible to give a general rate of return valid in all markets. A theoretical starting point could be the rate of return of risk-free investments, which has to be corrected with the capital market and entrepreneurial risk premiums.

594. The delimitation of costs (expenses) from profits raises conceptual problems, due to the terminological difference between competition law and economic costs. In accounting, the risk premium and opportunity costs are part of the profit, while in economics these are the costs of the capital. The terminology of Hungarian competition law is closer to accounting.

B. Comparative Analyses

595. The different methods of comparative analyses (benchmarking) centre around a reference market sufficiently competitive to be used (after corrections) as a proxy of competitive price. The reference market is the result of changing one of the coordinates of the scrutinized market (geographical location, temporal dimension, product dimension). Accordingly, the competition authority may use geographical, temporal (historical) and product or customer group comparisons. In terms of practice, geographical and temporal comparisons are the most important methods of inquiry. Of course, the comparative method (benchmarking) may be reasonably applied only if there is a reference market the prices of which can be used as a reference with relatively minor corrections. If the reference market (counter-factual) differs, in terms of costs or

---

500. In Case *Vj-27/2005 Antenna Hungária*, one of the focal points of the cost-price analysis was the question of cost-effectiveness (i.e., whether certain cost elements were justified). The CC established as to several cost elements that they were connected to other operations and identified expenditures that were unjustified because they could not have been made part of the price under competitive circumstances. Likewise, a cost-based price-analysis was accomplished in Case *Vj-33/2004 MOL*.
501. *Cf.* Case *Vj-54/2000*.

Part II, Ch. 2, Dominant Undertakings' Prohibited Practices

other factors, considerably from the market under scrutiny, a comparison will yield no benchmark for assessing the prices.

1. Territorial Comparisons

596. In essence, there are three types of territorial comparisons: comparison between domestic markets, comparison with export/import prices and comparison with prices in another national market.

597. In case the undertaking's dominant position is confined to certain parts of Hungary and there is a non-dominated local market in the country, the latter's prices may be used as a reference, in most cases without correction.[502]

598. Export/import prices may also be used as a reference.[503]

599. In principle, prices prevailing in other countries may also be used as a reference; however, as market circumstances are normally very different, this method's use is normally very limited.[504]

2. Temporal/Historical Comparisons

600. An earlier stage of the same market may also be used as a reference market, provided there was workable competition in the market, so the price prevailing in this earlier period can be regarded as competitive. In the CC's decisional practice, this analytical method has been quite often used in cases concerning cable-television enterprises. In several decisions, the CC established that earlier market prices are the best benchmarks.[505]

601. In cases where the earlier price's price-cost structure is not an appropriate reference-base, a price increase above inflation may be justified in respect of non-quantifiable costs. For instance, if the undertaking suffers losses and increases the price in order to make a profit, or the earlier profit was insufficiently low and this is why the price is raised, a price increase over inflation can be acceptable. Furthermore, certain costs may not change in step with inflation.[506] Likewise, technical and

---

502. András Bodócsi, *Az árak megítélése a versenytörvény alapján*, (10) Versenyfelügyeleti Értesítő 368 (1998). The abuse was established through this method in Case *Vj-64/1991*.
503. This method was used in Case *Vj-72/1993. See* Case *Vj-73/1991*.
504. *See* András Bodócsi, *Az árak megítélése a versenytörvény alapján*, (10) Versenyfelügyeleti Értesítő 368 (1998). *Cf.* Case *Vj-8/1994*; Case *Vj-73/1991*.
505. Case *Vj-17/1998*.
506. Case *Vj-99/1998*. Cf. Case *Vj-17/1998*. (It amounts to the change of the economic conditions, if the enterprise has to increase its profit as compared to the earlier period in order to remain operational.); Case *Vj 20/1998*; Case *Vj-15/1998*.

organizational restructuring may also justify the increase of the price. This principle was followed by the CC in numerous cases concerning cable-television enterprises, where it was found that certain technical changes justified a price increase higher than inflation.[507] These expenses have to be reasonably divided between the service provider and the consumers; the dominant undertaking cannot shift the expenses unilaterally onto consumers.

602. In Case *Vj-17/1998*, the defendant raised the argument that the margin was increased with the purpose to use the extra-profits to acquire new customers. The service provider charged small entry fees but increased the subscription fees subsequently, thus shifting the loss resulting from the low entry fees; this strategy aimed at attracting new consumers (where the undertaking had no dominant position) at the cost of the old, captive consumers (where the undertaking enjoyed economic dominance). The CC condemned the undertaking.

3. Comparison between Product Markets or Customer Groups

603. The price prevailing on a closely related product market can also be used as a reference-base. The relevant product may be a close substitute.

II. Discrimination

604. Unequal treatment of equivalent transactions is prohibited by section 21(g) CA, if this entails business partners a competitive disadvantage and it has no objective justification.[508] Apparently, section 21(g) CA prohibits only secondary line discrimination; however, primary line discrimination may also be condemned on the basis of the general prohibition of abusive conduct set out in section 21 CA. Accordingly, the prohibition embedded in section 21(g) may be boiled down to the following conceptual elements: the compared transactions are equivalent, unequal treatment is afforded, the unequal treatment entails a competitive disadvantage to the customer and there is no objective justification.[509]

605. Accordingly, unequal treatment is not outright prohibited. It falls foul of the CA only if it has a negative impact on competition in the market. If the business partners treated differently are not present in the same relevant market, i.e., they are not competitors, unequal treatment will not go counter to section 21(g) CA, albeit, at least theoretically, it might still breach the general prohibition of abusive conduct.

---

507. HCO's Annual Report of 1999.
508. On EU competition practice *see* C-85/76 *Hoffmann la Roche* ECR [1979] 461; C-27/76 *United Brands* ECR [1978] 207; C-7/82 *GVL v. Commission* ECR [1983] 483; T-228/97 *Irish Sugar* ECR [1999] II-2969; T-219/99 *British Airways*, C-95/04P *British Airways* ECR [2007] I-2331. Numerous discrimination cases emerged in the aviation sector; however, these had very special fact, *see* T-128/98 *Alpha Flight service* ECR [2000] I-9297; C-163/99 *Portuguese Airports* ECR [2001] I 2613.
509. *See* Case *Vj-7/2007 TV2/DigiTV*.

Part II, Ch. 2, Dominant Undertakings' Prohibited Practices

This proposition was confirmed in numerous telecommunications cases where the undertaking discriminated between end-consumers (mainly private persons). Although it was established that there was clear and unjustified discrimination, the customers were not competing with each other and, hence, suffered no competitive disadvantage as a result of the unequal treatment.[510]

606. The principle that competition law protects competition and not competitors, and that the HCO shall intervene only if the practice has a negative impact on competition in the market governs also the treatment of discrimination cases. In numerous cases, the CC found that the discriminatory practice is of minor importance and, as such, is not susceptible of appreciably affecting competition in the market.[511]

607. In Case *Vj-7/2007 TV2/DigiTV*, the alleged unequal treatment amounted to 2% of the price (the allegedly discriminatory programme fee charged by TV2 amounted merely to 2% of the overall income of DigiTV). The same point was raised in Case *Vj-97/2004 FilmJus*, where the CC came to the conclusion that the difference between the fees was so small that it was not susceptible of entailing a competitive disadvantage.[512] In Case *Vj-186/2007 Magyar Posta*, the CC refused to condemn the Hungarian Post for a blatant discrimination, because it considered that it was 'not likely that (...) [that the disparate treatment] caused consumer harm'.[513] (para 35).

608. Accordingly, if the value covered by the alleged discrimination is small as compared to the totality of the enterprise's purchases, even a blatant discrimination may avoid antitrust condemnation. Likewise, if the allegedly discriminatory practice concerns only a small portion of the market (a few customers only) and, as such, has no palpable effect on competition in the market, competition law condemnation is unlikely; the CC may consider that the practice would entail no significant consumer harm in terms of higher prices or lower output. If there is effective competition in the market, occasional unequal treatment may not be an enforcement priority for the HCO.[514]

609. In Case *Vj-124/2003 Matáv and Axelero*, the CC considered an arrangement affording disparate treatment based on purchase volumes to be acceptable.[515]

---

510. See Case *Vj-18/2002 UPC*; Case *Vj-37/2002 Fibernet*; Case *Vj-14/2003 Vidanet*; Case *Vj-17/2003 MatávKábelNet*; Case *Vj-22/2003 Kábelduó Szolgáltató*; Case *Vj-83/2003 Zalaegerszegi Elektromos Karbantartó*; Case *Vj-93/2003 Kábelszat*; Case *Vj-36/2004 Bodor and his sons*; Case *Vj-88/2007 T-Kábel*.
511. See Case *Vj-7/2007 TV2/DigiTV*, where the allegedly discriminatory fees charged by TV2 represented 2% of the budget of DigiTV. A similar argument emerged in Case *Vj-97/2004 FILMJUS*.
512. Paragraphs 51–53.
513. Paragraph 35.
514. See by analogy Case *Vj-7/2007 TV2/DigiTV*, para. 63.
515. Paragraphs 52–54.

610. In *Vj-23/1999 Kábeltel/Elektra*, the CC found that unequal treatment between the undertaking's owners (cable-television network) and other subscribers as to prices was justified.[516] Nonetheless, it is rather questionable whether this approach is of general application and whether undertakings do have the general possibility to treat group members and unconnected enterprises differently; such a proposition would clearly go counter to the Commission's decisional practice.[517]

§2. EXCLUSIONARY PRACTICES

611. While the direct victims of a dominant undertaking's exclusionary practices are rivals, Hungarian competition law is not meant to shield competitors but to protect competition. According to the 'Fundamental principles followed by the HCO concerning the freedom of competition', which is a policy document summarizing the HCO's competition policy, competition law protects competition and not competitors (market operators), and especially not a particular competitor.[518] The policy document stresses that an exclusionary abuse if not an abuse against actual or potential competitors or direct contracting partners, even if one of them suffers a detriment due to the abuse; a conduct is considered to be an abuse from the point of view of the final consumers and their general interest.[519]

612. The above approach has permeated the CC's decisional practice on exclusionary practices and is a general principle of interpretation in dominant position cases.

I. **Predatory Pricing**

613. The legal test of predatory pricing centres around five questions:

– the relationship between costs and price;
– the calculation of costs in case of multi-product firms (how to share the common costs of different products);
– the issue of 'recoupment';
– the requirement of anti-competitive foreclosure; and
– objective justification.

614. It is to be noted that Hungarian decisional practice differs from EU competition law as regards certain questions. For instance, under Hungarian law, predatory pricing can be established only if the possibility of recoupment is proved: predatory pricing cannot be established if the market is contestable.

---

516. *See* Case *Vj-23/1999 Kábeltel/Elektra*, s. II.
517. *See e.g.*, T-228/97 *Irish Sugar* [1999] ECR II-2969.
518. Paragraph 3.199.
519. Paragraph 3.129.

A. The Relationship between Costs and Price

615. Under EU and Hungarian competition law, two cost concepts have emerged as regards predation: average total costs (ATC) and average variable costs (AVC). ATC is the cost element, which contains the fixed costs (such as rental fees of premises, management costs, labour costs, fixed service charges, etc.) and the variable costs incurred. AVC varies depending on the quantity produced: AVC designates the expenses incurring when producing one incremental unit (additional cost of raw materials, energy, etc.). AVC is, in other words, one item within the ATC.

616. In the famous *AKZO* judgment,[520] the CJEU held that:

> *prices below average variable costs (that is to say, those which vary depending on the quantities produced) by means of which a dominant undertaking seeks to eliminate a competitor must be regarded as abusive. A dominant undertaking has no interest in applying such prices except that of eliminating competitors so as to enable it subsequently to raise its prices by taking advantage of its monopolistic position, since each sale generates a loss, namely the total amount of the fixed costs (that is to say, those which remain constant regardless of the quantities produced) and, at least, part of the variable costs relating to the unit produced.*[521]

617. The CJEU regards prices below AVC as predatory, since each unit of sale causes loss to the undertaking. This was confirmed in *Tetra Pak II* in which the ECJ unequivocally established that:

> *prices below average variable costs must always be considered abusive. In such a case, there is no conceivable economic purpose other than the elimination of a competitor, since each item produced and sold entails a loss for the undertaking.*[522]

618. In *AKZO*, the CJEU also addressed prices between AVC and ATC, holding that:

> *[...] prices below average total costs, that is to say, fixed costs plus variable costs, but above average variable costs, must be regarded as abusive, if they are determined as part of a plan for eliminating a competitor. Such prices can drive from the market undertakings which are perhaps as efficient as the dominant undertaking but which, because of their smaller financial resources, are incapable of withstanding the competition waged against them.*[523]

---

520. C-62/86 *AKZO Chemie BV v. Commission of the European Communities*, [1991] ECR I-3359.
521. Paragraph 71.
522. C-333/94 P *Tetra Pak International SA v. Commission*, [1996] ECR I-5951. para. 41.
523. Paragraph 72.

619. Accordingly, prices between AVC and ATC cannot be regarded automatically as predatory. In this regard, it is to be proved that the pricing policy is part of a plan of driving the competitor out from the market. Prices above ATC are, as a general rule, not abusive.[524] Recent Commission documents have essentially confirmed the principles emerging from the above CJEU case law.[525]

620. The decisional practice of the CC mainly uses the concept of direct costs; however, the above classification of expenditures (i.e., AVC and ATC) also appears in the decisional practice.

621. In Case *Vj-168/2004 Auchan and Tesco*, the CC held that it is the direct costs that have to be taken into consideration in the application of the test of predatory pricing. In this regard, direct costs cover all expenditures that are directly related to the sale of the product or to the provision of the service. In this sense, it certainly encompasses variable costs and it involves some fixed costs. Nevertheless, it is rather dubious how the CC draws the line between direct and indirect costs.

622. In Case *Vj-168/2004 Auchan and Tesco*, the CC held that it is primarily the direct costs that are to be taken into account, while indirect costs normally have to be disregarded. It is interesting that once it was established that the prices were higher than the average of the direct costs, the CC 'excluded the presumption of predatory pricing without further inquiry'.[526]

623. The HCO also translated the above analysis to the terms of AVC and ATC, holding that it is 'very probable' that prices under AVC, if applied permanently, are predatory in nature, while such a conclusion may be 'certainly excluded' if the prices are higher than ATC. If the price is between AVC and ATC, 'additional factors have to be taken into account'.[527]

B. Cost Tests in Respect of Multi-product Enterprises

624. In case of multi-product activities, where certain common fixed costs are shared by different products or services, the calculation of the relevant costs may be uncertain. In such cases, the Commission applies the long-run average incremental costs test (LRAIC).

---

524. Unless, very exceptionally, the pricing above ATC still form part of a clearly exclusionary plan including loyalty agreements, targeted and selective price reductions. This was established by the ECJ only in two very specific cases involving maritime transportation. *See* Joined cases C-395/96 P and C-396/96 P. *Compagnie maritime belge transports SA (C-395/96 P), Compagnie maritime belge SA (C-395/96 P) and Dafra-Lines A/S (C-396/96 P) v. Commission of the European Communities*, [2000] ECR I-01365.
525. *See* Guidance on Art. 102. *See also* 2005 DG Competition Discussion Paper on the application of Art. 82 of the Treaty to exclusionary abuses, available at http://ec.europa.eu/competition/antitrust/art82/discpaper2005.pdf.
526. Paragraph 21.
527. Paragraph 9.

Part II, Ch. 2, Dominant Undertakings' Prohibited Practices   625–628

625. In *Deutsche Post AG*,[528] the Commission dealt with a case where the undertaking had a legal monopoly in one of the markets, while facing competition in another market. The case raised the question of cross-subsidisation. The Commission considered that:

> *when establishing whether the incremental costs incurred in providing mail-order parcel services [i.e. the competitive services] are covered, the additional costs of producing that service, incurred solely as a result of providing the service, must be distinguished from the common fixed costs, which are not incurred solely as a result of this service.*[529]

626. In order to avoid competition law condemnation, Deutsche Post AG was:

> *required only to cover the costs attributable to the provision of [the competitive service, meaning that] these operations [were] not burdened with the common fixed cost of providing network capacity that [Deutsche Post AG] incur[red] as a result of its statutory universal service obligation.*[530]

627. Accordingly, the Commission regarded LRAIC as '*the additional costs incurred in providing [the new service]*' and took the position that a competition law violation occurs if the incremental revenue, normally the price of the new service, does not cover incremental costs.

628. In *Wanadoo*,[531] in a margin squeeze case, the Commission confirmed the use of the LRAIC method for the calculation of the costs[532] and gave a definition in this regard:

> *The long run incremental cost of an individual product refers to the product-specific costs associated with the total volume of output of the relevant product. It is the difference between the total costs incurred by the firm when producing all products, including the individual product under analysis, and the total costs of the firm when the output of the individual product is set equal to zero, holding the output of all other products fixed. Such costs include not only all volume sensitive and fixed costs directly attributable to the production of the total volume of output of the product in question but also the increase in the common costs that is attributable to this activity.*
> *Since the long run incremental cost of the individual product also includes the increase in the common costs resulting from the provision of the product in question, the mere fact that one cost is common to different operations does not necessarily imply that the long run incremental cost due to the activity in question is zero for any individual product. One must assess whether such common*

---

528. OJ [2001] L 125/27.
529. Paragraph 7.
530. Paragraph 10.
531. Commission decision in Case Comp/38.784 *Wanadoo v. Telefónica* of 04 Jul. 2007.
532. Paragraph 318.

cost would have been incurred, partially or totally, if the company would have decided not to provide the product in question.[533]

629. The above approach is summarized in the Guidance on Article 102 as follows:

A multi-product rebate may be anti-competitive on the tied or the tying market if it is so large that equally efficient competitors offering only some of the components cannot compete against the discounted bundle.
In theory, it would be ideal if the effect of the rebate could be assessed by examining whether the incremental revenue covers the incremental costs for each product in the dominant undertaking's bundle. (...) [I]n its enforcement practice the Commission will in most situations use the incremental price as a good proxy. If the incremental price that customers pay for each of the dominant undertaking's products in the bundle remains above the LRAIC of the dominant undertaking from including that product in the bundle, the Commission will normally not intervene since an equally efficient competitor with only one product should in principle be able to compete profitably against the bundle. Enforcement action may, however, be warranted if the incremental price is below the LRAIC.[534,535]

630. A parallel tendency can be perceived in Hungarian competition law. In Case *Vj-168/2004 Auchan and Tesco*, the CC announced that if the undertaking is engaged in different activities, indirect costs cannot be apportioned among the different operations and 'the undertaking in question can define the principle of division freely'.[536] In case of multi-product undertakings, it does not amount to

---

533. Paragraphs 319–320.
534. Paragraphs 59–60. 'The cost benchmarks that the Commission is likely to use are average avoidable cost (AAC) and long-run average incremental cost (LRAIC). Failure to cover AAC indicates that the dominant undertaking is sacrificing profits in the short term and that an equally efficient competitor cannot serve the targeted customers without incurring a loss. LRAIC is usually above AAC because, in contrast to AAC (which only includes fixed costs if incurred during the period under examination), LRAIC includes product specific fixed costs made before the period in which allegedly abusive conduct took place. Failure to cover LRAIC indicates that the dominant undertaking is not recovering all the (attributable) fixed costs of producing the good or service in question and that an equally efficient competitor could be foreclosed from the market.' Guidance on Art. 102, para. 26.
535. The Guidance on Art. 102 also gives an explanation on the concept of LRAIC: 'Long-run average incremental cost is the average of all the (variable and fixed) costs that a company incurs to produce a particular product. LRAIC and average total cost (ATC) are good proxies for each other, and are the same in the case of single product undertakings. If multi-product undertakings have economies of scope, LRAIC would be below ATC for each individual product, as true common costs are not taken into account in LRAIC. In the case of multiple products, any costs that could have been avoided by not producing a particular product or range are not considered to be common costs. In situations where common costs are significant, they may have to be taken into account when assessing the ability to foreclose equally efficient competitors.' Para. 26, fn 2.
536. Paragraph 15.

Part II, Ch. 2, Dominant Undertakings' Prohibited Practices 631–633

predatory pricing if the price is lower than the total costs, provided it is higher than the average direct costs.[537]

C. The Requirement of Recoupment

631. There is a remarkable difference between EU and Hungarian competition law as to the requirement of recoupment. While under EU competition law this seems clearly not to be a pre-condition, under Hungarian competition law predatory pricing can be established only if the possibility of recoupment is proved.

632. In *Tetra Pak II*,[538] the CJEU held that in order to establish predatory pricing it is not necessary to prove that the undertaking in question has a real possibility to offset its losses.[539] Accordingly, the realistic chance of recoupment is not a necessary prerequisite of establishing predatory pricing in EU competition law. In *Wanadoo*[540] the CJEU – while endorsing the *Tetra Pak II* – stressed that the reason behind this approach is that prices below AVC prove the undertaking's predatory intent and, hence, it is unnecessary to prove the possibility of recoupment.[541] It follows from the above that if prices are between AVC and ATC, recoupment may serve as a factor when examining whether the prices are implemented in the frame of a general strategy to eliminate rivals. This is, however, undecided yet.

633. Contrary to EU competition law's above judicial practice, the requirement of recoupment is part of the Hungarian test on predatory pricing. The CC held in numerous decisions that in Hungarian competition law predatory pricing can be established only if there is a reasonable chance of recoupment. In Case *Vj-159/2003 MOL Rt., OTP Bank Rt., Matáv Rt. and Fotex Rt.*, the CC held that predatory pricing can be

---

537. Paragraph 18.
538. C-333/94 P. *Tetra Pak International SA v. Commission of the European Communities*, [1996] ECR I-05951.
539. '[I]t would not be appropriate, in the circumstances of the present case, to require in addition proof that Tetra Pak had a realistic chance of recouping its losses. It must be possible to penalize predatory pricing whenever there is a risk that competitors will be eliminated. The Court of First Instance found (...) that there was such a risk in this case. The aim pursued, which is to maintain undistorted competition, rules out waiting until such a strategy leads to the actual elimination of competitors.'
'it would not be appropriate, in the circumstances of the present case, to require in addition proof that Tetra Pak had a realistic chance of recouping its losses. It must be possible to penalize predatory pricing whenever there is a risk that competitors will be eliminated. The Court of First Instance found (...) that there was such a risk in this case. The aim pursued, which is to maintain undistorted competition, rules out waiting until such a strategy leads to the actual elimination of competitors.' para. 44.
540. C-202/07 P. *France Télécom SA v. Commission of the European Communities*, paras 29–38.
541. 'Accordingly, contrary to what the appellant claims, it does not follow from the case-law of the Court that proof of the possibility of recoupment of losses suffered by the application, by an undertaking in a dominant position, of prices lower than a certain level of costs constitutes a necessary precondition to establishing that such a pricing policy is abusive. In particular, the Court has taken the opportunity to dispense with such proof in circumstances where the eliminatory intent of the undertaking at issue could be presumed in view of that undertaking's application of prices lower than average variable costs (*see*, to that effect, *Tetra Pak v. Commission*, paragraph 44).' para. 110.

established only if the market is non-contestable.[542] In Cases *Vj-94/2000 Greiner Csomagolástechnika Ipari és Szolgáltató Kft.* and *Vj-76/1999 Microsoft Magyarország Kft.*, the CC mentioned entry barriers and the perspective of recoupment as the necessary elements of the assessment. In Case *Vj-138/2003 ISOPLUS Távhővezetékgyártó Kft.*, the CC expressly pointed out that predatory pricing can be established only if there are high entry barriers that thwart the re-entry of the undertakings and, thus, recoupment is possible.

D. *Anti-competitive Foreclosure*

634. The decisional practice of the CC suggests that allegedly abusive conducts, including predatory pricing, are not subject to automatic condemnation but the competition authority intervenes only if they produce negative effects on competition in the market. This is in line with the Commission's approach.

635. The Guidance on Article 102 provides that 'the Commission will normally intervene under Article 102 where, on the basis of cogent and convincing evidence, the allegedly abusive conduct is likely to lead to anti-competitive foreclosure'.[543] The Guidance also enumerates several factors that are to be taken into account when analysing the existence or non-existence of anti-competitive foreclosure, referring, among others, to the position of the dominant undertaking, the entry and expansion conditions on the market, the position of the dominant undertaking's competitors and the extent of the allegedly abusive conduct. As to the extent of the allegedly abusive conduct, the Guidance provides that:

> *in general, the higher the percentage of total sales in the relevant market affected by the conduct, the longer its duration, and the more regularly it has been applied, the greater is the likely foreclosure effect.*[544]

636. In the context of predatory pricing, the Guidance seems to make clear that the analysis of the cost-price ratio is, in itself, not sufficient for establishing an abuse, but it also has to be investigated whether there is anti-competitive foreclosure.[545] The Guidance mentions, among others, that albeit the perspective of recoupment is not a prerequisite of establishing predatory pricing, anti-competitive foreclosure is likely to exist 'if the undertaking is likely to be in a position to benefit from the sacrifice' (i.e., losses suffered from the low prices) and 'can reasonably expect its market power after the predatory conduct comes to an end to be greater than it would have been had the undertaking not engaged in that conduct in the first place'.[546]

---

542. Case *Vj-159/2003 MOL Rt., OTP Bank Rt., Matáv Rt. and Fotex Rt.*
543. Paragraph 20.
544. Paragraph 20.
545. Paragraphs 67–68.
546. Paragraphs 70–71.

Part II, Ch. 2, Dominant Undertakings' Prohibited Practices

637. In line with the above, the CC stated in numerous decisions that predatory pricing can be established only if the low-price strategy is applied for a sufficiently long period of time.[547] Similarly, in Case *Vj-76/1999 Microsoft Magyarország Kft.*, the CC also held that predatory pricing can be established only if there is a real chance of eliminating one or more competitors: the application of low prices restricted in terms of time or quantity cannot be regarded as predatory. All these statements suggest that under Hungarian competition law a conduct, even if involving below-cost sales, can be condemned only if it is capable of actually eliminating competitors.

E. Objective Justification

638. There is no specific Hungarian decisional practice on the question of objective justification in case of predatory pricing. However, it is probable that the CC would follow the very restrictive approach of the Commission's Guidance on Article 102, which provides that:

> in general it is considered unlikely that predatory conduct will create efficiencies. However, (...) the Commission will consider claims by a dominant undertaking that the low pricing enables it to achieve economies of scale or efficiencies related to expanding the market.[548]

II. Bundling/Tying

639. According to section 21(f) CA, an undertaking abuses its dominant position if it makes the sale of the product or service (tying product) dependent on the purchase of another product or service (tied product) or makes the conclusion of the contract subject to the acceptance of obligations that, by their nature or according to commercial customs, do not belong to the subject of such contracts.

640. The legal test of tying, apart from the existence of dominance, normally consists of the following four conditions:

– there are two separate products;
– the purchase of the tied product is coerced;
– there are detrimental effects on competition in the market (foreclosure); and
– there is no objective justification (efficiency).

---

547. *See* Case *Vj-168/2004. Auchan Magyarország Kft. and Tesco Globál Áruházak Rt.*; Case *Vj-159/2003 MOL Rt., OTP Bank Rt., Matáv Rt. and Fotex Rt.*; Case *Vj-76/1999 Microsoft Magyarország Kft.*
548. Paragraph 74.

641. Tying pre-supposes the existence of two separate products that are not connected taking into account the products' nature and the customary contractual practice.

642. The notion of tying implies that the tying product is sold on the condition that the customer also buys the tied product; it also covers sales in package (bundling).

643. Coercion may occur in different forms: it may comprise in a contractual stipulation, warning or technical tying. EU competition law's concept of de facto tying would also be followed in Hungarian competition law, that is, when the two products are not tied expressly but the dominant undertaking uses its pricing policy to tie them. By way of example, it may reduce the discount concerning the tying product if the customer fails to buy the tied product. Such a practice may have the same effect as if the undertaking sold the tied product on the condition that the customer purchases the tying product as well.[549]

644. There is no detailed practice in Hungarian competition law as to tying; nonetheless, EU competition law's approach may provide guidance in this regard.[550]

645. The Commission's Guidance on Article 102 may be relied on in respect of the detrimental effects on competition[551] and objective justification.[552]

III. Refusal to Deal

646. According to section 21(c), it amounts to an abuse if a dominant undertaking refuses, without objective justification, to establish or maintain a business relation conformable with the transaction's characteristics.[553] This provision has been applied by the CC on numerous occasions.[554] According to the decisional practice, refusal alone is not necessarily abusive, it is also required that it has a negative impact on competition in the market. In other words: no one has a normative right to contract or to maintain contractual relations with a dominant undertaking. This is in line with the principle (followed by the CC) that competition law protects competition and not competitors.

---

549. Richard Whish, *Competition Law* 727 (OUP, 2009).
550. *See* Commission Decision 88/138/EEC (*Eurofix-Bauco v. Hilti*) OJ [1988] L 65/19, para. 75; Commission Decision 92/163/EEC (*Tetra Pak II*) OJ [1992] L 72/1, paras 108–112.; Comp/E-2/36.041/PO – *Michelin*. 2002/405/EC OJ [2002] L 143/1.; *De Post/La Post* OJ [2002] L 61/32, para. 55.
551. Paragraphs 20 and 53–54.
552. Paragraphs 62 and para. 30.
553. In respect of refusal to deal and essential facilities *see* Csongor István Nagy, *Nélkülözhetetlen eszközök koncepciója az amerikai, a közösségi és a magyar versenyjogban*, in *Európai Jogi Tanulmányok* 125–156 (Miklós Király ed., ELTE ÁJK, Nemzetközi Magánjogi és Európai Gazdasági Jogi Tanszék 2006); Csongor István Nagy, *Refusal to Deal and the Doctrine of Essential Facilities in US and EC Competition Law. A Comparative Perspective and a Proposal for an Analytical Framework* 32(5) Eur. Law Rev. 664–685 (2007).
554. *See e.g.*, Case *VJ-61/1994 Burial Services* and Case *VJ-39/2002 UPC Hungary Kft.*

Part II, Ch. 2, Dominant Undertakings' Prohibited Practices

647. The legal test the CC developed for refusal to deal cases can be boiled down to four conjunctive conditions. In Case *Vj-10/2002/16*, the CC held that refusal to deal infringes competition law if:

- the undertaking has a dominant position in the relevant market;
- refuses or ceases to do business or binds it to abnormal conditions;
- the conduct has an appreciably negative impact on competition in the market and its efficiency, beyond impairing the interests of the undertaking concerned; or
- the dominant undertaking cannot prove that the conduct has objective and economically reasonable justifications.[555]

648. Due to the principle that competition law protects competition and not competitors, refusal to deal is not considered to be abusive if it has no palpable repercussions on consumers. Accordingly, the dominant undertaking does not infringe the law if it refuses to enter or maintain a contract, if this entails no considerable restriction of competition.

649. In Case *Vj-186/2007 Magyar Posta*, the CC ended the procedure against the Hungarian Post ('*Magyar Posta*') in a case where the Post's conduct prevented a competitor from entering the market. The CC held that although the Post had a dominant position and refused to deal (which was the pre-condition of entering the market of cash-transfer services) and the new entrant, in case of market entry, would have been the Post's actual competitor, there were several enterprises present in the market segment in question and, hence, the refusal did not restrict competition and, as a consequence, did not fall foul of the CA.

650. The Hungarian Post had a legal monopoly in different services. The Post also provided cash-transfer services, i.e., it delivered cash to addressees named by the client. For initiating such a cash-transfer, a special blank (cash-transfer blank) was needed, the technical details of which were determined by the Post. The production of blanks was liberalized, but producers had to obtain a licence from the Post. The corresponding regulation specified that the Post issued the licence once certain technical requirements were met. Licences could relate to two different activities: production of blanks and personalization of blanks, i.e., printing the name and identification data of a particular person or undertaking on blanks so the latter was not to be filled-out manually. Between 2004 and 2007, the Post refused to issue a licence for production to four undertakings mainly with reference to its own business interests, even though the applicants met the technical requirements established by the corresponding regulation. At the same time, the Post issued licences to several other undertakings. Dozens of undertakings were issued personalization licences. Some undertakings also received licences to produce and distribute blanks; however, the Post's business code provided that the Post issued production licences only if it did not have sufficient capacity to satisfy the demand. Before issuing a production licence, the Post examined the utilization rate of its own capacities.

---

555. Paragraph 36; this proposition was confirmed by the CC in Case *Vj-98/2003/26*, para. 20.

651. The CC found that although the Post failed to grant, due to economic considerations, a production licence in four cases (and in one case due to technical reasons), numerous undertakings were present in the market of producing blanks and these enterprises were significant competitors for the Post and generated intensive competition.[556] According to the CC, the conduct at stake was not general and did not restrict competition in the market for the production of blanks or in any other segment of the market. What is more, the Post was not the most significant operator in the market for personalized blanks. The CC emphasized that although the behaviour of the Post may have impeded the entry of certain market operators, it was not systematic and had no restrictive effects on competition and on consumers.[557] The undertakings already present in the market disposed of sufficient free capacity. The CC considered that the CA does not protect the existence or contracting possibilities of market operators but it protects market competition.[558] Since it was not proven that the conduct of the Post endangered competition in the market for the production of blanks or in any other market, it could not be assumed that consumers were injured. Hence, the CC concluded that the public interest did not justify the HCO's procedure. Nevertheless, it was also stressed that in case of demonstrated negative market effects the conduct of the Post would have amounted to a competition law violation.

652. According to the CC's decisional practice, the requirements against refusal to deal by dominant undertakings are more relaxed if this targets one of the dominant undertaking's distributors.[559]

653. In Case *Vj-6/2005*, the CC held that the producer has a wide discretion as to how it organizes its distribution system. For consumers, the relevant field of rivalry is inter-producer competition, while it is of slight importance whether the producer cuts out a reseller from the distribution system. The dominant producer's freedom in respect of its distribution policy and the business policy towards its traders is considerable. The question to be inquired is whether the exclusion of a trader and the inclusion of a new one impair inter-product competition. If this is not the case, the restriction or lack of intra-brand competition (i.e., competition between different distribution channels or different traders of the same brand) is not problematic.[560]

654. Accordingly, no distributor has a normative right to be on the market. Since in case of refusal the principal question is whether this is detrimental to consumers, competition law is not meant to ensure that a particular distributor can appear on the market or can stay on it under certain conditions, provided this entails no benefit to consumers.[561]

---

556. Paragraphs 33–35.
557. Paragraph 33.
558. Paragraph 34.
559. Case *Vj-105/2001*, para. 32; Case *Vj-6/2005*, para. 73; Case *Vj7/2005*, para. 68.
560. Paragraphs 71 and 74.
561. Case *Vj-105/2001*, para. 32. point; Case *Vj-7/2005*, para. 68.; Case *Vj-6/2005*, para. 73.

Part II, Ch. 2, Dominant Undertakings' Prohibited Practices

655. The dominant undertaking can prove that the refusal is based on objective justifications. This requirement is met, if the refusal is based on objective, economically reasonable grounds. The undertaking, including dominant enterprises, cannot be compelled to act to the prejudice of its legal interests or to cause itself extra-costs.[562]

656. In Case *Vj-89/1998/17*, a cable television switched off some of its customers. The CC held that this occurred in individual matters and, as such, had no effects on the market; it found that this was a civil matter. This case concerned final consumers; it is assumed that this approach is *a fortiori* applicable to undertakings. The CC's decision suggests that the notion of abuse cannot be used to solve individual civil disputes.

657. The CC examined the undertaking's motivations and assumed that the switching-off had reasonable grounds. It advanced that a service provider is not interested in excluding its customers from the service, since this entails a decrease in its subscription clientele. It is unlikely that it excludes consumers with no arrears from the service. However, the CC also noted that if this practice is widespread, it may qualify as abusive.

IV. Price Squeeze

658. There have been only a few price squeeze cases in Hungary. The test applied by the CC is similar to the approach of EU competition law, which can be used as a reference point in these matters.

659. In *Napier Brown – British Sugar*,[563] the British Sugar (BS) had a dominant position in the sugar wholesale market, while being in competition with Napier Brown (NB) in the retail market. British Sugar was condemned for increasing the wholesale prices and decreasing the retail prices in a way that forced the retail competitor to operate at loss. The legal test applied by the Commission was the following: assuming that NB matched BS's efficiency, the Commission examined the margin left to NB or any other retail competitor if using industrial sugar purchased from BS. The Commission held that the retail prices did not enable competing repackagers as efficient as BS to earn a sufficient margin, 'even without trying to make a profit'.[564]

---

562. Case *Vj-105/2001*, para. 32; Case *Vj-98/2003/26*, para. 21; Case *Vj-6/2005*, para. 73; Case *Vj-7/2005*, para. 68; Case *Vj-117/2005*, para. 38; this approach was confirmed by the judicial practice, see Case *FB. 2.K.32366/1993.*; Case *FB. 2.K.32527/1992.*
563. Commission Decision 88/518/EEC *Napier Brown – British Sugar.* OJ [1988] L 284/41.
564. Paragraph 30 ('The pricing information indicated above shows that BS has engaged in a price cutting campaign leaving an insufficient margin for a packager and seller of retail sugar, as efficient as BS itself in its packaging and selling operations, to survive in the long term.')

660. The Commission established that where an undertaking is dominant in the markets for both the raw material and the derived products, if amounts to an abuse, if the difference between the prices the dominant undertaking charges for the raw material and for the derived product is 'insufficient to reflect that dominant company's own costs of transformation'; that is, the difference between the dominant enterprise's wholesale and retail prices has to be compared to its own repackaging costs. Accordingly, the retail costs to be taken into account are those of the dominant undertaking; this is meant to ensure that only competitors as efficient as the dominant undertaking receive protection from competition law. The Commission noted that the above pricing policy, if maintained in the long term, was susceptible of driving the competitor out of the market.[565] Nevertheless, the entry barriers and the perspectives of re-entry were not an issue. It is to be noted that in this case the profit, calculated on the basis of the above formula, was negative.

661. In *Deustche Telekom*,[566] the Commission also investigated a case where the dominant undertaking left a negative profit to its retail distributors. The Commission placed emphasis on the fact that Deutsche Telekom's (DT) retail competitors 'even if they are at least as efficient as DT, can never make a profit, because on top of the wholesale charges they pay to DT they also have other costs such as marketing, billing, debt collection, etc.'[567] The Commission rephrased the legal test established in *Napier Brown – British Sugar*.[568]

662. In *Wanadoo España v. Telefónica*,[569] the Commission also condemned a price squeeze where the margin left to the retail competitors was negative. The margin between the wholesale and retail prices was insufficient to cover the costs that an operator as efficient as Telefónica would incur to provide retail broadband access. The Commission summarized the legal test of price squeeze as follows:

> *In accordance with established case law the methodology applied for establishing the existence of a margin squeeze consists in assessing whether Telefónica's downstream arm would operate profitably on the basis of the upstream charges levied by Telefónica's upstream arm.*[570]

663. In Case *Vj-100/2002 Magyar Távközlési Rt.*, the Hungarian telecommunications incumbent (MATÁV, now called Magyar Telekom) set the (wholesale) prices of access services and the retail telecommunications prices at a level triggering a 'negative

---

565. Commission Decision 88/518/EEC *Napier Brown – British Sugar.* OJ [1988] L 284/41, para. 66.
566. Commission Decision 2003/707/EC *Deutsche Telekom AG*). OJ [2003] L 263/9.
567. Paragraph 102.
568. Paragraphs 106–108.
569. Commission Decision of 4 Jul. 2007 relating to a proceeding under Art. 82 of the EC Treaty (Case COMP/38.784 – *Wanadoo España v. Telefónica*).
570. Summary of Commission Decision of 4 Jul. 2007 relating to a proceeding under Art. 82 of the EC Treaty (Case COMP/38.784 – *Wanadoo España v. Telefónica*).

margin'. As a result of this, the matter was a 'simple' price squeeze case, yet the CC stressed that an abuse may be established even if the margin is 'positive' but too small. The CC held that it has to be analysed whether the margin of the dominant undertaking on the downstream market covers both the wholesale price and the retail costs. The CC stressed that the wholesale costs are expected to be equal to those of the competitors, otherwise the dominant undertaking would be condemned for discrimination. A negative margin amounts to the violation of competition law but in case the margin is relatively small, a more detailed cost analysis may be necessary. Nevertheless, the CC also added that the foregoing is only one of the prerequisites of price squeeze and the establishing of an infringement also pre-supposes that the practice lasts for a long period of time and there are considerable entry barriers in the market. It is to be emphasized that in this case the abuse took place during the period the telecommunications market was opened (from January 2002 onward).

664. In *Vj-101/2002 Vivendi Telecom Rt.*, the defendant charged a high price in its (wholesale) ADSL contracts, while pushing down its prices in the retail market for access services to ADSL-based Internet. The CC found that although the retail margin the foregoing pricing policy entailed was rather small and objectionable, the market was contestable and partly due to the competitive pressure on the part of cable broadband Internet, the defendant could not have increased its prices without attracting new entrants.[571]

665. In *Vj-73/2003 Magyar Távközlési Rt.*, essentially the same issues emerged (this was also a telecommunications case). The CC stressed that if the dominant undertaking achieves cost-savings through efficiency, it may certainly include it into the final price without committing a price squeeze. The CC established no abuse, since the alleged price squeeze in 2002 was the result of price-regulation (which concerned both wholesale and retail prices), whilst in 2003 the margin left to the retail segment was considered to be reasonable.

666. In sum, in accordance with EU competition law, the CC's decisional practice suggests that price squeeze can be established even in case the competitor is left some margin, provided the margin is unreasonably low. It is assumed that the test of EU competition law can be applied also in Hungarian competition law: the relevant question is whether the dominant undertaking's downstream arm could operate profitably taking into account the prices the upstream arm charges. Furthermore, a practice can be condemned only if it is performed for a long period of time and it is capable of driving competitors out of the market. Even in this case (similarly to predatory pricing) the potential of autotherapy has to be taken into account: price squeeze can be established only if considerable entry barriers exist, that is, if the market is not contestable. Finally, competition law protects only those downstream competitors

---

571. The HCO conceptualized the applicable test as follows: whether 'P' is equal or higher than 'A' + 'C', where 'P' is retail price charged by the dominant undertaking, 'A' is the wholesale input price of the commodity and 'C' is the retail costs (the cost of converting the input into a final product).

that are at least as efficient as the dominant undertaking: if the dominant undertaking, in its retail level operations, achieves cost-savings through efficiency, it may certainly include these into the final price without committing a price squeeze.

V. Exclusivity and Long-Term Agreements

667. The structure of the analysis in matters concerning exclusivity arrangements used by dominant enterprises was summarized in Case *Vj-22/2005/145 MÁV*, where the CC referred to the test[572] applied by the CJEU in *Hofmann-La Roche*.[573] In this case, the CJEU held that exclusivity clauses applied by dominant undertakings are, in principle, abusive,[574] except the exclusivity can be justified on the basis of Article 101(3) TFEU, i.e., it enhances efficiency, it is proportionate, a fair share is allotted to consumers and competition is not eliminated completely.[575]

668. Long-term agreements may be treated in the same manner as exclusivity (non-compete) clauses, if they entail similar effects; e.g., the long-term supply agreement covers a substantial part or the totality of the buyer's purchases. Hence, the analysis of exclusivity clauses (non-compete obligations, exclusive purchasing) and of agreements having similar effects (quantity forcing, requirements contracts) converges.

669. Although it was not made express in the above decision, the CC subjects exclusivity clauses (as alleged abuses of dominant position in general) to effects-analysis[576] and, when evaluating such practices, takes additional factors into account.

---

572. Paragraphs 288–289.
573. Case 85/76 *Hoffmann-La Roche & Co. AG v. Commission* [1979] ECR 461.
574. '*An undertaking which is in a dominant position on a market and ties purchasers – even if it does so at their request – by an obligation or promise on their part to obtain all or most of their requirements exclusively from the said undertaking abuses its dominant position within the meaning of Article 102 of the Treaty, whether the obligation in question is stipulated without further qualification or whether it is undertaken in consideration of the grant of a rebate.*' Para. 89.
575. '*Obligations of this kind to obtain supplies exclusively from a particular undertaking, whether or not they are in consideration of rebates or of the granting of fidelity rebates intended to give the purchaser an incentive to obtain his supplies exclusively from the undertaking in a dominant position, are incompatible with the objective of undistorted competition within the common market, because – unless there are exceptional circumstances which may make an agreement between undertakings in the context of article 101 and in particular of paragraph (3) of that article, permissible – they are not based on an economic transaction which justifies this burden or benefit but are designed to deprive the purchaser of or restrict his possible choices of sources of supply and to deny other producers access to the market.*' Para. 90.
576. *See* Guidance on the Commission's enforcement priorities in applying Art. 82 of the EC Treaty to abusive exclusionary conduct by dominant undertakings. OJ [2009] C 45/7, paras 19–20; Case T-65/89 *BPB Industries Plc and British Gypsum Ltd v. Commission* [1993] ECR II-00389, para. 66.

Part II, Ch. 2, Dominant Undertakings' Prohibited Practices 670–675

670. Accordingly, in the first step, it is to be analysed whether the arrangement has actual or potential anti-competitive effects (foreclosure). If the answer to this question is in the affirmative, in the second step it is to be examined whether there are objective justifications warranting the restriction.

A. Anti-competitive Effects

671. The level of dominance has a significant role in the competition law analysis of the restraint. For instance in *Repsol*,[577] where the dominant firm's market share ranged from 30% to 50%, a five-year-long duration was accepted.[578] This suggests that the Commission balanced the duration and the level of the supplier's market dominance. This approach may also be followed by the CC.

672. The ratio (percentage) of the customer's demand that is tied under the long-term commitment is also taken into account, i.e., what percentage of the customer's consumption is covered by exclusivity.[579]

673. When examining the tied part of the customer demand, it has to be taken into consideration that transaction costs may become too high in respect of small quantities, making alternative sources less economic. Recent decisions seem to suggest that 20% of the customer's requirement is the threshold, at or over which there is incentive to find a second source of supply.[580]

674. It is also examined how much of the market is covered by the tied sales. The bigger the tied part of the market is, the higher the risk of foreclosure is.

675. In *MÁV*, the exclusivity clauses covered approximately 30%–40 % of the market.[581] The CC emphasized that the exclusivity arrangement practically foreclosed a considerable part of the relevant market.[582] In *DÉMÁSZ II*,[583] the HCO terminated a procedure against a local incumbent electricity service provider on the basis that the 'best offer' clauses covered only a small portion of the purchases of the buyers on the market.[584]

---

577. Case *Repsol CPP SA*, OJ [2004] C 258/7.
578. Paragraphs 11–12.
579. A. de Hauteclocque & J.-M. Glachant, *Long-term Energy Supply Contracts in European Competition Policy: Fuzzy not Crazy*, 37(12) Energy Policy 15 (2009), available at http://web.mit.edu/ceepr/www/publications/workingpapers/2008-016.pdf.
580. A. de Hauteclocque & J.-M. Glachant, *Long-term Energy Supply Contracts in European Competition Policy: Fuzzy not Crazy*, 37(12) Energy Policy 15 (2009), available at http://web.mit.edu/ceepr/www/publications/workingpapers/2008-016.pdf.
581. Paragraphs 286 and 293(b).
582. Paragraphs 293(e) and 293(g).
583. Case *Vj-106/2006/69*.
584. Paragraph 59.

676. Likewise, in *Budapesti Elektromos Művek*,[585] the CC closed the competition proceeding against an electricity producer on the basis that the 'best offer' provisions had no appreciable foreclosure effect on the market: these contractual arrangements concerned only 38% of the turnover of the seller's customers and 10% of the entire market. The CC also considered the declarations of the consumers, who confirmed that the contract did not restrict them in finding an alternative supplier.[586] The CC terminated the proceeding in *E.ON Tiszántúli Áramszolgáltató* on the basis of similar arguments: only 10% of the supplier's customers were covered by long-term 'best offer' agreements.[587] In *E.ON Dél-dunántúli Áramszolgáltató*, 30% of the supplier's big purchasers was covered by 'best offer' clauses and this represented approximately 5% of the market.[588] In *E.ON Észak-dunántúli Áramszolgáltató*,[589] 15% of the big purchasers and approximately 5% of the market was covered.[590] In *Észak-magyarországi Áramszolgáltató*,[591] 15%–20% of the big purchasers and small part (a few percent) of the market was covered.[592]

677. It is to be noted that in *Distrigas*,[593] where the Commission accepted the commitments of Distrigas and terminated the proceeding, the undertaking, among others, promised that on average 70% of the gas, which it has contracted to supply to resellers and large gas customers, would return to the market every year (in principle, because the contracts ended). Distrigas had some flexibility to meet this average; however, each year at least 65% of the contracted volumes had to be liberated.

678. The duration of the exclusivity is also a crucial aspect of competition analysis.

679. In *TITÁSZ*, the CC objected to the duration of the exclusivity clauses inserted in the public lighting contracts of a local incumbent electricity service provider. The average duration was ten years, but in certain cases it was fifteen years.[594] It is to be emphasized that this case emerged in the context of market liberalization. Similarly, in *DÉMÁSZ*,[595] the CC condemned the electricity purchase agreement concluded by the local incumbent electricity service provider providing for a fifteen years long duration. The CC emphasized that it was not the duration of the agreement but the length of the exclusivity that raised concerns. Although the buyer (a city) could terminate

---

585. Case *Vj-104/2006/130*.
586. Paragraphs 55–56.
587. Paragraph 55.
588. Paragraph 55.
589. Case *Vj-107/2006/76*.
590. Paragraph 56.
591. Case *Vj-105/2006/66*.
592. Paragraph 57.
593. Press Release of the European Commission, IP/07/1487, Brussels, 11 Oct. 2007.
594. Paragraphs 96–97.
595. Case *Vj-176/2001*.

the contract, this could be done only if paying liquidated damages.[596] It is to be emphasized here as well that this case emerged in the context of market liberalization.

680. It is to be noted that in *Distrigas*, the Commission accepted the commitments of Distrigas and terminated the proceeding. The Commission's main concern was that the long-term supply agreements, allegedly, foreclosed competition from the Belgian gas market because new entrants could have no access to customers. The commitment provided that Distrigas would not conclude gas supply contracts with gas resellers with a duration of more than two years; while the maximum duration of new contracts with other large gas customers (industrial consumers and electricity generators) would be five years (with the exception of new gas fired power plants).

681. The features of the buyer may also be relevant for the competition law analysis.

682. In *MÁV*, the HCO stressed that the buyers covered by exclusivity were the most significant customers in the industry, which were the most important targets of new entrants (the case emerged in the context of market liberalization[597]).[598]

683. This is in line with the Commission's approach in *Distrigas*, where the duration of the exclusivity varied according to the identity of the purchaser (gas resellers, other large customers).

684. As to the question of objective justification, in *MÁV* the CC held that although exclusivity employed by a dominant undertaking is normally anti-competitive, under certain conditions it may be justifiable. The reason is that such vertical restraints may have not only negative but also positive effects on the market. Hence, the competition law assessment has to embrace also the positive effects on competition and balance the negative and the positive implications.[599]

685. In this regard, the CC would likely follow the Commission's decisional practice. In *Synergen*, for instance, the Commission accepted an agreement where an electricity plant concluded a gas supply contract (exclusivity) with a fifteen years duration covering 100% of its needs and sold 50% of its output to the electricity incumbent. The Commission recognized that investment and project financing requires predictability and security in terms of input supply and output sales.[600] In *Exeltium*, a consortium of energy intensive users concluded an electricity supply agreement with EDF for a period of more than twenty years. The parties argued thatthe agreement was efficient, providing

---

596. Paragraphs 88–91.
597. This was considered to be very important by the CC. Para. 293(e).
598. Paragraphs 293(a) and 293(c).
599. Paragraph 292.
600. European Commission's Press Release, IP/02/792 Brussels, 31 May 2002.

for security of supply and hedging for buyers. The Commission, after a while, closed the proceeding, but the parties were required to delete certain resale restrictions and to insert an opt-out clause in order to mitigate the anti-competitive effects.[601]

---

601. A. de Hauteclocque & J.-M. Glachant, *Long-term Energy Supply Contracts in European Competition Policy: Fuzzy not Crazy*, 37(12) Energy Policy 15 (2009), available at http://web.mit.edu/ceepr/www/publications/workingpapers/2008-016.pdf. *See* European Commission: MEMO/08/533 of 31 Jul. 2008.

Chapter 3. Concentrations

686. The comprehensive assessment of a concentration can be accomplished only on the basis of the extensive and detailed examination and evaluation of market data.[602] In respect of the merger assessment of concentrations, section 30(2) CA adopts the 'effects on competition' test. The HCO authorizes the concentration if it does not lessen competition in the market significantly, in particular as a result of creating or strengthening a dominant position. In case the object or effect of the joint venture defined in section 23(1)(c) CA is to coordinate the market conduct of the founding undertakings, the concentration has to be adjudicated on the basis of section 17 CA.

687. Accordingly, the question to be answered in the frame of the merger analysis is whether the concentration substantially lessens competition.[603] The Hungarian 'effects on competition' test is the counterpart of the 'substantial lessening of competition' (SLC) test and the rough equivalent of the 'significant impediment to effective competition' (SIEC) test, as used in EU merger control law. A typical instance where the concentration would lessen competition significantly is the creation or strengthening of a dominant position; however, a concentration may lessen competition substantially even in case no dominance is created or strengthened.[604]

688. The 'effects on competition' test replaced the dominance test as from 1 July 2009.[605] The consideration behind the new approach is that a concentration may lessen competition not only in case of dominance, by way of example, the increase of market concentration may facilitate cartelization or tacit collusion. For example, in case there are three enterprises in the market of roughly equal size and two of them merge, the transaction might not entail a dominant position, albeit the competitive pressure on market operators, presumably, decreases and the market power of the two remaining enterprises increases; this may trigger the increase of the prices.[606]

689. A concentration may have horizontal and non-horizontal effects.

690. Section 30(1) CA contains an illustrative list of the factors to be taken into consideration when assessing the advantages and disadvantages of the concentration.

---

602. HCO's 'Communication on the analytical methods applied by the HCO in procedures for the authorization of concentrations, as well as on the circle of data necessary for these and on the requirements against these data', 1.
603. HCO's 'General Methodology: the methodological approach of the analysis of concentrations', para. 1.1.
604. HCO's 'General Methodology: the methodological approach of the analysis of concentrations', para. 1.2.
605. Act XIV of 2009.
606. *See* HCO's 'General Methodology: the methodological approach of the analysis of concentrations', para. 4.

- The structure of the relevant markets: the actual or potential competition in the relevant markets; the procurement and sales possibilities; the costs, risks and technical, economic and legal conditions of entering and leaving the market; the concentration's expected impact on competition in the relevant market.
- The market situation and strategy of the undertakings concerned, their economic and financial capacity, business conduct, competitiveness in the domestic and foreign market and the expected change of these.
- The concentration's impact on suppliers and business customers.

691. The potential negative effects on competition can be counterbalanced by certain factors. When assessing the concentration, the CC takes both the detrimental and the counterbalancing factors into consideration.

- Entry: if due to the higher prices new enterprises can enter the market quickly and in a cost-effective manner, this may lessen the merging parties' ability and incentives to increase prices.
- Buyer power: if there are buyers, the conduct of which entails a price decrease as to a considerable part of the market, this may lessen the merging parties' ability to increase prices.
- Efficiency benefits: if the concentration lessens the participating undertakings' production-related costs, this may have a price-decreasing effect; in respect of this counter-veiling factor, it has to be taken into account whether these efficiency benefits are concentration-specific, can be quantitatively demonstrated and an appropriate part of these benefits accrue to consumers.
- Failing firm: if it is proved that the competitive pressure effected by the target enterprise (the firm to be acquired) would disappear from the relevant market even in the absence of the concentration (i.e., there is no less restrictive alternative), the concentration would have no impact on the market.[607]

692. The assessment of the concentration is based on a prospective analysis. The concentration's effect is the future change the concentration entails that would not emerge in the absence of the concentration. The assessment focuses on those effects that would emerge in the 'not too far future', that is, between the end of the adaptation period after the implementation of the concentration and the moment when the market's structure would considerably change.[608]

693. It has to be noted that in general, in the assessment of concentrations, the HCO normally follows the methods and techniques of EU competition law and, as far as substantive analysis is concerned, no significant differences from EU merger control can be perceived.

---

607. HCO's 'General Methodology: the methodological approach of the analysis of concentrations', para. 3.
608. HCO's 'General Methodology: the methodological approach of the analysis of concentrations', para. 4.

Part II, Ch. 3, Concentrations

§1. HORIZONTAL MERGERS

694. Horizontal effects emerge between competitors active in the same relevant market. Horizontal effects may be unilateral (non-coordinated) and coordinated. The unilateral effects accrue from the disappearance of one of the competitors from the market (which becomes part of another competitor); this mitigates the competitive pressure on the undertakings remaining in the market. The concept of coordinated effects encompasses the risk of tacit collusion: the transaction may ease the collusion between the undertakings remaining in the market.

695. The HCO established in Case *Vj-118/2010*[609] that competition may be considerably deteriorated even in case a smaller competitor falls out of the market, especially in case the undertakings participating in the merger have high market shares, are close competitors, as well as the concentration switches off one of the important factors of competition (i.e., the enterprise dropping out is considered to be a maverick firm). In case of concentrated markets, it is especially important to ascertain the role the target enterprise played in the competition.

696. In Case *Vj-153/2009*,[610] the HCO listed certain circumstances that may qualify as indicia of coordinated effects: the ability to control coordinated behaviour; the feasibility of a certain punishment, deterrent mechanism, as a result of which the participants may not unilaterally diverge from the coordinated conduct; there is no external actor that could and would be interested in destabilizing the coordination (maverick firm). At the same time, it is not necessary to prove a pre-existent tacit collusion in the market or that market mechanisms would entail a cartel. Tacit collusion as a possible outcome does not necessarily imply that the parties conclude a restrictive agreement or engage in active concerted practice; negative effects on competition caused by tacit collusion may emerge even absent these.

§2. VERTICAL AND CONGLOMERATE MERGERS

697. Non-horizontal effects may be vertical, portfolio or conglomerate. Vertical effects may emerge, if the groups of undertakings concerned operate on the different levels of the value chain (production-distribution chain) and there is or could be a seller-purchaser relationship between them. Portfolio effects may accrue from the circumstance that due to the concentration the new undertaking's product portfolio expands, in particular if these products are complementary.[611]

698. In Case *Vj-71/2010*,[612] the HCO established that the partial or complete foreclosure of the market may occur in two ways. First, downstream competitors may be excluded from access to the inputs produced or distributed by the merging groups of undertakings

---

609. *See also* HCO's Position Statement No. 30.15.
610. *See also* HCO's Position Statement No. 30.16.
611. Notice 1/2014, para. 11.
612. *See also* HCO's Position Statement No. 30.14.

(refusal in the upstream market). Second, the undertaking having market power in the downstream market may restrict its upstream competitors' access to buyers (refusal in the downstream market). In the frame of the merger assessment, as to vertical effects, the HCO, in line with EU competition law, examines, first, whether the group of undertakings coming into existence as a result of the concentration is capable of foreclosing the market (i.e., restricting access to inputs or buyers), second, whether it is interested in pursuing such an anti-competitive strategy, that is, whether the loss of profit entailed by the refusal is outweighed by the profit caused by the deterioration of competition (due to the increase of the number of sales and/or of the prices), third, whether this has a detrimental impact on downstream competition and final consumers, as well as whether the occasional negative effects on competition are counterbalanced by equalizing buying power, the possibility of market entry or the enhancement of efficiency brought about by the vertical integration. A concentration qualifies as restrictive only if the foregoing three conditions are met.

§3. Pure Conglomerate Mergers

699. There is no specific Hungarian practice as to pure conglomerate mergers; so far, the HCO has opened no full investigation specifically due to conglomerate effects.

Part III. Administrative Procedure

Chapter 1. Administrative Investigations before the Antitrust Authority

§1. INITIATIVE

I. General Sector Inquiries

700. The HCO has two tools to assess market trends, without launching a competition proceeding: market surveys and sector inquiries.

701. The inputs to market surveys are publicly available information and data collection based on voluntary data-conveyance. In the frame of market surveys, the HCO examines the operation of particular markets, market trends and certain market practices and their effects on competition and business customers, in particular final business customers.[613] The HCO makes both the opening and the results of the market survey public.[614]

702. In case the change of prices or other market circumstances suggests that competition is restricted or distorted in a market, the HCO, by order, starts a sector inquiry so as to discover and assess processes in the market. The order has to indicate the circumstances that made the launch of the sector inquiry necessary. The order has to be published on the HCO's website.[615]

703. In the frame of the sector inquiry, the HCO may collect information and request data; the conveyance of the requested data is mandatory, the HCO may impose a fine in case the undertaking fails to convey the data (or does not convey it within the deadline) or submits false data.[616]

704. The HCO prepares a report on the results of the sector inquiry.[617]

---

613. Section 43/C(1) CA.
614. Section 43/C(2)-(3) CA.
615. Section 43/D(1) CA.
616. Section 43/D(3) CA.
617. Section 43/E(1) CA.

705. It has to be ensured that the undertakings operating in the sector concerned have the chance to comment on the report; for this purpose, the draft report has to be sent to these undertakings[618] or in case these undertakings cannot be identified or the number of the enterprises active in the sector is high, the HCO holds a public hearing.[619]

706. If, as a result of the market survey or the sector inquiry, the HCO identifies market distortions that cannot be (or can only partially be) rectified through a competition proceeding, the HCO informs the Parliament's competent committee or the competent minister or authority on this, issues a non-mandatory public recommendation for market operators as to best practices and recommended market conduct and, if necessary, it may initiate the adoption or amendment of a rule of law at the competent body.[620]

II. Ex Officio Investigations

707. Procedures in antitrust cases (restrictive agreements, dominant position) are always launched ex officio, even if the procedure is opened as a result of a formal or informal complaint. In contrast, procedures in merger control cases are launched upon request, with the exception of cases where an undertaking fails to fulfil its duties under the merger control rules (e.g., it implements a concentration without prior authorization).

708. According to section 70(1) CA, not all violations have to be investigated by the HCO, only those where the protection of the public interest warrants this. The case-handler, by order, opens an investigation if he perceives a likely illegal action, conduct or situation coming under the HCO's competence, provided the protection of the public interest demands the carrying out of the investigation. In the order, the circumstance, conduct or situation serving as the investigation's subject-matter has to be spelled out.

709. The HCO has a certain margin of appreciation as to whether the investigation would be warranted by the protection of the public interest and, hence, whether it launches an investigation or not. However, this decision is subject to judicial review in case of a formal complaint. If a formal complaint is submitted to the HCO, the case-handler has to decide within two months whether it opens the competition proceedings or whether the pre-conditions of opening the procedure are not fulfilled. If the case-handler refuses to start a procedure, this order can be attacked before the court within eight days from the service of the order. If the court considers that the conditions set out in section 70(1) CA are met, enjoins the case-handler to launch the investigation within thirty days.[621]

---

618. Section 43/D(2) CA.
619. Section 43/D(3) CA.
620. Section 43/F CA.
621. Section 43/H(7) CA and s. 43/H(10) CA.

Part III, Ch. 1, Administrative Investigations

III. Complaints

710. With the obvious exception of merger applications, antitrust proceedings are always instituted ex officio. However, anyone may submit a formal complaint ('bejelentés') or an informal complaint ('panasz') reporting on circumstances that may fall foul of EU or Hungarian competition law, provided the case comes under the HCO's competence. It is noteworthy that anyone may submit a complaint: the complainant does not have to prove legal interest and there are no restrictions as to who may submit a complaint. The procedure concerning formal and informal complaints is not part of the competition proceeding; they HCO may ex officio open the competition proceeding as a consequence of the complaint or if the conditions of the institution of the competition proceeding are not met, it may reject the complaint. If the competition proceeding is opened, this will be a procedure independent of the procedure within which the complaint was assessed.

711. If a document submitted does not meet the requirements of a formal complaint, it is treated as an informal complaint. The procedural rules on the handling of informal complaints are rather simple. In case an informal complaint is submitted to the HCO, the case-handler has to take the necessary measures; the case-handler is not obliged to take any measure if the same complainant re-submits an earlier informal complaint (submits a new complaint that has the same content as his earlier complaint) or if an anonymous informal complaint is submitted. The case-handler may hear both the complainant and the undertaking against whom the complaint was submitted and may request information. The complainant may ask the HCO not to reveal his personal identity and the fact that he submitted a complaint to the HCO.[622] If the HCO institutes a competition procedure or a procedure is already pending in the matter, the complainant is to be informed about this fact.[623]

712. Formal complaints have to be submitted in the form published by the HCO. The proceeding concerning the adjudication of formal complaints is a formal procedure, though, as noted above, not part of the competition proceeding. In order to make a decision on the formal complaint, the case-handler may collect information and may hear the persons concerned. However, if the person concerned refuses to cooperate, no fine can be imposed and no coercive measure may be adopted. The complainant may ask the HCO to conceal his personal identity and the fact that he submitted a formal complaint to the HCO.

713. As noted, the procedure on adjudicating the formal complaint is formal, the case-handler has to adjudicate the complaint in a formal decision (order):

- it may institute a competition proceeding;
- it may establish that on the basis of the information included in the formal complaint and collected during the procedure on the adjudication of the formal complaint

---

622. Section 43/G(3) CA.
623. Section 43/I CA.

the conditions of instituting a competition proceeding, as set out in section 70(1) CA, are not met;
- it terminates the procedure, if, as to the subject-matter indicated in the formal complaint, there is a pending competition proceeding against the organization or person concerned by the complaint or if the HCO, as to the subject-matter indicated in the formal complaint, has already adjudicated the allegations included in the formal complaint (on the basis of the same fact pattern as the one set out in the formal complaint and of unchanged legal regulation);
- if the matter comes under another authority's competence, it has to transfer the complaint to the competent authority.[624]

714. The above order is to be rendered within two months; if necessary, the deadline may be extended by two months.[625]

715. If the case-handler refuses to launch a competition proceeding – that is, it comes to the conclusion that the conditions of instituting a competition proceeding set out in section 70(1) CA are not met –, it adopts an order. The order has to be served on the complainant, who made the formal complaint; it also has to be served on the undertaking against whom the complaint was made, in case the latter took part in the procedure.[626]

716. The case-handler's order rejecting the institution of the competition proceeding can be attacked before the court by the complainant (who made a formal complaint). The deadline for submitting the application is eight days. The adjudication of the application is governed by the rules applicable to the judicial review of orders adopted in an administrative proceeding with the difference that if the court establishes that the case-handler should have instituted the competition proceeding (because the preconditions of this were met), it enjoins the case-handler to open the competition procedure within thirty days.[627]

717. The Act on Public Procurement provides that if during the public tender procedure the tenderer perceives the obvious violation of section 11 CA (the Hungarian equivalent of Article 101 TFEU) or that of Article 101 TFEU or has good reason to assume that this occurs, it has to submit a formal or informal complaint to the HCO.[628]

IV. Informant's Award

718. Under Hungarian law, the natural person who gives to the HCO written evidence indispensable for proving a cartel or helps the HCO to find such evidence in the frame of a dawn raid is entitled to 'informant's award'. The amount of the

---

624. Section 43/H(7) CA.
625. Section 43/H(7)-(8) CA.
626. Section 43/H(9) CA.
627. Section 43/H(10) CA.
628. Section 28(2) of the Act on Public Procurement.

Part III, Ch. 1, Administrative Investigations

informant award is 1% of the fine but cannot exceed HUF 50 million.[629] This institution of Hungarian competition law seems to be rather idiosyncratic.

719. The rules on the informant's award entered into force on 1 April 2010 and are meant to intensify the influx of information on secret cartels. However, it is to be noted that this institution has caused no boom as to cartel investigations, probably due to the same reasons that may entail the non-success of the leniency policy in Hungary.

A. The Conditions of the Informant's Award

720. The informer is entitled to an award only in case it reveals a cartel, i.e., a horizontal hardcore agreement; accordingly, it does not cover vertical restrictions and abuses of dominant position. The award is available in case of price-fixing, market division and quota cartels (agreements between competitors that are directly or indirectly aimed at fixing the purchase or sales prices, sharing of markets – including bid-rigging – or at the allocation of production or sales quotas).[630]

721. As to the value of the evidence to be provided, the requirement is that it has to be indispensable and written.[631] The evidence meets the former requirement both if it is indispensable for establishing the violation and if it helps the HCO to obtain the evidence proving the violation (i.e., on the basis of the evidence, the court authorizes the dawn raid, where the HCO obtains the evidence proving the violation). As the informant often does not have the whole set of evidence at hand but knows where the evidence can be found, he may also be entitled to the award if he brings the HCO in the situation where it can find the indispensable evidence. If the informer knows where the evidence is and helps the HCO to receive a court warrant for dawn raid, and the HCO, in fact, finds the evidence on the spot, the evidence submitted qualifies as indispensable.[632] The court grants a search warrant (dawn raid order) if the HCO substantiates that the source of information concerning the violation can be found on the spot; the HCO also has to substantiate that other means of investigation would be unsuccessful and it can be assumed that the source of information would not be submitted voluntarily or would be made useless.[633]

722. The explanatory report of the amendment inserting the informant's award into the CA provides that the evidence meets the requirements of the law, if it is indispensable for proving the fact (commission) of the violation; however, evidence relevant as to the determination of the fine does not meet this requirement. Accordingly, if the evidence submitted by the whistle-blower reveals an unknown cartel or proves that the known cartel covered more enterprises or a wider territory, the informant

---

629. Section 79/A(3) CA.
630. Section 79/A(1) CA.
631. Section 79/A(1) CA.
632. Section 79/A(2) CA.
633. Section 65/A(4) CA.

may be eligible for an award; however, if the evidence only proves, in respect of a cartel known to the HCO, that the cartelist companies acted maliciously and did know how serious their mischief was, the informant will not be entitled to an award.

723. The explanatory report also establishes that the question whether the evidence is indispensable can be assessed only in the light of the entire proceeding, the evidence collected and the final decision that provides the competition law characterization of the acts committed. It is to be noted, however, that from the perspective of the entitlement to the informant's award, the evidence remains indispensable even in case later on the HCO obtains evidence that can substitute the evidence submitted by the informant.[634]

B. The Amount of the Informant's Award and the Legal Guarantees of the Entitlement

724. The CA is fairly generous as to the amount of the informant's award: the informer can claim 1% of the fine imposed in the CC's decision in the merits; however, the award cannot exceed HUF 50 million.[635] It is to be stressed that the calculation of the award is based on the amount of the fine imposed by the CC and not on the amount affirmed by the court, which may reduce the fine or quash the decision imposing the fine. That is, the entitlement to the award is independent from the fate of the administrative decision; the informant is entitled to the award once the administrative decision is rendered and it cannot be claimed back if the HCO fails to defend its decision before the court. Likewise, the award cannot be claimed back if the court quashes the administrative decision and this deprives the evidence of its indispensable character; i.e., in the light of the judgment the evidence no longer qualifies as indispensable.[636] According to the explanatory report of the amendment inserting the informant's award, it would not be fair to place the risk related to the judicial review of the CC's decision on the informant. The informant's contribution to the discovery of the cartel and the CC's decision are useful in themselves; hence, the final result of the procedure should not affect his award.

725. Nonetheless, the award can be claimed back if the judicial annulment or amendment of the administrative decision is due to the illegality of the evidence and this illegality issues from the informant's conduct.[637] As provided in the explanatory report of the amendment introducing the informant's award, this is the case if the informer submits forged evidence, that is, the defendant proves that the document is not connected to it and it is probably forged. The re-vindication of the award on the basis of this would occur, very probably, only rarely, since such problems

---

634. Section 79/A(2) CA.
635. Section 79/A(3) CA.
636. Section 79/A(7) CA.
637. Section 79/A(7) CA.

would come to light during the administrative proceeding where the defendant has the chance to impeach the evidence.

726. The informant has a statutory right to the award. That is, it does not come under the HCO's discretion whether it awards it or not. Although it may have some margin of appreciation when interpreting the rules and assessing the facts, the decision rejecting the claim for an award can be attacked before the court. The CC has to render an order on the informant's claim for the award, not later than thirty days after the adoption of the decision at the end of the competition proceeding. This order can be attacked before the court. The payment of the award is due within thirty days after the order becomes final.[638]

C. The Payment of the Informant Award in Case of More Than One Informant; the Exclusion of the Award's Accumulation

727. Albeit one natural person can receive only one informant's award (in the same case), more than one natural person may submit evidence, and in such cases, all of them may be entitled to the award.[639] In order to obviate the accumulation of the award by the same person, the CA provides that in case of more than one informer, the HCO shall not pay multiple awards, if it can be established that the different pieces of evidence originate from a single source and they were split so as to multiply the amount of the award. In such cases, a single award is to be paid, which is to be apportioned equally among the informants.[640]

728. If more than one informant submits evidence, the question emerges how these can qualify as indispensable. Since the CA does contain provisions on the case when more than one informant submits evidence, providing that more than one person may receive an award, the conclusion can be drawn that the submission of indispensable evidence does not imply that no other evidence can qualify as indispensable. The term 'indispensable' implies that the evidence is necessary but not necessarily sufficient for establishing the violation. Hence, the submission of indispensable evidence does not exclude that other pieces of evidence may equally qualify as indispensable. However, if the evidence at the HCO's disposal is necessary and sufficient, no further informant may be entitled to an award. Accordingly, evidence representing an added value, which may strengthen the proof of the cartel or may contain relevant information as to the considerations governing the setting of the fine, does not qualify as indispensable and triggers no entitlement to the informant's award. This is reinforced by the explanatory report: a piece of evidence is indispensable if it is necessary for proving the fact (commission) of the violation; however, evidence relevant as to the determination of the fine does not meet this requirement.

---

638. Section 79/B(4)-(5) CA.
639. Section 79/A(3) CA.
640. Section 79/A(6) CA.

D. *Restraints on the Entitlement to the Informant's Award*

729. The CA establishes two restraints on the entitlement to the informant's award: the informant's award and the immunity (full or partial) under the leniency policy cannot be accumulated and the informant is not entitled to the award if the evidence was obtained as a result of a crime (felony or misdemeanour) or an offence.

730. The executive officers, members, supervisory board members, employees and agents of the undertaking that submitted a leniency application are not entitled to informant's award.[641] The purpose of this provision is to obviate the accumulation of the benefits, that is, to avoid cases where the cartelist enterprise receives full or partial immunity from the competition fine (due to the successful leniency application), while the executive receives an award.

731. Furthermore, no award shall be paid for evidence obtained as a result of a crime or an offence.[642] It is to be stressed that this does not apply to the case where the disclosure of the evidence qualifies as a crime or offence. Furthermore, the mere violation of the law (e.g., breach of secrecy) does not lift the entitlement to the award, as long as it does not qualify as a criminal act or an offence. The explanatory report reinforces this proposition, stressing that the violation of the rules of employment or civil law does not justify the exclusion of the informant's award; this is warranted only in case of serious violations of the law. According to the explanatory report, the public interest in the discovery of the cartel justifies the ignorance of the infringement of civil and employment law.

E. *The Protection of the Informant*

732. The CA ensures the protection of the informant's interests. The HCO has to ensure that potential informants, without disclosing their personal identity, can make inquiries about the details of the requirements applicable to the informant's award and about whether the documents they have may meet these requirements.[643] Furthermore, the informant may request the HCO to handle his personal data and place of living separately; this request cannot be rejected.[644]

F. *The Refund of the Informant's Award*

733. The CC may order that the award has to be refunded within thirty days after the decision justifying the refunding becomes final; the CC's order can be attacked

---

641. Section 79/A(4) CA.
642. Section 79/A(5) CA.
643. Section 79/B(1) CA.
644. Section 79/B(2) CA.

Part III, Ch. 1, Administrative Investigations

before the court.[645] This provision, through setting the starting date of the deadline, suggests that refunding may occur if the circumstance justifying this is confirmed in a final decision. This may happen in two cases. First, if the informer obtains the evidence through committing a crime or an offence, he is not entitled to the award. If the criminal procedure is started before the payment of the award, the payment has to be suspended until the criminal procedure ends; if the commission of the award is finally established, the award is to be paid back to the HCO.[646] Second, the award may be claimed back if the court quashes or amends the CC's decision due to the illegality of the evidence and this illegality issues from the informant's conduct. As noted, the amount of the award is calculated on the basis of the fine set in the CC's decision, and the subsequent fate of the administrative decision (its judicial annulment or amendment), in principle, does not affect the entitlement to and the amount of the informant's award.[647] It is to be noted that although the entitlement to the award is restricted in case more than one person submits evidence that originates from the same source and the pieces of evidence were divided in order to multiply the award (a single award is to be paid and the amount has to be divided equally), the CA contains no provision on the case when this circumstance is discovered only after the award has been paid.[648] It is rather uncertain whether and how the HCO may claim back part of the award in such cases, as the provision on the award's refunding refers to cases where the circumstance justifying the refunding is established in a formal decision (e.g., commission of a crime or offence). In case of multiple submissions, there is no such formal decision.

V. Limitation Period

734. No investigation can be started where five years have elapsed since the infringement of the provisions on cartels, abuse of dominant position and merger control.[649] In case the violation is continuous, the limitation period starts at the time the violation ends. If the violation relies in the non-termination of an unlawful situation, the limitation period starts when the unlawful situation ends. If the concentration is implemented without permission, the limitation period starts from the moment the concentration is implemented.[650]

735. The limitation period in respect of the antitrust violations (i.e., restrictive agreements, abuse of dominant position and infringement of the rules on merger control) is five years. This period is in line with the general rule: in civil and administrative matters the general limitation period is, apart from several exceptions, normally five years. Section 67(4) CA provides that no proceeding can be started if more than

---

645. Section 79/B(6) CA.
646. Section 79/A(5) CA.
647. Section 79/A(7) CA.
648. Section 79/A(6) CA.
649. Section 67(3) CA.
650. Section 67(3)-(4) CA.

five years have elapsed since the violation of the competition rule.[651] This language makes it clear that the limitation period is firm.

736. The CA adds that this rule does not apply to the administrative proceeding that has to be repeated due to a court judgment; that is, if the court quashes the administrative decision for the HCO's violation of certain procedural rules and remands the case to the HCO, the competition authority will have to repeat the proceeding; it will not be barred from conducting the repeated procedure by the fact that more than five years have elapsed between the violation of competition law and the start of the repeated administrative proceeding. Unfortunately, the CA does not set a deadline for the institution of the repeated proceeding: that is, formally, no limitation period applies to these cases and theoretically the HCO may start the repeated competition procedure at any time.

737. If the illegal conduct is continuous, the limitation period starts from the moment the violation ceases. Likewise, if the violation consists of not putting an end to a certain situation or plight, the limitation deadline does not start until this situation or plight subsists.[652]

738. For instance, if certain undertakings operate a price-fixing cartel, regularly meeting and setting the price of a commodity between 2003 and 2012, the term of limitation starts at the time the cartel is dissolved (i.e., 2012). The concept of institutionalized cartels (single complex and continuous infringements) plays a very important role in this context. As noted above, if the undertakings conclude more than one agreement (e.g., they regularly divide the public tenders), their conduct may be regarded not simply as a series of individual agreements but also as a general framework-agreement aimed at colluding at public tenders (institutionalized cartels or single complex and continuous infringements). In such cases, the HCO investigates the institutionalized cartel (i.e., the framework agreement) and not the individual agreements. In case of an 'institutionalized cartel', the term of limitation, since the 'institutionalized cartel' qualifies as a 'single complex and continuous infringements', starts only when the violation ends, hence, the events at the outset of the collusion may also be investigated.

739. It is worth comparing the calculation of the limitation period in administrative and civil matters. Although the term of the limitation period is the same both in administrative and private enforcement, five years in both cases,[653] there are considerable differences concerning the starting point of the limitation period. Likewise, there are considerable differences concerning the suspension of the limitation period.

---

651. Section 67(3) CA.
652. Section 67(4) CA.
653. *See* Section 6:22(1) CC.

Part III, Ch. 1, Administrative Investigations 740–744

740. In civil matters, the limitation period commences on the day when the claim becomes due;[654] claims for recovery become due when the damages occur.[655] The limitation period may be both suspended (*dormit*) and interrupted (*interrumpitur*). If the obligee cannot enforce the claim due to excusable reasons, the claim remains actionable for one year from the termination of the hindrance even if the limitation period expired or less than one year is left.[656] Accordingly, the CC does not provide for a suspension properly called, but merely grants a restricted extension to the limitation period, ensuring that the obligee has at least one year after the termination of the hindrance.

741. The flow of the limitation period is interrupted if the obligor acknowledges the debt, the parties amend the claim through an agreement or reach a settlement concerning it, an action is commenced before the court, if the court adopts a final decision in the merits ending the procedure and if the claim is submitted in an insolvency procedure.[657] After the interruption, the limitation period starts from the beginning.[658]

742. Accordingly, there are three points of divergence between administrative law and civil law limitation.

743. The first is the starting point of the limitation period. There could be a divergence if in a particular case the commission (or termination) of the infringement and the occurrence of the plaintiff's damages do not coincide. For instance, the starting dates of the limitation period may fall apart also in case the plaintiff is an indirect purchaser, since there could be a time lag between the conclusion and enforcement of the cartel and the occurrence of damages to the indirect purchasers.

744. The second point of divergence is entailed by the fact that the provisions on the administrative limitation period contain a rule on continuous infringements, while such a rule is missing regarding civil claims. For instance, assume that undertakings conspire to divide the construction projects of different municipalities in a bid-rigging cartel. From the point of view of the administrative limitation period, the five-year term starts when the undertakings terminate the agreement, while from the point of view of the civil limitation period, the claims of the individual municipalities may start once the particular municipality paid or agreed to pay a higher price, i.e., the starting point regarding the different tenders is different. Another example for divergence is when there is a cartel lasting for several years and the injured person purchases from one of the cartelist firms on numerous occasions during that period. In this case, the administrative limitation period starts at the end of

---

654. Section 6:22(2) CC.
655. Section 6:532 CC.
656. Section 6:24(2) CC; it is to be noted that in cases where the initial limitation period is one year or less, the extended deadline is three months.
657. Section 6:25(1) CC.
658. Section 6:25(2) CC.

the infringement, while the starting points of the limitation of the individual claims for damages caused by the individual purchases are different.

745. The third point relates to the rule on suspension. The limitation period under administrative (competition) law cannot be suspended; it expires at the end of the five years term even if the cartel remains covert during the entire period. At the same time, if the obligee has not been aware, nor should have been aware, of the infringement, he will have a one-year long period from the time he learns about the infringement for enforcing the claim. Having no information about the infringement would probably amount to an excusable reason to justify why the obligee could not enforce his claim. However, it is unsettled when the injured person gets into the situation to enforce the claim (from the perspective of the suspension of the period of limitation): the time when the procedure is launched, provided public notice is given on this (e.g., press release), or the time when the administrative decision is adopted; or more generously, when the condemning decision is finally affirmed by the court or the deadline of appeal expires.

§2. Powers

746. The HCO has various tools of investigation and sources of information to establish the facts of the case, in particular, the declarations, information and documents submitted by the parties, the interrogation of witnesses, the declarations and documents submitted by other persons, dawn raids (on the spot investigations without prior notice).

747. The CA establishes only a few restrictions against the HCO's powers of investigation and it is also hard-fisted as to the protected information: apart from the legal privilege (attorney-client communication), which is protected under certain circumstance, there is no information that would be inadmissible due to its nature (of course, it might be inadmissible for other reasons).

748. The HCO has the power to learn the personal data of the party and other participants of the procedure (e.g., witnesses) and to seize the register or database containing these data.[659] Furthermore, the HCO has the power to collect information and evidence containing business secrets and to use these in the competition procedure; however, concerning these, access to the file can be restricted or excluded.[660] The party and its representative, after the end of the investigation phase, have access to the administrative file and may make copies and take notes. However, the party and the participants of the procedure can request the HCO to restrict access to the file with reference to the protection of its business secrets. If making such a request, the party can be called to prepare and submit a non-confidential version of the document.[661]

---

659. Section 65(7) CA.
660. Sections 55-55/A CA.
661. Section 43/D(3) CA.

Part III, Ch. 1, Administrative Investigations

I. Requests for Information

749. The parties have a duty to disclose the information requested by the case-handler. The case-handler and the CC can request the party to disclose the information that is necessary for the decision in the merits, including personal data.[662]

750. The HCO has a wide discretion in drafting the questions of information requests. The party has to submit the information and documents requested by the HCO; this duty is very wide and it has only some restrictions. First, the party does not have to disclose the information or submit the document if the information or document is obviously not connected to the investigation's subject-matter or it is impossible to submit it.[663] Second, the prohibition of self-incrimination applies to the duty of disclosure: the party does not have to admit the commission of the violation. However, it must not refuse to submit the incriminating evidence;[664] accordingly, if the case-handler or the CC requests information or evidence that proves the commission of the competition law violation, the party may not reject the submission of this. Third, as noted above, attorney-client communication is privileged.

751. The party has to submit the information and documents even if they contains personal data or business secrets, albeit the party may request the HCO to restrict access to the file; in such cases, the original confidential document will be part of the administrative file, while the non-confidential version (which does not contain the business secrets) is accessible by the parties.

752. Not only the parties are subject to the duty to disclose the information requested: all persons and organizations have to provide, verbally or in writing, the information necessary for establishing the facts and to submit the documents connected to the investigation's subject-matter.[665]

II. Investigating and Search Powers

753. The most significant tools of investigation are the interrogation of witnesses (testimonies) and dawn raids.

754. An important limit on the case-handlers' investigating and search powers is the legal privilege providing immunity for the communication between the attorney and the client.

755. Hungarian competition procedure does not follow the principle that evidence can used only for the purposes of the investigation in the frame of which it was

---

662. Section 64/B(1) CA.
663. Case *2.Kpk.45980/2007/14* (Budapest Court); Case *3.Kpk.46.368/2009/2* (Budapest Court); Case *3.Kpk.45.935/2011/7* (Budapest Court); Case *3.Kpk.45122/2012/5* (Budapest Court).
664. Section 64/B(1) CA.
665. Section 64/B(4) CA.

obtained: although fishing expeditions are, legally speaking, not allowed and the case-handlers can conduct the dawn raid only within the limits of the competition proceeding's subject-matter, section 65/A(9) CA expressly provides that if they obtain unrelated evidence (i.e., evidence not related to the competition proceeding's subject-matter) that proves another violation of antitrust rules (restrictive agreements, abuse of dominant position), they can collect it and, if they acquire the court's posterior authorization for this, they can use it. Hungarian competition (procedural) law distinguishes between the seizure of evidence on dawn raids and the use of this evidence. The requirement that the investigation has to remain within the limits of the subject-matter established in the search warrant (court order authorizing the dawn raid) applies only to the case-handlers' operations on the spot and it is virtually a 'lex imperfecta', since the law establishes no sanction for the case the case-handler transgresses, even if deliberately, its powers and collects evidence that is unrelated to the matter set out in the search warrant. As noted above, in such cases the court authorization has to be requested posteriorly: the HCO has to submit a request within sixty days; failing posterior judicial authorization (i.e., if the court's authorization is no requested within the deadline or the authorization is rejected), the evidence is not admissible.

756. According to the CC's decisional practice, the evidence collected by the case-handler on the dawn raid can be used (if posterior court authorization is requested) even if the case-handler transgressed the subject-matter established in the court authorization. In this regard, it has no relevance whether the case-handler transgressed the search warrant's subject-matter deliberately, in bad faith or against the undertaking's express objections. The case-handler collects the documents available on the spot indiscriminately and selects the relevant documents only after analysing the collected materials. According to the CC, under Hungarian competition law the case-handler is expressly allowed to search for and collect documents that are obviously and blatantly unrelated to the matter at stake; the only limitation that applies in such cases is that he has to request the court's authorization subsequently.[666]

757. This decisional practice seems to go counter to section 65/A CA and to reduce the requirement of prior court authorization to a mere formality. Section 65/A(9) CA addresses the case where the case-handler finds the unrelated piece of evidence by accident: in such cases he has the power to collect it and request the court's posterior authorization. However, section 65/A(9) CA does not empower the case-handler to actively and deliberately search for unrelated evidence, especially in case the undertaking expressly indicates that the file, dossier or database contains unrelated data. The requirement of prior court authorization reinforces this interpretation, and section 65/A CA makes it explicit that that the dawn raid can be conducted only with the purpose of acquiring evidence related to the violation serving as the procedure's subject-matter.

---

666. Case *Vj-11-17/2014*, paras 40–41.

Part III, Ch. 1, Administrative Investigations

758. Unfortunately, this practice enables case-handlers to conduct finishing expeditions, since in the phase of the dawn raid it frees the case-handler from any limit, while it is highly unlikely that the court would reject the subsequent authorization if relevant evidence is found; it is to be noted that in such cases the court does not analyse whether the evidence was, in any sense, related to the search warrant's subject-matter; the legal test is whether the conditions of prior authorization are met.

759. One of the most important pieces of evidence is witness testimonies.[667] It is important to distinguish witness testimonies from 'party interrogations' (or 'party declarations'). The declarations of the party and that of the person acting on behalf of the party do not qualify as a witness testimony. Thus, although the party has the duty to convey all the information requested, the breach of this duty does not amount to a perjury but may be penalized with a procedural fine. The practice of the HCO is that if a natural person has the right of representation (power of attorney), he cannot be interrogated as a witness, since the two statuses are incompatible. In this regard, it is irrelevant whether the person's right of representation is based on the statute (statutory representative, e.g., directors) or on the party's authorization (power of attorney). Until 1 July 2014, section 54(2) CA listed those persons who may be granted a power of attorney (who could act as the party's agent); this list covered the fellow parties and their statutory representatives and agents, attorneys and law firms, the officers of the state body regarding the activities of the state body, the managing members and the employees of economic organizations in the organization's matters, interest representing organizations in their sectors of operation and persons authorized by the law. As from 1 July 2014, this provision was repealed and sections 40-40/A of the APA apply, which contain no such enumeration as to whom can be granted a power of attorney.

760. The foregoing implies that the statutory representatives of the parties (executives, managing partners, etc.) cannot be interrogated as a witness. Likewise, agents are not interrogated as a witness but as a party representatives ('party interrogation').

761. In restrictive agreement and dominance cases, irrespective of whether the proceeding is based on Hungarian or EU competition law, the HCO may hold on the spot inspections without prior notice (dawn raids). In the course of these inspections the case-handlers may search and enter any premise (whether the owner, possessor or the person in the premise provides access voluntarily or not), may open closed territories, buildings and premises,[668] may request verbal and written information and explanation and may collect information on the spot in any other manner.[669]

---

667. *See* ss 53–54 APA.
668. Section 65/A(1) CA.
669. Section 65/A(1) CA.

762. It is noteworthy that the case-handlers may conduct inspection also as to private premises (e.g., private dwellings, holiday houses), private vehicles, other private territories and private data carriers, provided the premise, vehicle, territory or data carrier is in the use of a person who – at the time of the procedure or during the period covered by the investigation's subject-matter – is or was the party's executive officer, employee, agent or belonging to a person who exercises or exercised de facto control over the party.[670]

763. Dawn raids can take place only on the basis of a prior court order (warrant). These orders are to be requested in writing from the Budapest Administrative and Labour Court; the court has to adopt a decision within 72 hours. The request is adjudicated in a non-contentious procedure; the court's order cannot be appealed (or attacked with a plea for supervision).[671] The prerequisite of the judicial authorization is that the HCO demonstrates that it is likely that other acts of investigation would not be successful and it is reasonably supposable that the evidence related to the violation is available on the site indicated in the request, and it can be assumed that it would not be conveyed voluntarily or would be made unusable. The court may also give partial authorization, specifying the person against whom the inspection can be made and the act of inspection that can be carried out. The judicial authorization is in force for three months: the HCO can carry out the inspection within three months after the issuance of the order.[672]

764. The competition investigation (competition procedure) has to be instituted at the latest when starting the dawn raid. If the competition procedure was not started before the dawn raid, the order instituting the proceeding shall be conveyed to the party present on the spot. Likewise, at the beginning of the inspection the party shall be informed about the court order and the purpose of the inspection.[673] Since at the dawn raid the party might obstruct the inspection, the HCO may avail itself of the assistance of the police.[674]

765. Section 65/A(9) CA addresses an important problem concerning the admissibility of evidence; the adoption of this provision was inspired by the anomalies of an earlier case.[675] Section 65/A(9) CA provides that if at the dawn raid the case-handler finds evidence that is not covered by the judicial authorization and is not connected to the investigation's subject-matter but may be related to a violation of Hungarian or EU law on restrictive agreements or dominant position, he can collect this (making a copy or seizing it). Nonetheless, the judicial authorization as to this evidence has to be gained subsequently; the HCO has to submit the request for this within sixty

---

670. Section 65/A(2) CA.
671. Section 65/A(3) CA.
672. Section 65/A(4)-(5) CA.
673. Section 65/A(6)-(7) CA.
674. Section 65/A(1) CA.
675. Case *Vj-27/2003* (administrative case) and Case *IV.39.399/2007/28* (Supreme Court).

Part III, Ch. 1, Administrative Investigations 766–768

days after the inspection was carried out.[676] The evidence is not admissible in the absence posterior judicial authorization.

766. In sum, on the spot inspections without prior notice can be conducted only on the basis of judicial authorization and the inspection has to remain within the scope of the court order (these requirements are made explicit by section 65/A CA); in particular, the inspection can cover only those sources of information that are connected to the competition procedure's subject-matter. The court authorizes on the spot inspections without prior notice only if the HCO shows, among others, that it can be reasonably assumed that the source of information related to the violation is available on the site indicated in the request. As noted above: although fishing expeditions are not allowed, the requirement that the dawn raid has to remain within the subject-matter of the investigation is a 'lex imperfecta', the ignorance of which triggers no legal sanction. If the case-handler collects evidence that is not connected to the investigation's subject-matter, this evidence is admissible (provided, posterior court permission is requested and granted) and although the collection of such evidence is contrary to the procedural rules, the HCO can use it and can institute a new competition procedure on the basis of this. This concern is mirrored in the HCO's practice: case-handlers may collect all evidence available on the spot and search for and gather documents that are obviously and blatantly unrelated to the matter at stake; the law establishes no sanction for the case he transgresses his powers.

767. In line with EU competition law, Hungarian competition procedure protects the communication between the attorney and the client (legal privilege). Documents prepared for the sake of or within the frame of the exercise of the right of defence by the party that came into existence during the communication between the client and the attorney, were created for the purpose of such a communication or fixes the statements made during this communication are privileged, provided the foregoing characteristics can be ascertained directly from the document itself. The legal privilege implies that such documents are not admissible as evidence, cannot be inspected, seized, in the course of inspections the document's possessor, with some exceptions, cannot be enjoined to show them. The party may waive this privilege.[677]

768. It is to be noted that a document may be covered by the legal privilege not only in case it comes into existence in the course of a pending competition procedure but also in case it is created before the institution of the competition procedure, provided the conditions set out in the CA are met.[678] For instance, the document may qualify as privileged if, before the competition proceeding, the attorney prepares a memorandum or legal opinion on the competition law assessment of an agreement and submits proposals for the sake of minimizing the competition law risks.

---

676. Section 65/A(10) CA.
677. Section 65/C(1)-(2) CA.
678. Case *BH2009.364*.

769. A document complying with the above requirements may lose the legal privilege in two cases.

770. First, the document is not covered by the legal privilege if it is not in the possession of the party or the attorney concerned, save they prove that the document got out of their possession in an illegal manner.[679]

771. Second, the document ceases to be privileged if the party fails to 'act promptly', i.e., it fails to raise the legal privilege objection on spot or, in some cases, subsequently within the deadline set by the CA.[680] In principle, the party has to raise the legal privilege objection (i.e., make a declaration that the document is covered by the legal privilege) at the time when the case-handler takes possession over it. However, in certain cases, the party is not expected to submit the objection on the spot: in case none of the persons present on the spot have a right of representation (power of attorney) to make a declaration as to whether the document was made with the purpose of exercising the right of defence and in case the case-handler makes a 'seizure copy' of the data and documents of a data carrier (this occurs if the volume of the data on the data carrier is so huge that on the spot it cannot be inspected within reasonable time or the party agrees to this),[681] the party has to be called to submit a declaration as to whether the seized documents or data (or part of them) is covered by the legal privilege; the party has to be granted at least eight days to submit its declaration.[682] If the party fails to make a declaration within the deadline set by the case-handler, the evidence is to be regarded as not privileged.[683]

772. The CA establishes a procedure for the case the case-handler impugns the privileged nature of the evidence: in such cases the Administrative and Labour Court of Budapest, upon the request of the HCO, has to decide, after hearing the party, on whether the evidence is covered by the legal privilege or not.[684]

§3. Right of Defence

I. Content and Notification of Opening Decisions

773. In antitrust matters (restrictive agreements and dominant position cases) the competition proceeding is started ex officio, irrespective of whether it was antedated by a formal or informal complaint. In merger matters, the proceeding is launched upon request, except the HCO institutes a proceeding because the parties breached the rules of merger control, e.g., they failed to notify a merger or implemented it without prior authorization.

---

679. Section 65/C(2) CA.
680. Section 65/C(8) CA.
681. Section 65/B(1) CA.
682. Section 65/C(6) CA.
683. Section 65/C(8) CA.
684. Section 65/C(10) CA.

Part III, Ch. 1, Administrative Investigations

774. Ex officio proceedings are started by the case-handler's order.

775. The case-handler has to open a competition proceeding if the following two conditions are met: (1) he perceives a likely illegal action, conduct or situation coming under the HCO's competence (perception of relevant violation) and (2) the protection of the public interest demands the carrying out of the investigation.[685] The order opening an investigation has to specify the circumstances, conducts and situations that gave rise to the competition proceeding.[686] Accordingly, the HCO does not have to investigate each and every violation or case suggesting the occurrence of a violation; one of the prerequisites of launching the competition procedure is that its institution is necessary to safeguard the public interest. The HCO has the possibility not to investigate cases that due to their range or the gravity of the alleged infringement do not merit the use of the competition authority's scarce resources. However, albeit that the HCO has a margin of appreciation, its decision not to open an investigation is subject to judicial review: if a formal complaint is submitted and the HCO decides not to launch an investigation, the complainant can attack this order before the Administrative and Labour Court of Budapest.[687]

776. The order opening the competition procedure has an important function: it defines the proceeding's subject-matter. In principle, the investigation's purview is confined to the subject-matter set out in this order. It is to be noted, however, that although the competition proceeding has to remain within the limits set by the order opening the procedure, this principle limits the case-handler's investigating powers only slightly. It is settled judicial practice that the undertaking has to answer all information requests issued by the case-handler and it may refuse to supply the requested data only if the information or document is obviously not connected to the investigation's subject-matter or it is impossible to submit it.[688]

777. The investigation may be extended in three directions.

778. First, if the case-handler considers that the activity, conduct or situation investigated may violate or may also violate another provision of competition law than the one specified in the order opening the procedure, he shall extend the investigation by order. By way of example, the case-handler starts a proceeding against two enterprises for an alleged horizontal collusion and subsequently comes to the conclusion that the defendants' conduct does not come under the scope of section 11 CA (the national equivalent of Article 101 TFEU) but may amount to an abuse of collective dominance under section 21 CA (the national equivalent of Article 102 TFEU).

---

685. Section 70(1) CA.
686. Section 70(1) CA.
687. Section 43/H(7) CA and s. 43/H(10) CA.
688. Case *2.Kpk.45980/2007/14* (Budapest Court); Case *3.Kpk.46.368/2009/2* (Budapest Court); Case *3.Kpk.45.935/2011/7* (Budapest Court); Case *3.Kpk.45122/2012/5* (Budapest Court).

779. Second, the case-handler may also extend the competition investigation to activities, conducts or situations that are connected to those indicated in the order opening the procedure.[689]

780. Third, the competition proceeding can be extended to another undertaking, if on the basis of the available data it appears to be likely that this undertaking was also part of the conduct serving as the proceeding's subject-matter or that another undertaking may also be liable for the investigated conduct.[690]

781. The case-handler may split the competition proceeding launched against more than one undertaking and the competition proceeding launched against the same party or parties for more violations, and conduct the investigation in separate proceedings, if the case can be adjudicated separately in respect of the individual enterprises or violations.[691]

II. Proceedings: Hearings, Access to File

782. The administrative competition procedure comprises two phases: the investigation phase conducted by the case-handler and the decision-making phase coming under the responsibility of the CC.

783. During the investigation phase, the case-handler collects information and evidence and may send information requests to the defendant undertakings, which they are obliged to answer. Although a party may submit substantive arguments during the investigation phase, and may request the HCO to terminate the proceeding due to the lack of illegal conduct, substantive defence is normally submitted after the party receives the CC's preliminary position: at the time the preliminary position is served on the party, the CC calls the undertaking to submit its remarks on that within the deadline fixed by the CC. Before the issuance of the preliminary position, the party can hardly submit comprehensive legal arguments, since it is the preliminary position that reveals what the 'indictment' is.

784. Likewise, although theoretically the case-handler may hear the parties, the hearing occurs in the decision-making phase before the CC, after the party received the preliminary position. Unfortunately, albeit that at the end of the investigation the case-handler prepares a report and submits it to the CC, this report is not served automatically on the parties; however, the CC may decide to send out the case-handler's report to the parties before preparing its preliminary position; in this case, it also calls the parties to comment on the report within a certain deadline.[692]

---

689. Section 70(4) CA.
690. Section 53(4) CA.
691. Section 70(5) CA.
692. Section 73(3) CA.

Part III, Ch. 1, Administrative Investigations

785. The party can access the procedure's file (i.e., the documents that came into existence during the procedure).[693] In case the proceeding is instituted ex officio (i.e., in all matters apart from merger applications[694]), the party can access the documents as from the time the file is opened, i.e., after the completion of the investigation, after the CC's preliminary position or (if the CC sends out the case-handler's report before that) after the case-handler's report is dispatched to the parties.[695] At the same moment, the CC may grant the parties access to the file before the foregoing point of time, if this does not endanger the procedure's success,[696] in particular, the party can be granted access to those documents that are necessary for exercising its right of appeal against an order that can be appealed separately. For instance, if a procedural fine is imposed on the party for an allegedly false declaration and for conveying false information, the party can have access to the documents the case-handler's allegation of false declaration is based on.[697]

786. Access to certain data can be restricted (e.g., protected data, business secrets, etc.).[698]

787. The request to have access to the file is adjudicated in an order; if access is rejected, the applicant can appeal the order.[699]

788. In Case *Kfv.VI.37.232/2011/13*,[700] the Hungarian Supreme Court pronounced that documents acquired from an unspecified source are, in principle, admissible as evidence.

789. The HCO established that the defendants engaged in bid-rigging concerning certain tenders published by the Municipality of Budapest for construction and renovation works (roads, bridges) and imposed fines. The key evidence was a hand-written document that contained references to the defendants and the tenders. During the proceeding, the author of the document acknowledged that he wrote the document (he refused to acknowledge some of the notes; the HCO disregarded these notes and did not use them as evidence). The HCO intimated that it acquired the document before the institution of the competition proceeding but did not specify how and under which circumstances it was obtained. The defendants advanced that this impaired their right of defence.

790. The defendants attacked the HCO's decision, alleging that the authority violated, among others, the rules of evidence, the right of defence and the right to a fair trial. Both the Budapest Court and the Budapest Court of Appeals rejected the

---

693. Section 55(1) CA.
694. Including the applications for the prolongation of the period under s. 25 during which no merger authorization is needed s. 67(1)-(2) CA.
695. Section 55(5) CA.
696. Section 55(6) CA.
697. Section 55(5) CA.
698. Section 55/A CA.
699. Section 55/B CA.
700. The administrative case' number: *Vj-25/2004/103*.

appeal. The defendants submitted a plea for supervision (an extra-ordinary appeal, limited to points of law) to the Hungarian Supreme Court.

791. The Hungarian Supreme Court rejected the plea for supervision and confirmed the HCO's decision.

792. It held that the authority has to establish the facts under the 'free-evidencing' system. It may use any evidence (both direct and indirect) that proves the relevant facts. In this case, the key evidence was the above-mentioned document. The defendants advanced that it was unknown for them how and under which circumstances the HCO obtained the document, hence, they could not examine whether the document was acquired lawfully, thus, their right of defence and the right to a fair trial were impaired.

793. The Supreme Court considered that it does not qualify as unlawful evidence if the document comes from an unknown person prior to the institution of the proceeding. The HCO cannot disregard if it receives a document that proves a violation, provided that the document is authentic, there is no doubt as to its genuineness and the authority can ascertain its authenticity. In this case, the HCO interrogated the author of the document and the latter acknowledged that the document was prepared by him.

794. The circumstance that during the competition preceding the HCO did not inform the defendants about how it acquired the document may breach the right of defence. However, a mere reference to the breach of the right of defence is not sufficient. The defendant is expected to demonstrate a causal link between the fact that it did not know the source of the document and the impairment of the right of defence. The defendants had the chance to examine the document and to challenge its authenticity and genuineness.

795. The standard of proof in Hungarian cartel cases is rather low. The Supreme Court's judgment seems to be balanced; however, it is to be noted that the adjudication of the case was simplified by the circumstances that the document was hand-written and the document's author could be clearly identified.

III. Case-Handler's Report

796. After the completion of the investigation, the case-handler has to prepare a report, which contains the conclusions of the competition investigation. The case-handler's report and the file of the case have to be submitted to the CC.[701]

797. The report is not served automatically on the parties; however, the CC may decide to send it out to the parties before preparing its preliminary position; in this case, the CC also calls the parties to comment on the report within a certain deadline

---

701. Section 71(1) CA.

Part III, Ch. 1, Administrative Investigations

and prepares its preliminary position afterwards (taking into consideration the remarks and comments of the parties).[702]

798. The case-handler's report contains the definition of the subject-matter of the case, the facts established by the case-handler and the supporting evidence, the case-handler's proposal as to the further course of the proceeding and – in case of necessity – his proposal for the adoption of interim measures.[703] The case-handler can propose the adoption of interim measures before the completion of the investigation; in this case, he has to submit a separate report.[704]

IV. The CC's Preliminary Position

799. On the basis of the case-handler's report, the CC prepares a preliminary position, which is delivered to the party. Since the institution of statement of objections as such is unknown to Hungarian competition procedural law, the CC's preliminary position fulfils some of the functions of the statement of objections. Although the order opening the competition proceeding defines the subject-matter of the competition proceeding, it lacks the details that are normally included in a statement of objections in EU competition procedure. The order opening the proceeding merely establishes the general frame of the competition procedure. On the contrary, the CC's preliminary position is a quasi draft decision the defendant can comment on before the final decision is adopted.

800. After having received the case-handler's report, the CC has the following options.

801. First, it can return the documents, if it considers the case-handler's report to be defective, i.e., it finds that further investigation is needed to establish the facts, it considers that it is justified to extend the procedure or to call a new party into the proceeding.[705]

802. Second, it can adopt interim measures:

– it may prohibit the pursuance of the conduct that is likely to infringe the CA or order the elimination of the situation that is likely to infringe the CA, provided this is urgently necessary to protect the legal or economic interests of the person concerned or due to the coming into existence, maintenance or development of economic competition;[706]
– it may adopt, to the extent it is necessary, control-restricting measures to mitigate the concentration's detrimental effects on competition and to ensure the feasibility

---

702. Section 73(3) CA.
703. Section 71(1)-(2) CA.
704. Section 71(3) CA.
705. Section 72(1) CA.
706. Section 72/A(1)(a) CA.

of the measures under section 31 CA, in case the concentration was implemented despite the prohibition embedded in section 29 (and it is likely not susceptible of being authorized under section 30), the CC's decision prohibiting the concentration or without the fulfilment of the condition set out in the authorization;[707]
– if the CC, on the basis of section 29/A(1) CA, permitted that the acquirer obtains control over the target undertaking before the decision on the authorization of the concentration is made, it can withdraw the permission on the basis of section 29/A(3) CA or amend the control-restricting measure adopted in the permission if it is likely that the concentration would considerably lessen competition in the relevant market.[708]

803. The order providing for an interim measure can be appealed separately under section 82 CA.[709]

804. It is to be noted that the CC may provide guidance to the case-handler as to the method and direction of the investigation even before the completion of the investigation.[710]

805. Third, if the CC neither has to return the case file, nor has to adopt interim measures, nor terminates the procedure, it prepares its preliminary position on the matter and sends it to the party. The preliminary position contains the facts of the case (fact pattern) as established by the CC, the supporting evidence, the assessment of the facts and the description of the aspects and conclusions necessary for the adoption of the decision and the presentation of the factors to be taken into consideration when setting the fine.[711]

806. The CC does not have to prepare a preliminary position if the proceeding was instituted upon request, i.e., the party submitted a merger application,[712] the CC agrees with the request's content, and the concentration can be authorized without the need to prescribe conditions or obligations, as provided in section 30(3) CA.[713]

V. Final Hearing and Decision

807. The CC holds a hearing if the party requests so or the CC considers it necessary. When dispatching the preliminary position to the party, the CC calls the party to inform the CC on whether it requests a hearing.[714]

---

707. Section 72/A(1)(b) CA.
708. Section 72/A(1)(c) CA.
709. Section 72 (3)-(4) CA.
710. Section 47(2) CA.
711. Section 73(1) CA.
712. Section 68 CA.
713. Section 73(2) CA.
714. Section 74(1) CA.

Part III, Ch. 1, Administrative Investigations

808. The CC holds no hearing if the proceeding was instituted upon request, i.e., the party submitted a merger application,[715] the CC agrees with the request's content, and the concentration can be authorized without the need to prescribe conditions or obligations, as provided in section 30(3) CA.[716]

809. The CC's hearing is public; however, the CC, upon its own motion or upon request, can exclude the public from the hearing or part of it with a reasoned order, if this is unconditionally necessary for the protection of certain data.[717]

810. The CC's preliminary position plays a crucial role in the defendant undertakings' right of defence, since this is the document that conveys to them the 'indictment' and the underlying evidence and legal argumentation. Accordingly, it is essential that the undertakings have the chance to comment on the preliminary position and that the major points of the subsequent decision appear in the preliminary position so as to enable the undertakings to exercise their right of defence concerning each point of the 'indictment'.

811. In Case *Kfv.II.37.268/2013/8.*, the Supreme Court established that it is a serious procedural error if the CC's final decision departs from the preliminary position as to substantial points, because in this case the parties are deprived of the right of defence, i.e., the possibility to learn the 'indictment' and to submit their remarks and arguments in respect of it. If the CC changes its position, it has to adopt a supplemental preliminary position. In this matter, the preliminary position concluded that the vertical block exemption regulation applied to the agreements at stake (agreements between insurance companies and brokers setting sales target bonuses), while the CC's final decision departed from this position and established that these agreements are not covered by the vertical block exemption regulation *ratione materiae*.

VI. Legal Remedies against the HCO's Acts, Orders and Decisions

812. In the HCO's procedure, the parties can avail themselves of three types of remedies: appeal against the decision in the merits to the Administrative and Labour Court of Budapest, appeal against orders rendered in the course of the procedure and investigation objections against procedural acts not covered by the foregoing.

813. The CC's decision in the merits can be attacked before the court. The statement of claim has to be submitted at the HCO and be addressed to the Administrative and Labour Court of Budapest.[718]

---

715. Section 68 CA.
716. Section 73(2) CA.
717. Section 74(3) CA.
718. Sections 83-84 CA.

814. The orders of the case-handler and of the CC adopted in the course of the competition proceeding can be appealed only if the CA or the APA specifically allows such an appeal. The case-handler's order can be attacked before the CC, while the CC's order can be attacked before the Administrative and Labour Court of Budapest.[719]

815. The party can object to the investigation's irregularity within five days. If the case-handler rejects the objection, he has to give his reasons in his report; if the CC rejects the objection, it has to give its reasons in the final decision.[720]

---

719. Section 82 CA.
720. Section 81 CA.

Chapter 2. Voluntary Notifications and Clearance Decisions Merger Control

§1. PRELIMINARY FILING OBLIGATIONS

I. Criteria and Thresholds

816. In line with international practice, only concentrations above a certain threshold are notifiable to the competition authority; mergers under this size are presumed not to raise competition concerns.

817. Under Hungarian competition law, a transaction is notifiable (i.e., the HCO's merger permission has to be requested) if it qualifies as a concentration and the CA's turnover thresholds are exceeded.

818. Section 23(1) CA distinguishes between three categories of concentrations. Accordingly, a concentration between undertakings occurs if:

– two or more undertakings independent of each other amalgamate (they amalgamate creating a new legal person) or one of them merges into another one (incorporation: the former becomes part of the latter and loses its legal personality), or part of an undertaking becomes part of another undertaking independent from the one containing the part of undertaking;
– an undertaking or more undertakings jointly acquire direct or indirect control over an undertaking that is independent from the former undertaking(s), or over more undertakings that are independent from it (them) but not independent from each other;
– more than one undertaking independent from each other jointly establish an undertaking controlled by them that is capable of pursuing, on a lasting basis, all the functions of an independent undertaking (full-function joint venture).

819. In each case, it is a fundamental requirement that the transaction occurs between undertakings that are independent from each other. Section 15(1) CA defines the case when two undertakings cannot be regarded as independent from each other. Accordingly, undertakings forming part of the same group and undertakings that are controlled by the same undertakings are not independent from each other. Section 15(2) CA defines the concept of 'group of undertakings' as follows: undertaking 'A' is part of the same group of undertakings as undertaking 'B':

– if 'A', individually, directly or indirectly, controls 'B';
– if 'B', individually, directly or indirectly, controls 'A';
– if the undertaking controlling 'A', individually, directly or indirectly, controls 'B'; and
– if two or more from the undertakings that are in a controlling relationship with 'A' as specified in the preceding points and undertaking 'A' control 'B' jointly.

820. The concept of control is defined in section 23(2)-(3) CA.

821. As a general consideration, the quantitative measure established in this regard has to fulfil two requirements. First, it has to screen out those concentrations that, due to their small size, are not susceptible of substantially affecting competition. Second, it has to establish clear criteria that can be applied easily. Since market share data, which would probably be the best proxy of the potential of competition problems, do not meet the latter requirement, taking into account the uncertainties related to the definition of the relevant market and the availability of market data, the merger threshold is based on the undertakings' turnover, which is, however, a rather imperfect filter. The excessive width of the scope of the notification duty is corrected in the merger procedure: if the concentration, obviously, raises no competition concerns, the CC will clear it in a simplified procedure.[721,722]

822. A concentration is notifiable if the joint net turnover of the groups of undertakings concerned (i.e., the sum of the net turnover of the groups between which the concentration occurs) is higher than HUF 15 milliard, and each of at least two of the groups concerned have (severally) a net turnover higher than HUF 500 million. If only two groups are involved in the concentration, both groups have to have a net turnover higher than HUF 500 million.[723] In this context, the term 'net' refers to the income excluding sales taxes (VAT, excise tax and similar taxes).

823. The turnover thresholds established in section 24(1) CA combine two facets. The joint turnover threshold measures whether the concentration's absolute size is significant enough to have a real impact on competition in the market and a realistic potential to raise competition concerns. The purpose of the individual turnover threshold is to screen out concentrations, where the high joint turnover is due solely to one of the groups concerned, while the other group's turnover is very low. In such cases, the concentration increases the already existing high turnover only slightly; hence, it is needless to subject it to competition law scrutiny.[724]

824. In order to decide, whether the concentration exceeds the above turnover thresholds, first of all, the 'groups of undertakings concerned' have to be identified and delimited. A 'group of undertakings concerned' consists of a direct participant and the indirect participants connected to this direct participant.[725]

825. In the first step, the direct participant (participants) is to be identified. The direct participants are those between which the concentration occurs. The following qualify as direct participants:

– in case of amalgamation: the amalgamating undertakings;
– in case of incorporation: the incorporating and the incorporated undertakings;

---

721. *See* s. 63(3) CA.
722. Csongor István Nagy, *III. Rész: Antitröszt jog*, in *Magyar versenyjog* 261-262 (Kinga Pázmándi ed., HVG-Orac 2012).
723. Section 24(1) CA.
724. Csongor István Nagy, *III. Rész: Antitröszt jog*, in *Magyar versenyjog* 262 (Kinga Pázmándi ed., HVG-Orac 2012).
725. Section 26(5) CA.

Part III, Ch. 2, Voluntary Notifications

– in case a part of an undertaking becomes part of another undertaking: the receiving undertaking;
– in case of acquisition of control: the undertaking(s) acquiring direct control, the undertaking(s) acquiring indirect joint control (undertaking(s) controlling the first undertaking jointly with one or more members of another group of undertakings), and the undertaking(s) getting under control; and
– in case of establishing a joint-venture: the founders.[726]

826. Once the direct participants have been identified, the indirect participants can be singled out accordingly. The indirect participants are the members of the group of undertakings the direct participant is part of (excluding the direct participant).[727]

827. Section 26(4) CA contains an important rule: when delimiting the circle of indirect participants, the undertaking whose right of control ceases to exist due to the concentration and the undertaking controlled by this undertaking (provided the former does not qualify as a direct participant) are to be disregarded. For instance, if undertaking 'A' has control over undertaking 'B' (e.g., it is the sole shareholder) and sells its shares to undertaking 'C', the direct participants are 'B' (the undertaking getting under direct control) and 'C' (the undertaking acquiring direct control). Although 'B' and 'A' are part of the same group, 'A' is to be disregarded when delimitating the circle of indirect participants, as 'A' loses its right of control due to the concentration. According to section 26(4) CA, not only 'A' but its entire 'bloodline' has to be disregarded (i.e., the undertakings controlled by 'A'). Furthermore, it is submitted that according to the above provision also the undertaking (or undertakings) controlling 'A' have to be disregarded. Although section 26(4) CA does not address this issue specifically, it provides that the undertaking that loses its right of control (irrespective of whether this is direct or indirect) has to be disregarded; this implies that the undertaking controlling 'A', as it loses indirect control, has to be ignored too. In sum, both undertakings controlled by 'A' and undertakings controlling 'A' have to be ignored.

828. The legal test enshrined in section 24(1) CA could be abused by means of 'salami tactics'. The individual turnover threshold of HUF 500 million could be used to transfer assets between two (or more) groups bit by bit, until one of the groups absorbs the entire target.[728] Section 24(2) CA addresses this risk, and provides that when calculating the individual turnovers for the purpose of applying the HUF 500 million threshold, the non-notifiable concentrations between the acquiring group and the group of undertakings losing its controlling rights that occurred within a period of two year preceding the concentration have to be taken into account

---

726. Section 26(2) CA.
727. Section 26(3) CA.
728. Csongor István Nagy, *III. Rész: Antitröszt jog*, in *Magyar versenyjog* 263 (Kinga Pázmándi ed., HVG-Orac 2012).

829. Section 24(3) CA establishes special rules in respect of the calculation of the net turnover of certain insurance companies, investment service providers, credit institutions and financial undertakings. In case of concentrations between insurance companies, instead of the net turnover, the value of the gross insurance fees is to be taken into account; in case of the concentration of investment service providers, the relevant figure is the income from the investment services, and in case of funds, the relevant figure is the value of the contributions. In case of credit institutions and financial undertakings, the sum of the following income elements is to be taken into account: (a) interests and interest-like income, (b) income from investment papers (securities in stock corporations, other investment papers yielding a variable return, income from shares, income from shares in connected undertakings, (c) commissions, (d) the net profit of financial operations, and (e) income from other business activities.

830. It would be unreasonable to count in the turnover realized from transactions between undertakings belonging to the same group, since this 'in-house' (or internal) turnover would not provide any indication as to the group's real market position; the concept of 'economic unit' also underpins this rule, i.e., undertakings forming part of the same group have to be treated as one unit. Accordingly, in Hungarian merger control law, when calculating the relevant net turnover, the transactions between the groups concerned have to be ignored. According to section 27(1) CA, in the application of section 24(1) CA, when calculating the net turnover, the turnover between undertakings belonging to the group and their parts shall be disregarded. This approach is in line with EU merger control law.[729]

831. It is to be noted that before 1 July 2014, Hungarian merger control law contained a wider exception in this regard and, thus, was not in accordance with EU merger control law. According to the old rule, the turnover that occurred between the undertakings (groups of undertakings) concerned was to be disregarded.[730] This rule went further than the one applicable as from 1 July 2014 and excluded not only internal turnover (e.g., transactions between parent and subsidiary or between sister companies) but also the turnover between the groups concerned (e.g., transactions between the acquiring company and the target company).[731]

832. Accordingly, old section 27(1) CA provided that not only intra-group turnover but the entire turnover between the undertakings concerned was to be disregarded; that is, this rule applied also in cases where the undertakings between which

---

729. Jurisdictional Notice, paras 167–168.
730. Section 27(1) CA.
731. Articles 5(1) and 5(4) of the Merger Control Regulation, Jurisdictional Notice, para. 167 ('The aim is to exclude the proceeds of business dealings within a group so as to take account of the real economic weight of each entity in the form of market turnover. Thus, the 'amounts' taken into account by the Merger Regulation reflect only the transactions which take place between the group of undertakings on the one hand and third parties on the other.'). For a criticism on the Hungarian rule, *see* Álmos Papp, *Az összefonódással érintett vállalkozások*, 4(4) Versenytükör 28–29 (2008). For an analysis in favour of the Hungarian rule *see* András Bodócsi, *Észrevételek a cikkhez…*, 4(4) Versenytükör 29 (2008).

Part III, Ch. 2, Voluntary Notifications 833–834

the turnover occurred were part of two different groups of undertakings, provided both were concerned by the concentration. By way of example, a concentration between a supplier of spare parts and a producer (e.g., the producer took over the supplier) may have needed not to be notified to the HCO, if all or most of the supplier's output was supplied to the producer. Since in this case the turnover realized between the supplier and the producer was to be disregarded (this qualified as turnover between two undertakings concerned), the supplier might have had no substantial net turnover beyond the sales made to the producer; hence, there might not have been two groups of undertakings that each had a net turnover of at least HUF 500 million. This overly wide exception was repealed as from 1 July 2014.

833. As noted above, Hungarian competition law follows the effects-doctrine as to antitrust law's territorial scope (restrictive agreements, abuse of dominant position, merger control), while other provisions of the CA, i.e., the rules on unfair competition and on the prohibition on unfair manipulation of business decisions come under the effects-principle only if the act was committed in the European Economic Area.[732] That is, the purview of Hungarian competition rules covers all conducts that may affect the Hungarian market and this applies also to concentrations: mergers between foreign enterprises may be notifiable also to the HCO. Theoretically, all concentrations are potentially notifiable if they exceed the turnover thresholds.

834. Section 27(2) CA establishes a special rule for foreign undertakings: when calculating the turnover of undertakings of foreign domicile, the relevant figure is the foreign undertaking's turnover in Hungary (i.e., 'the net turnover realized from the products sold on the territory of Hungary in the preceding business year'). Accordingly, a concentration between two foreign enterprises may be notifiable in Hungary, if the groups concerned (through their subsidiaries, branches or cross-border sales) realize turnover in Hungary. The CC has applied section 27(2) CA in numerous cases.[733] It is to be stressed that the term 'products sold on the territory of Hungary' is to be interpreted broadly: it also covers sales effected from abroad towards Hungary (Hungarian buyers).[734]

---

732. Section 1(1) CA.
733. Case *Vj-56/2005 Villas Austria and Heraklith Consulting & Engineering*; Case *Vj-29/2005 Europolis and others*; Case *Vj-202/2004 General Electric and Ionics*; Case *Vj-188/2004 General Electric Edwards Systems Technology*; Case *Vj-106/2003 Samsung General Chemicals and Total Holdings*; Case *Vj-177/2001 GlaxoSmithKline and Humán Oltóanyagtermelő*; Case *Vj-170/2001 Pantel Novumés MOL*; Case *Vj-139/2001 Saminaés SCI Systems*; Case *Vj-124/2000 AB Volvo*; Case *Vj-143/1999 Hoechst Aktiengesellschaft and Rhone-Poulenc*; Case *Vj-107/1999 Exxon Corporation and Mobil Corporation*; Case *Vj-101/1999 Renault and Nissan*; Case *Vj-99/1999 BayWa and RWA Raiffeisen*; Case *Vj-7/1999 ICN Magyarországés Fúzió-Pharma*; Case *Vj-170/1998 Phoenix Pharma and Dunapharma*; Case *Vj-155/1998 ENSO and STORA*; Case *Vj-82/1998 B.A.T. Industries and Zürich Insurance*; Case *Vj-42/1998 Compaq Computer and Digital Equipment*; Case *Vj-163/1997 Stora Merchant AB and Papírker Kereskedelmi Rt.*; Case *Vj-27/1997 Bank Austria and Creditanstalt-Bankverein*; Case *Vj-26/1997 Bayernwerk, Electricité de France and Északdunántúli Áramszolgáltató*.
734. Csongor István Nagy, *III. Rész: Antitröszt jog*, in *Magyar versenyjog* 265 (Kinga Pázmándi ed., HVG-Orac 2012).

835. It is to be noted that the special rule embedded in section 27(2) CA applies only to foreign undertakings (undertakings of foreign domicile); that is, the text suggests that in case of Hungarian undertakings the entire turnover is to be taken into account, irrespective of whether it emerges from domestic sales or export.

836. Special rules apply to the calculation of the turnover of public enterprises. Since the state is the majority owner of numerous undertakings (i.e., it disposes of the majority of the voting rights), due to the general definition of control in section 23(2) CA, all these undertakings would belong to the same group. This would go counter to the reality of control. Hence, the CA provides that if a public enterprise has an autonomous decision-making power as to its market conduct, it has to be regarded as an independent entity.[735] In respect of restrictive agreements, this exception is included in section 15(3) CA; as regards merger control, this principle is included in section 27(3) CA, which provides that when calculating the net turnover of undertakings whose the majority owner is the state or a local self-government (municipality), the turnover of the undertaking shall be taken into account that forms an economic unit and has autonomous decision-making power as to its market conduct.

837. As noted above, in the absence of this rule, all state-owned public enterprises would be considered to be a part of the same group; this could be hardly reconciled with the realities of control and decision-making; hence, section 27(3) of the CA provides that enterprises with independent decision-making power qualify as independent undertakings. This rule is in line with section 15(3) of the CA, which establishes the same principle as to restrictive agreements, providing that a public undertaking (whose majority owner is the state or a local self-government) has to be regarded as independent if it has autonomy in deciding on its market conduct.

838. A special rule is warranted for cases where a part of an undertaking becomes part of another (independent) undertaking; in such cases, when calculating the relevant net turnover, not the entire selling undertaking has to be taken into account but only the turnover connected to the part of undertaking sold. According to section 27(4) CA: 'in case of a part of undertaking, the net turnover realized in the preceding business year through the utilization of the assets and rights sold is to be taken into account'.

839. The calculation of the turnover in case of joint control is addressed in section 27(5) CA, which provides that the turnover of the undertaking under joint control shall be divided equally between the controlling undertakings. Undertakings belonging to the same group are regarded as one unit from the perspective of the controlling proportion. Accordingly, if an undertaking has two 50% shareholders, which control it jointly, half of the undertaking's net turnover is to be allotted to one of the controlling undertakings, while the other half to the other controlling undertaking. If the undertaking has a 50% and two 25% owners and the latter belong to

---

735. *See* Case *Vj-85/2013 MMBF Földgáztároló Zrt.*, paras 15–19.

Part III, Ch. 2, Voluntary Notifications 840–845

the same group, half of the turnover has to be allotted to the 50% shareholder, while the other half goes to the group containing the two 25% shareholders.

840. The CA establishes certain exceptions to the duty to notify.

841. Conceptually, the first case is not an exception to the notification duty but an exclusion from the notion of concentration. Section 23(4) CA establishes an exception to the definition of concentration: the activity of a liquidator or receiver (irrespective of whether it acts in a winding-up or insolvency proceeding) does not qualify as a concentration.

842. Furthermore, the CA provides in respect of certain transactions that even if they qualify as a concentration under section 23(1) CA, they do not need to be notified to the HCO. According to section 25 CA, the temporary acquisition of control (for a period not longer than one year) of certain organizations (insurance companies, credit institutions, financial holding companies, holding companies with mixed operation, investment companies, trustee organizations etc.) does not entail a notification duty, if the purpose of the acquisition of control is to prepare the resale of the enterprise, and the undertaking acquiring control does not exercise its controlling rights or it does only to the extent inevitably necessary. The HCO, upon the request of the enterprise acquiring control submitted before the end of the one-year-long transitory period, can prolong the transitory period on one occasion by, at most, one year, if the enterprise proves that the sale, for a reason it was not responsible for, was not possible within one year.

843. Finally, section 24/A CA authorizes the government to exempt a concentration from the notification duty, if this is warranted by the public interest: the government – if this is justified by the public interest, especially the preservation of the workplaces for the sake of the security of supply – may pronounce a concentration to have a national strategic significance; such concentrations, contrary to section 24 CA, do not have to be notified to the HCO.

II. Turnover Calculation

844. According to section 24 CA, the HCO's permission is to be requested for the concentration, if the joint net turnover realized in the preceding business year by all the groups of undertakings concerned (as defined in section 26(5) CA) and by the undertakings jointly controlled by the members of the groups of undertakings concerned and other undertakings exceeds HUF 15 billion and among the groups of undertakings concerned there are at least two groups of undertakings whose individual net turnover, including the undertakings jointly controlled by the members of the groups of undertaking and other undertakings, exceeds HUF 500 million.

845. In this context, the term 'net' refers to the income excluding sales taxes (VAT, excise tax and similar taxes).

846. Section 24(2) CA provides that when calculating the individual turnovers for the purpose of applying the HUF 500 million threshold, the non-notifiable concentrations between the acquiring group and the group of undertakings losing its controlling rights that occurred within a period of two year preceding the concentration are to be taken into account. Accordingly, if the acquiring group of undertakings, in the preceding two years, purchased one or more undertakings or parts of undertaking from the selling group and these concentrations were not notifiable due to their remaining under the turnover threshold, these turnovers are to be counted in.

III. The Notification Duty's Addressee and Deadline

847. Section 28 CA identifies the holder of the duty to notify. The concentration has to be notified, in case of amalgamation, incorporation and the foundation of a joint venture, by the direct participant, in all other cases, by the acquirer of the part of undertaking or the acquirer of the direct right of control or the undertaking having direct control over the acquiring undertaking.

848. As from 1 July 2014, the CA sets no deadline for the submission of the merger application. However, section 28(3) CA provides that in case of the concentration of credit institutions and insurance companies, the merger application has to be submitted at the same time when the application for the permission of the Hungarian National Bank is submitted.

849. Earlier, the CA provided that the merger application had to be submitted within thirty days of the publication of the public offer, the conclusion of the contract or the acquisition of the right of control; if more than one of these occurs, the deadline starts from the one that occurs earlier. In case of agreements concluded during the insolvency proceeding of an enterprise having a special significance for the national economy as defined in section 65 of Act XLIX of 1991 on the reorganization and insolvency proceedings that resulted in the acquisition or change of control over the undertaking or part of undertaking having a special significance for the national economy, the deadline was fifteen days. With the introduction of the express prohibition of implementation, the foregoing deadlines were repealed.

IV. The Consequences of the Failure to Notify

850. If the addressee of the notification duty fails to notify the concentration to the HCO, it may face both civil and administrative law consequences.

A. The Consequences of the Failure to Notify before 1 July 2014

851. According to section 79 CA (as effective before 1 July 2014), if the undertaking failed to notify the concentration within the deadline, the HCO imposed a fine, the daily maximum of which was HUF 200,000.

Part III, Ch. 2, Voluntary Notifications 852–856

852. The CA did not make it clear whether it was prohibited to implement the concentration before the HCO cleared it. In Hungarian competition law, the majority opinion in the scholarship and in the transactional practice was that Hungarian merger control did not prohibit prior implementation, as the CA contained no express provision enjoining the parties from implementing the merger.[736] At the same moment, it is submitted that this prohibition was reasonably deducible from the CA, and it would have gone counter to the legislative intent if such early implementations had been allowed. Be it as it may, the legal treatment of early implementations was uncertain and the parties ran a legal risk if they did not await the HCO's clearance.

853. As noted, the CA did not make it unequivocal whether early implementations were prohibited. Section 31 CA made it clear that if the HCO established in a competition proceeding that the concentration that was implemented without a clearance could not have been cleared, prescribed the concentration's dissolution and could establish obligations for the restitution of effective competition.[737] Nonetheless, if the HCO came to the conclusion that the concentration could have been cleared, it did not dissolve the merger.

854. It is submitted that the prohibition to implement the merger before clearance could be deduced from the CA, which provided in section 24(1) CA that 'the HCO's permission shall be sought to a concentration of undertakings' that meets the conditions of set out in the CA. One subset of the concentration is the acquisition of control,[738] which included the acquisition of de facto control.[739]

855. Consequently, the HCO's permission had to be sought also in case de facto control was acquired; e.g., the acquirer in fact took over the target's management before obtaining it legally (before receiving the voting rights). The language of 24(1) CA could be reasonably interpreted in a way that the concentration, that is, the implementation of the concentration, pre-supposed the HCO's permission. Section 24(1) did not state that the permission was need 'in case of a concentration' but it provided that it was need 'to a concentration'.

856. This interpretation was underpinned by some obiter dicta in the CC's decisional practice and the teleological interpretation of the CA. In Case *Vj-146/2008 Strabag SE and Cemex Austria AG*, the CC noted that before the clearance the parties were prohibited from implementing those concentrations that were to be notified to the HCO. The CC cleared a merger with preliminary (suspensive) conditions; since in a certain region, the parties' joint market share was high, the concentration was cleared with the condition that the parties divested one of the plants. The CC advanced that it did not consider it necessary to prescribe a condition or obligation

---

736. *See* Gábor Fejes, Zoltán Marosi & Lia Szabó, *Miben áll az összefonódást tilalmazó GVH-határozat polgári jogi joghatása – dilemmák a versenyjog és a polgári jog határmezsgyéjén*, 61(11) Jogtudományi Közlöny 401-416 (2006).
737. Section 31 CA.
738. Section 23(1)(b) CA.
739. Section 23(2)(d) CA.

in respect to the plant to be divested for the period until it is sold, as the prescribed condition was preliminary (suspensive); hence, the concentration could not be implemented before the divestiture took place.[740] In other words: the CC stated that the concentration could not be implemented before the clearance entered into force (note that in case of a preliminary condition, clearance enters into force only once the condition is fulfilled).[741]

857. This was confirmed by section 29/A CA, which provided that in case of acquisition or change of control concerning enterprises in liquidation that have a special relevance from the perspective of the national economy, the acquirer can exercise its right of control, to the extent this is unconditionally necessary for the normal management operations, before obtaining the HCO's merger permission (clearance). A contratio, in the absence of this special provision, the right of control cannot be exercised, and the management of the target enterprises cannot be taken over.

858. In case of implementing the merger without a clearing permission, the sanctions the enterprise faced were twofold: dissolution and fine.

859. According to section 31 CA, if it was established during the competition proceedings that the notifiable concentration implemented without a permission could not have been cleared, the HCO, in its decision, prescribed the dissolution of the merged undertakings or assets (or shares of business) or the termination of the joint control within a particular deadline, or could establish any other obligation for reinstating efficient competition.

860. The status of the fine the HCO could impose was uncertain. Thus much is certain: if the duty to notify was not observed (the merger permission was not requested within the deadline established in the CA), the competition authority could impose a fine, the maximum of which was HUF 200,000 per day.[742] Nonetheless, the fine imposed for the circumstance that the merger was implemented without permission (irrespective of whether this occurred before or after the submission of the notification) had an uncertain status. The CA's provision in section 78(1) dealing with the fine in the merits provided that the CC 'may impose a fine against the person who violates the provisions of this Act'. In other words, a fine in the merits could be imposed if any of the CA's provisions were infringed, while it was assumed that if the CA determined a special fine concerning a particular type of violation, the principle of *lex specialis derogate legi generali* prevailed. By way of example, the CA contained special provisions on the violation of the duty to provide information during a sector inquiry,[743] on the procedural fine,[744] on the failure to notify the concentration.[745] As there was no special

---

740. Paragraph 61.
741. Section 30(4) CA.
742. Section 79 CA.
743. Section 43/C CA.
744. Section 61 CA.
745. Section 79 CA.

Part III, Ch. 2, Voluntary Notifications   861–863

fine established for the implementation of unpermitted concentrations, the language of section 78(1) CA suggested that a fine in the merits could be imposed in such cases. Namely, the provision included in section 79 CA applied to the failure to notify and not to the implementation of the concentration without permission.

861. The decisional practice of the CC was, however, much milder than what the above provisions would suggest: the CC imposed a fine in numerous cases where the concentration was not notified; however, in all cases solely the special fine applicable to the failure to notify was imposed (section 79 CA), taking into account the maximum daily amount,[746] and no fine in the merits was imposed (section 78 CA). While section 79 CA applied to the failure to notify, it did not cover the implementation without permission (provided of course that the implementation without permission was prohibited); however, in the non-notification cases the CC did not consider that the imposition of a fine in the merits would be warranted. It is to be stressed that in all of these cases, although the notification duty was breached, the concentration was cleared posteriorly in each and every matter. The CC's attitude may have been different if the parties had failed to notify and implemented a concentration that could not be cleared.

862. The civil law consequences of the implementation without authorization were included in section 29 CA, which provided that the coming into existence of the contract resulting in the concentration of undertakings (provided the concentration was notifiable) pre-supposed the HCO's permission (i.e., the HCO's permission was necessary for the coming into existence of the contract underlying the concentration). According to section 29/A(4) CA, if the HCO did not authorize the concentration, all legal acts and declarations that infringed the prohibition of implementation embedded in section 29 CA or a control-restricting provision adopted under section 29/A(2) CA were automatically invalid. However, the undertaking violating the prohibition of implementation or the control-restricting provision could not refer to the foregoing provision and this undertaking was responsible for the damages emerging from the application of the legal consequence of automatic invalidity.

B. *The Consequences of the Failure to Notify after 1 July 2014*

863. The new provision that entered into force as from 1 July 2014 introduced a clear prohibition as to the implementation of concentrations without authorization, thus bringing Hungarian competition law in line with EU merger control;[747] this did

---

746. Case *Vj-162/2005/11 Bonitás and MFS*, paras 13–14; Case *Vj-195/2005/10 Bonitás and Multireklám*, para. 35; Case *Vj-205/2005/9 Bonitás*, paras 18–21; Case *Vj-125/2008/16 Tendre and Bábolna*, paras 25–27; Case *Vj-124/2008/16. Bonitas, Forrás and Tendre* ügy, paras 25–29; Case *Vj-100-8/2009 Tendre and Foring*, paras 18–20; Case *Vj-109-8/2009 CSIM and Tendre*, paras 12–15.
747. Article 7 and recital 31 of the Merger Control Regulation.

away with the above uncertainties as to the existence and non-existence of the prohibition of implementation. However, it seems that the new provisions entail no significant change as compared to the CC's decisional practice in respect of non-notified concentrations, with the exception that they establish the minimum of the daily fine (HUF 50,000). On the contrary, for concentrations implemented after the submission of the merger applications, the new rules create an uncertain situation with the risk of a potentially high fine.

864. According to section 78(1)(d) CA, the CC may impose a fine against the person who fails to request the HCO's permission for a concentration as defined in section 24 and the concentration is implemented, even if the CC, subsequently, authorizes it in its decision.

865. Two limits apply to the fine governed by section 78(1)(d) CA.

866. Section 78(1b) CA sets a general cap on all fines in the merits: the fine is imposed by the CC and (in line with EU competition law) it may range up to 10% of the annual turnover the undertaking or (where the undertaking is part of a group of undertakings and the group is identified in the decision) the group of undertakings the perpetrator is part of realized in the previous business (calendar) year (i.e., the calendar year preceding the date of the decision establishing the violation).[748]

867. Section 78(1c) CA establishes a restriction in terms of amount applicable specifically to section 78(1)(d) fines. The fine has to be calculated on a daily basis and the daily fine may range from HUF 50,000 to HUF 200,000. The relevant period ranges from the publication of the public offer, the conclusion of the contract or the acquisition of the right of control (depending on which of these occurs earlier) to the launch of the competition proceeding. When calculating the amount of the fine, the transitory period established by section 25 CA (applicable to the temporary acquisition of control by certain organizations) has to be disregarded.

868. Although the above provisions entered into force on 1 July 2014 and, thus, have not been tested in practice, it seems that the new rules applicable as from 1 July 2014 did not increase the risks of fine as to concentrations implemented without the HCO's authorization. Such fines range from HUF 50,000 to HUF 200,000, similarly to the CC's decisional practice before 1 July 2014. What is more, the new provisions do lessen these risks: before 1 July 2014, it had been uncertain whether the foregoing range applies solely to the failure to notify and the implementation of a concentration that cannot be authorized may warrant the imposition of the fine in the merits, which could range up to 10% of the net turnover. The new rules make it clear that if the concentration is implemented without prior authorization, a daily fine has to be imposed and the amount of this ranges from HUF 50,000 to HUF 200,000 per diem.

---

748. Section 78(1b) CA.

Part III, Ch. 2, Voluntary Notifications

869. Perversely, section 78(1)(d) CA and the lenient rule of fines applies only to cases where the concentration is implemented without a notification. From a statutory perspective, section 78(1)(d) CA does not cover cases where the concentration is implemented after the merger application is submitted. Such cases would be covered by section 78(1)(a) CA, where the only limit is that the amount of the fine cannot exceed 10% of the net turnover acquired in the preceding business year. This is a contradictory situation, since implementation without notification appears to be a graver violation than implementation after notification.

870. As far as civil law consequences are concerned, section 29 CA provides that notifiable concentrations cannot be implemented without the HCO's authorization, in particular the voting rights and the rights as to the appointment or election of the executive officers cannot be exercised; in the course of the business relations between the acquirer and the target, the pre-merger situation has to prevail. This prohibition does not apply to the conclusion of the contract serving as the basis of the concentration or to the issuance of the public offer, as well as to such legal acts and declarations that are necessary for creating the concentration but do not entail that the acquirer can exercise controlling rights.

§2. STRUCTURE OF PROCEEDINGS

I. Preliminary Assessment, Simplified Procedure and Full Investigation

871. The fact that the concentration is notifiable does not entail the presumption that it raises competition concerns. The duty to notify rests on a formula based on net turnover, which cannot be used to predict the potential competition effects. The turnover formula is a filter; here, the primary purpose is to meet the requirement of predictability; hence, the filtering test has to be based on a measure that can be easily calculated. Although market share would be a more efficient filter, the definition of the relevant market and the calculation of market share is too uncertain and requires data that may not be easily available to the applicant. Accordingly, the CA uses a turnover filter. Nonetheless, the rules on merger procedure correct the imperfections of the turnover filter, which is more flexible (and hence somewhat less predictable) and is largely based on market share: the concentration is to be adjudicated in a simplified procedure, if it raises no substantial competition concerns. If the simplified procedure cannot be applied, the concentration is subjected to a more time-consuming full-blown inquiry.

872. Section 63 CA establishes two deadlines for adjudication of concentrations. A deadline of thirty days applies to 'simple' merger cases[749] (if justified, this can be extended by twenty days);[750] if the CC decides that the concentration has to

---

749. Section 63(2)(d) CA.
750. Section 63(5) CA.

be subjected to a full-inquiry, the comprehensive analysis has to be accomplished in four months[751] (if justified, this deadline can be extended by two months).[752]

II. Simplified Procedure

873. The HCO issued a Notice on how to distinguish concentrations that can be cleared in a simplified procedure from those that cannot.[753] The Notice summarizes the HCO's decisional practice; the undertakings can expect that if the fulfilment of the conditions set out in the Notice is proved, the merger application will be assessed in a simplified procedure (which is more favourable to them).[754] However, it is to be noted that a concentration may still be assessed in a simplified procedure, even if it does not meet the requirements set out in the Notice, in case the merger permission obviously cannot be rejected.[755]

874. The Notice distinguishes between three types of concentrations that do not warrant a full inquiry.

– The concentration has neither horizontal, nor vertical, nor portfolio effects (Case A).
– The parties' market share is low (Case B).
– The merger increases market concentration only slightly (Cases C and D).

875. The Notice establishes information requirements as to all types of concentrations: the simplified procedure cannot be applied, if it is difficult to define the relevant market or the parties' market shares. Accordingly, a concentration may be assessed in a simplified procedure only if the market share is based on clear, objective and controllable data, and these data are available within the deadline set out for the handling of the case.[756]

876. The concentration has neither horizontal, nor vertical, nor portfolio effects (Case A), if:

– there is no relevant market where at least two of the groups of undertakings participating in the concentration would be competitors (there is no horizontal relationship between the parties);
– there is no relevant market where at least two of the groups of undertakings participating in the concentration would or could be in a vertical (seller-buyer) relationship (there is no vertical relationship between the parties);

---

751. Section 63(3) CA.
752. Section 63(5) CA.
753. Notice 1/2014 on the aspects of differentiating between concentrations subject to authorization in simplified and full procedure. This replaced, as from 1 Jul. 2014, Notice 3/2009.
754. Notice 1/2014, para. 5.
755. Notice 1/2014, para. 5. *See e.g.*, Case *Vj-3/2012 Budapest Főváros Önkormányzata et al.*
756. 17-19. Point.

Part III, Ch. 2, Voluntary Notifications 877–879

– the groups of undertakings participating in the concentration have no interest (production, distribution, etc.) in the markets of complementary products (there is no portfolio effect).[757]

877. There are horizontal and/or vertical and/or portfolio effects, but the parties' market share is low (Case B):

– the parties' joint market share exceeds 20% in none of the relevant markets;
– there is no relevant market where at least two of the groups of undertakings participating in the concentration would be in a vertical (seller-buyer) relationship and where the individual market share of either the group of undertakings acting as seller or the group of undertakings acting as buyer would exceed 30%; and
– there is no relevant market affected by portfolio effects, where the individual market share of one of the groups of undertakings concerned would exceed 30%.[758]

878. In case the parties overpass the above market share threshold established in respect of horizontal effects (the parties' joint market share exceeds 20% in one of the relevant markets) but the concentration increases market concentration only slightly, the concentration may still be assessed in a simplified procedure (Case C), if

– in the relevant market where the above market share thresholds are exceeded, the joint market share of the groups of undertakings concerned, with the exclusion of the group having the highest market share, is not more than 5%;
– in this relevant market, there is a competing undertaking that has a market share of a similar size as that of the largest group covered by the merger (i.e., the group having the highest market share from the groups covered by the concentration);
– the concentration does not entail the significant lessening of potential competition, as it can be reasonably assumed that the market share of the undertaking of low market share would not increase in the future perceivably.[759]

879. By way of example, if in the relevant market there are two groups of 30% and ten groups of 4% market share, the above conditions may be met, in case one of the groups of 30% acquires control over one of its competitors of 4%. The market share of the party not being the largest group covered by the concentration does not exceed 5%, and there is a competitor in the relevant market that has a market share of a similar size as the merger's largest participant. However, it is to be

---

757. Notice 1/2014, para. 14(a). Notice 3/2009, applicable until 1 Jul. 2014, also contained a fourth condition: there is no conglomerate effect: the concentration merits a full inquiry, even if it fulfils the above conditions, if the concentration the financial situation of a group of undertakings that previously had a weaker financial situation, this group's market share exceeds 30% in one of the relevant markets and on the basis of the characteristics of the market there is a real danger that on the basis of this stronger status it would apply strategies restricting competition (e.g., predatory pricing) Para. 16. This requirement was omitted in the currently effective Notice.
758. Notice 1/2014, para. 14(b).
759. Notice 1/2014, para. 14(c).

examined whether the group of 4% could increase its market share in the absence of the concentration.

880. Nonetheless, the above conditions are not met, if in the relevant market, there is a group of 40%, a group of 20% and ten groups of 4%, and the group of 40% wants to acquire control over one of the enterprises of 4%. In this case, there is no competitor in the relevant market that has a market share of a similar size as the merger's largest participant. Of course, this concentration might still be assessed in a simplified procedure; however, it will be probably subject to a full inquiry.

881. In case the parties overpass the above market share threshold established in respect of vertical and/or portfolio effects (the parties' individual market share exceeds 30% in one of these relevant markets) but one of the following sets of conditions are met (i.e., the following two sets of requirements are disjunctive) the simplified procedure may still be used (Case D):

– the market share of the other group of undertakings does not exceed 5%; furthermore, there is a competing undertaking that has a market share of a similar size as that of the largest group having a market share higher than 30% and it can be reasonably assumed that the market share of the undertaking of 5% or less would not increase in the future perceivably; or
– the group of undertakings of more than 30% market share had been present on the seller and purchaser side of the market affected by the vertical effects, as well as on both markets affected by the portfolio effect even before the concentration, provided that on the side of the relevant market where both groups are present, the concentration, from a horizontal perspective, fulfils the requirements of being assessed in a simplified procedure (i.e., the parties' joint market share exceeds 20% in none of the relevant markets or the conditions of Case C are met) and it is not the case that the group of more than 30% market share has less than 5% market share on the other side of the relevant market, while the other group has a higher market share than this.[760]

882. In case of undertakings under joint control, which are part of none of the groups of undertakings concerned, the market share is to be divided equally between the groups of undertakings controlling them.[761]

883. The market share, in principle, is to be calculated on the basis of the data of the year when the concentration occurs or the preceding year. However, if the market share is fluctuating considerably and there are huge differences between the individual years, the HCO may take into account the market shares of a longer period. This is the case when the undertakings compete for a few high-value contracts (e.g., tenders).[762]

---

760. Notice 1/2014, para. 14(d).
761. Notice 1/2014, para. 15.
762. Notice 1/2014, para. 16. *See* Case *Vj-103/2011 ABB/General Trafo.*

Part III, Ch. 2, Voluntary Notifications 884–887

III. Time Framework

884. The deadline established in merger cases (authorization of the concentration under section 24 CA and prolongation of the term under section 25 CA)[763] is of utmost importance, since if the CC fails to make a decision, the merger authorization shall be deemed as given.[764]

885. As to merger cases, the CA establishes four deadlines:

- In proceedings launched because of the implementation of the concentration despite the prohibition embedded in section 29 CA,[765] the final decision has to be adopted within six months from the launch of the investigation; this deadline can be extended by two months.[766]
- In case of merger applications in simple matters, the CC has to adopt a decision within thirty days[767] (and may be extended by twenty days if justified).[768]
- In case the party requests the prolongation of the period of one year set in section 25 CA for the temporary acquisition of control of certain organizations, the final decision has to be adopted within forty-five days.[769]
- In case of merger applications in complicated matters (i.e., if the CC decided, on the basis of section 72(3) CA, that a full-blown inquiry is necessary), the deadline for adjudicating matters that necessitate a full investigation is four months[770] (and may be extended by two months if justified).[771]

886. When calculating the deadline established in days, the administration holiday of section 33/B CA cannot be counted in. If the deadline established in months would expire during the time of the administration holiday, the deadline expires on the first day following the administration holiday.[772] The administration holiday covers ten working days preceding 20 August, and the period between 24 December and 1 January.[773]

887. It has to be noted that when calculating the above deadlines set by the CA, numerous periods have to be disregarded. By way of example, the time of information conveyances (the period between the information requests and their performance or the expiry of the deadline for performance),[774] the period between the

---

763. Section 67(1) CA.
764. Section 64 CA.
765. Section 67(2) CA.
766. Section 63(2)(c) CA.
767. Section 63(2)(d) CA.
768. Section 63(5) CA.
769. Section 63(2)(e) CA.
770. Section 63(3) CA.
771. Section 63(5) CA.
772. Section 63(7) CA.
773. Section 33/B CA.
774. Section 63(4)(f) CA.

dispatch of the CC's preliminary position and the submission of the party's remarks (or they expiry of the deadline),[775] the period of market testing of proposed conditions and obligations (the time between the publication of the call and the expiry of the deadline to submit comments) etc.[776] Hence, the actual length of the merger proceedings is normally significantly longer.

IV. Right of Defence

888. The merger procedure, like competition proceedings in general, comprises two phases: the investigation phase conducted by the case-handler and the decision-making phase coming under the responsibility of the CC.

889. The party can access the case file (i.e., the documents that came into existence during the procedure).[777] In case a proceeding is instituted ex officio (i.e., in all matters apart from merger applications[778]), the party can access the documents as from the time the file is opened, i.e., after the completion of the investigation, after the CC's preliminary position or (if the CC sends out the case-handler's report before that) after the case-handler's report is dispatched to the parties.[779] This rule suggests that no such time-bar exists as to merger procedures instituted upon request. However, if the merger procedure is instituted ex officio, for instance, because the parties failed to notify the merger, the above restriction applies.

890. Access to certain data can be restricted (e.g., protected data, business secrets, etc.).[780]

891. The request to have access to the file is adjudicated in an order; if access is rejected, the applicant can appeal the order.[781]

892. After the completion of the investigation, the case-handler has to prepare a report, which contains the conclusions of the competition investigation. The case-handler's report and the file of the case have to be submitted to the CC.[782]

893. The report is not served automatically on the parties; however, the CC may decide to send out the case-handler's report to the parties before preparing its preliminary position; in this case, the CC also calls the parties to comment on the report

---

775. Section 63(4)(g) CA.
776. Section 63(4)(h) CA.
777. Section 55(1) CA.
778. Including applications for the prolongation of the period under s. 25 CA during which no merger authorization is needed s. 67(1)-(2) CA.
779. Section 55(5) CA.
780. Section 55/A CA.
781. Section 55/B CA.
782. Section 71(1) CA.

Part III, Ch. 2, Voluntary Notifications

within a certain deadline and prepares its preliminary position afterwards (taking into consideration the remarks and comments of the parties).[783]

894. The case-handler's report contains the definition of the subject-matter of the case, the facts established by the case-handler and the supporting evidence, the case-handler's proposal as to the further course of the proceeding and – in case of necessity – his proposal for the adoption of interim measures.[784] The case-handler can propose the adoption of interim measures before the completion of the investigation; in this case, he has to submit a separate report.[785]

895. On the basis of the case-handler's report, the CC prepares a preliminary position, which is delivered to the party.

896. After having received the case-handler's report, the CC has the following options.

897. First, it can return the documents, if it considers the case-handler's report to be defective, i.e., it finds that further investigation is needed to establish the facts, and it considers that it is justified to extend the procedure or to call a new party into the proceeding.[786]

898. Second, it can adopt interim measures:

– it may prohibit the pursuance of the conduct that is likely to infringe the CA or order the elimination of the situation that is likely to infringe the CA, provided this is urgently necessary to protect the legal or economic interests of the person concerned or due to the coming into existence, maintenance or development of economic competition;[787]
– it may adopt, to the extent it is necessary, control-restricting measures for mitigating the concentration's detrimental effects on competition and for ensuring the feasibility of the measures under section 31 CA, in case the concentration was implemented despite the prohibition embedded in section 29 (and it is likely not susceptible of being authorized under section 30), the CC's decision prohibiting the concentration or without the fulfilment of the condition set out in the authorization;[788]
– if the CC, on the basis of section 29/A(1) CA, permitted that the acquirer obtains control over the target undertaking before the decision on the authorization of the concentration is made, it can withdraw the permission on the basis of section 29/A(3) CA or amend the control-restricting measure adopted in the permission

---

783. Section 73(3) CA.
784. Section 71(1)-(2) CA.
785. Section 71(3) CA.
786. Section 72(1) CA.
787. Section 72/A(1)(a) CA.
788. Section 72/A(1)(b) CA.

if it is likely that the concentration would considerably lessen competition in the relevant market.[789]

899. The order providing for an interim measure can be appealed separately under section 82 CA.[790]

900. It is to be noted that the CC may provide guidance to the case-handler as to the method and direction of the investigation even before the completion of the investigation.[791]

901. Third, if the CC neither has to return the case file, nor has to adopt interim measures, nor terminates the procedure, it prepares its preliminary position on the matter and sends it to the party. The preliminary position contains the facts of the case (fact pattern) as established by the CC, the supporting evidence, the assessment of the facts and the description of the aspects and conclusions necessary for the adoption of the decision and the presentation of the factors to be taken into consideration when setting the fine.[792]

902. The CC does not have to prepare a preliminary position if the proceeding was instituted upon request, i.e., the party submitted a merger application,[793] the CC agrees with the request's content, and the concentration can be authorized without the need to prescribe conditions or obligations, as provided in section 30(3) CA.[794]

903. The CC holds a hearing if the party requests so or the CC considers it necessary. When dispatching the preliminary position to the party, the CC calls the party to inform the CC on whether it requests a hearing.[795]

904. The CC holds no hearing if the proceeding was instituted upon request, i.e., the party submitted a merger application,[796] the CC agrees with the request's content, and the concentration can be authorized without the need to prescribe conditions or obligations, as provided in sections 30(3).[797]

905. The CC's hearing is public; however, the CC, upon its own motion or upon request, can exclude the public from the hearing or part of it with a reasoned order, if this is unconditionally necessary for the protection of certain data.[798]

---

789. Section 72/A(1)(c) CA.
790. Section 72 (3)-(4) CA.
791. Section 47(2) CA.
792. Section 73(1) CA.
793. Section 68 CA.
794. Section 73(2) CA.
795. Section 74(1) CA.
796. Section 68 CA.
797. Section 73(2) CA.
798. Section 74(3) CA.

Part III, Ch. 2, Voluntary Notifications

§3. CLEARANCE AND CONDITIONAL CLEARANCE

I. Substantive Merger Analysis

906. The comprehensive assessment of the concentration can be accomplished only on the basis of the extensive and detailed examination and evaluation of market data.[799] In respect of the merger assessment of concentrations, section 30(2) CA adopts the 'effects on competition' test. The HCO authorizes the concentration if it does not lessen competition in the market significantly, in particular as a result of creating or strengthening a dominant position. In case the object or effect of the joint venture defined in section 23(1)(c) CA is to coordinate the market conduct of the founding undertakings, the concentration has to be adjudicated on the basis of section 17 CA.

907. Accordingly, the question to be answered in the frame of the merger analysis is whether the concentration substantially lessens competition.[800] The Hungarian 'effects on competition' test is the counterpart of the 'substantial lessening of competition' (SLC) test and the rough equivalent of the 'significant impediment to effective competition' (SIEC) test, as used in EU merger control law. A typical instance where the concentration would lessen competition significantly is the creation or strengthening of a dominant position; however, a concentration may lessen competition substantially even in case no dominance is created or strengthened.[801]

908. The 'effects on competition' test replaced the dominance test as from 1 July 2009.[802] The consideration behind the new approach is that a concentration may lessen competition not only in case of dominance, by way of example, the increase of market concentration may facilitate cartelization or tacit collusion. For example, in case there are three enterprises in the market of roughly equal size and two of them merge, the transaction might not entail a dominant position, albeit the competitive pressure on market operators, presumably, decreases and the market power of the two remaining enterprises increases; this may trigger the increase of the prices.[803]

909. A concentration may have horizontal and non-horizontal effects.

910. Horizontal effects emerge between competitors active in the same relevant market. Horizontal effects may be unilateral (non-coordinated) and coordinated.

---

799. HCO's 'Communication on the analytical methods applied by the HCO in procedures for the authorization of concentrations, as well as on the circle of data necessary for these and on the requirements against these data', 1.
800. HCO's 'General Methodology: the methodological approach of the analysis of concentrations', para. 1.1.
801. HCO's 'General Methodology: the methodological approach of the analysis of concentrations', para. 1.2.
802. Act XIV of 2009.
803. *See* HCO's 'General Methodology: the methodological approach of the analysis of concentrations', 4. Point.

The unilateral effects accrue from the disappearance of one of the competitors from the market (which becomes part of another competitor); this mitigates the competitive pressure on the undertakings remaining in the market. The concept of coordinated effects encompasses the risk of tacit collusion: the transaction may ease the collusion between the undertakings remaining in the market.

911. Non-horizontal effects may be vertical, portfolio or conglomerate. Vertical effects may emerge, if the groups of undertakings concerned operate on the different levels of the value chain (production-distribution chain), and there is or could be a seller-purchaser relationship between them. Portfolio effects may accrue from the circumstance that due to the concentration the new undertaking's product portfolio expands, in particular if these products are complementary.[804]

912. Section 30(1) CA contains an illustrative list of the aspects to be taken into consideration when assessing the advantages and disadvantages of the concentration.

– The structure of the relevant markets: the actual or potential competition in the relevant markets; the procurement and sales possibilities; the costs, risks and technical, economic and legal conditions of entering and leaving the market; the concentration's expected impact on competition in the relevant market.
– The market situation and strategy of the undertakings concerned, their economic and financial capacity, business conduct, competitiveness in the domestic and foreign market and the expected change of these;
– the concentration's impact on suppliers and business customers.

913. The potential negative effects on competition can be counterbalanced by certain factors. When assessing the concentration, the CC takes both the detrimental and the counterbalancing factors into consideration.

– Entry: if due to the higher prices, new enterprises can enter the market quickly and in a cost-effective manner, this may lessen the merging parties' ability and incentives to increase prices.
– Buyer power: if there are buyers, the conduct of which entails a price decrease as to a considerable part of the market, this may lessen the merging parties' ability to increase prices.
– Efficiency benefits: if the concentration lessens the participating undertakings' production-related costs, this may have a price-decreasing effect; in respect of this counter-veiling factor, it has to be taken into account whether these efficiency benefits are concentration-specific, can be quantitatively demonstrated and an appropriate part of these benefits accrue to consumers.
– Failing firm: if it is proved that the competitive pressure effected by the target enterprise (the firm to be acquired) would disappear from the relevant market

---

804. Notice 1/2014, para. 11.

even in the absence of the concentration (i.e., there is no less restrictive alternative), the concentration would have no impact on the market.[805]

914. The assessment of the concentration is based on a prospective analysis. The concentration's effect is the future change the concentration entails that would not emerge in the absence of the concentration. The assessment focuses on those effects that would emerge in the 'not too far future', that is, between the end of the adaptation period after the implementation of the concentration and the moment, when the market's structure would considerably change.[806]

II. Conditions and Undertakings

915. If the HCO's merger investigation reveals competition concerns or the parties predict that such competition concerns may emerge, they may offer conditions or obligations to remedy these competition problems. According to section 30(3) CA, if the substantial lessening of competition in the relevant market resulting from the concentration can be eliminated in case of the occurrence of a particular preliminary or posterior condition – especially the sale of certain parts of undertaking or certain assets, the termination of control over an indirect participant – or in case of complying with certain behavioural rules, and the undertakings concerned in this regard undertake to appropriately amend the concentration according to such conditions, as well as to act accordingly during the concentration's implementation, the CC, instead of prohibiting the merger, authorizes the concentration with the prescription of the preliminary or posterior condition or obligation.

916. The fundamental difference between conditions and obligations is that structural remedies can be adopted only in the form of a condition, while behavioural remedies can be adopted solely in the form of an obligation.[807]

917. According to section 30(4) CA, in case of a preliminary condition, the authorization becomes effective only once the condition occurs (suspensive condition); in case of a posterior condition, the authorization is effective as from its adoption; however, it ceases to be effective in case the condition does not occur (resolutive condition).

918. There is an important difference between conditions and obligations as to the dynamics of the entering into force of the consequences. The consequences of conditions occur automatically and immediately (in case of a preliminary condition, the decision enters into force, while in case of a posterior condition, it abates when

---

805. HCO's 'General Methodology: the methodological approach of the analysis of concentrations', para. 3.
806. HCO's 'General Methodology: the methodological approach of the analysis of concentrations', para. 4.
807. Para 19 of Notice 2/2014.

the conditions is met). On the contrary, if the undertaking does not meet the obligation, the HCO withdraws the authorization under section 32(2)(b) CA and imposes a fine under section 78(1)(c) CA (or amends it, ex officio or upon request, in case the competitive conditions changed).[808]

919. The HCO's policy on conditions and obligations is summarized in Notice 2/2014. A remedy (irrespective of whether it is adopted in the form of a condition or an obligation) may be applied only if it is capable of solving the emerging competition problem, the notifying enterprises undertake it, the measure is effective, feasible and controllable, and the HCO and the notifying enterprises cooperate.[809]

920. Accordingly, in case of a condition, the merger applicant undertakes to do acts that change the structure of the market. The most frequently used structural remedy is divestiture: e.g., the party undertakes to sell its shares in one of its subsidiaries in order to do away with the competition problem. The HCO prefers structural remedies to behavioural ones.[810] In case of an obligation, the party undertakes to do something or to refrain from doing something. By way of example, it accepts the duty not to discriminate between its customers or to provide access to an asset or facility at cost-based prices.

921. For instance, a competition problem to be remedied emerges in case the overlaps between the operations of the merging undertakings are low in the various geographical markets, but there is a region where the joint market share is high. In such a case, the merger applicant(s) may undertake to sell some of the assets located on this market, thus doing away with the competition concerns, because otherwise there would be a danger that the permission is refused.

III. Ancillary Restraints

922. The implementation of the concentration often makes it necessary that the parties restrict competition between themselves outside the scope of the merger. Due to section 30(5) CA, the merger permission clears ancillary restraints as well: the merger permission covers all those restrictions of competition that are necessary for accomplishing of the concentration.

923. A typical ancillary restraint is the non-compete obligation. If the buyer, when buying the target undertaking, also purchases a circle of customers, the seller could easily deprive the target of its value if it re-entered the market and, using its business contacts and goodwill, re-gained its customers before the buyer could strike root in the market. As a consequence of this peril, the buyer may ask for an assurance that this will not happen; that is, the seller will not re-enter the market for a certain period of time.

---

808. Section 32(4)(b) CA.
809. Paragraphs 12-17.
810. Paragraph 21.

Part III, Ch. 2, Voluntary Notifications

924. A non-compete obligation stipulated at the time of the sale of an undertaking (or part of an undertaking) qualifies as justified, if it is restricted in time and does not extend beyond the products and the region covered by the activities of the undertaking (or part of undertaking) sold.[811] In this respect, the HCO normally uses the Commission's Notice on ancillary restraints as guidance.[812]

---

811. HCO's Position Statement No. 30.5, Case *Vj-19/1999*.
812. OJ [2005] C 56/24.

Chapter 3. Challenging of the Administrative Decision

§1. COMPETENT COURTS

925. The HCO's administrative decision can be attacked before the Administrative and Labour Budapest Court ('*Közigazgatási és Munkaügyi Bíróság*'), and the latter's judgment can be appealed before the Budapest Court ('*Fővárosi Törvényszék*'). The appeal from the Administrative and Labour Budapest Court to the Budapest Court is an ordinary appeal.

926. The Budapest Court's judgment can be challenged before the Supreme Court with a plea for supervision; the Supreme Court is the court of last instance. The plea for supervision is an extra-ordinary appeal limited to points of law.

§2. TIME LIMITS

927. The general deadline for challenging the HCO's administrative decision in the merits before the courts is thirty days.[813]

928. The deadline in respect of orders is eight days.[814]

§3. STANDING

929. Standing as to judicial review is rather limited. The treatment of decisions in the merits and procedural decisions (orders) is different.

930. As to administrative decisions in the merits, section 327(1) of the Code on Civil Procedure provides that the administrative decision can be challenged by the party of the administrative proceeding; other participants of the procedure (e.g., expert witnesses) may attack those parts of the decision that relate expressly to them.[815] Although the Act on Administrative Procedure defines the term 'party' broadly – providing that in administrative procedures all natural and legal persons qualify as a party if their rights or legal interests are affected by the matter[816] –, the CA's definition is fairly narrow: pursuant to section 52 CA, the following may qualify as a 'party' in the competition procedure.

---

813. Section 330(2) of the Code on Civil Procedure.
814. Section 82(3) CA.
815. Section 327(1) of the Code on Civil Procedure.
816. Persons subject to administrative control and persons the data of which is included in the administrative registry also qualify as a party. s. 15(1) APA.

Part III, Ch. 3, Challenging of the Administrative Decision 931–933

- In merger control cases, launched upon request, the applicant, the direct participant of the concentration, in case of the incorporation of a part of undertaking, the undertaking the part of undertakings was part of before the concentration qualify as a party.
- In merger control cases launched ex officio, the parties are the undertakings set out in the foregoing point, as well as the joint venture created by the concentration.
- In proceedings not covered by the preceding points, the undertaking against which the procedure was started ex officio qualifies as a party.[817]

931. The above definition of *locus standi* was inserted in the Code of Civil Procedure by Act LVI of 2009 and is effective as from 1 October 2009. As this provision restricts standing extremely, it may raise constitutional concerns, since according to section XXVIII(7) of the Fundamental Law, '[e]very person shall have the right to seek legal remedy against any court, administrative or other official decision which violates his or her rights or lawful interests.'

932. Procedural decisions (orders) are subject to somewhat dissimilar rules. Orders may be attacked only if the Act on Administrative Procedure or the HCA expressly provides so.[818] The orders of the case-handlers are to be attacked before the CC, while the latter's orders are to be attacked before the court. An order may be attacked by the party, by the other participants of the procedure so long as the order contains a measure relating to them and by the complainant (who submitted a formal complaint), provided the order is to be notified to him according to the CA.[819] Pursuant to section 60/A(2) CA, the order terminating the competition procedure on the basis of section 53(2)-(3) CA and of section 31(1)(e) or 31(1)(i) APA shall be delivered to the complainant (the person having made a formal complaint).

933. According to section 53(2) CA, the party's legal successor can be called into the proceeding; if this is not justified (taking into account the conditions of the launch of the competition proceeding as set out in section 70(1) CA), the case-handler or the CC puts an end to the proceeding. According to section 53(3) CA, if it can be established on the basis of the available data that the ex officio proceeding was not launched against the proper party, the proper party can be called into the proceeding; in the absence of this, the case-handler or the CC terminates the proceeding. According to section 31(1)(e) APA, the administrative procedure has to be terminated if the circumstance giving rise to the procedure no longer exists. According to section 31(1)(i) APA, in ex officio proceedings, the administrative procedure has to be terminated if the fact pattern could not be revealed to the extent necessary for adopting a decision and it cannot be expected that the further pursuance of the proceeding would be successful in ascertaining the facts.

---

817. Section 52 CA.
818. Section 82 CA.
819. Section 82(3) CA.

§4. SCOPE OF JUDICIAL REVIEW

934. The standard of review in Hungarian administrative and procedural law, including competition matters, is 'illegality'.[820] The HCO's decision may be attacked only if it violates the law. As to the application of the standard of review, four questions are to be distinguished: questions of fact, questions of law (general interpretation of the law), application of the law to the fact pattern and expert questions. In each case, the central question is whether the court can second-guess the decision (de novo review) or can only review it, being deferential to the authority's decision.

935. Below, the traditional Hungarian approach on the standard of judicial review will be presented and analysed. However, it has to be emphasized that the Supreme Court adopted a strikingly novel standard in Case *Kfv.III.37.690/2013/29 Railway Constructors*, which is – as the Court indicated – applicable only to cases covered by EU competition law. Nonetheless, it is expected that this jurisprudence will have a spillover effect on cases covered by Hungarian competition law and mark a new era of highly interventionist judicial review.

936. The Supreme Court held that the CC's decision must not have to be examined under the provision on discretionary acts, enabling a margin of appreciation (section 339/B CCP) but during the judicial review the CC's decision has to be treated as if it were an 'indictment'. In the court procedure, the plaintiffs need not demonstrate that the CC's decision assessed the evidence in a blatantly unreasonable manner or the legal assessment was obviously unreasonable; it suffices if they demonstrate that a more reasonable assessment of the evidence and a more reasonable legal balancing exists.

937. The Supreme Court deduced the above approach from Article 6 of the European Convention of Human Rights as interpreted in the judgment of the European Court of Human Rights in *Menarini*,[821] and declared that the above approach applies to cases where Article 101 TFEU is applied. Accordingly, the traditional Hungarian approach will be presented below with the caveat, that – at least as far as matters with an EU dimension are concerned – this appears to have been partially (or for the most part) overruled by the Supreme Court's judgment in Case *Kfv.III.37.690/2013/29 Railway Construction Companies*. However, as noted, this more interventionist judicial approach is expected to be extended to cases not affecting inter-state trade and coming solely under the purview of Hungarian competition law.

---

820. Section 109(1) APA; s. 339 CCP.
821. Judgment rendered in Case 43509/08 *Menarini Diagnostics S.R.L. v. Italy* on 27 Sep. 2011.

Part III, Ch. 3, Challenging of the Administrative Decision

I. Questions of Fact

938. The dominant view is that as to questions of fact the court reviews the authority's decision but cannot second-guess it.[822] The standard of review is 'illegality' and the court's function is to inquire whether the authority observed the procedural rules on proof. The authority is obliged to discover the facts;[823] it provides that it has to assess the pieces of evidence individually and in their entirety, and establish the fact pattern according to its conviction based on this assessment.[824] Accordingly, the authority's duties are twofold: it has to discover the facts and establish the fact pattern on the basis of its conviction resting on the assessment of the evidence. As the standard of review is 'illegality', the relevant question is whether the authority infringed these rules on proof. In other words: if the authority discovered the facts properly (it collected the available evidence, carried out the proving offered by the parties or gave reasons why it refused this motion[825]) and its balancing (or as the APA provides: conviction) is not unreasonable, the violation of the law cannot be established, provided the court did not conduct procedural acts of proof (taking new evidence) and did not repeat at least in part the procedural acts of proof (e.g., interrogating the witnesses who were interrogated also in the administrative procedure).

939. According to the rules on proof of the civil procedure, '[t]he court shall ascertain the fact pattern upon weighing the submissions (allegations) of the parties against the evidence obtained by the performance of taking of evidence. The court shall evaluate the evidence as a whole, and shall rule relying on its conviction'.[826] Although, as this provision suggests, the court establishes the fact pattern on the basis of its conviction, in the judicial review the relevant facts are not the facts of the case as such, but those circumstances that are necessary to decide on whether the authority violated the rules on proof. For instance, in case of a price cartel, the relevant factual question in the administrative proceeding is whether the undertakings agreed on the price; on the other hand, in the judicial review the relevant question is whether the HCO's establishing of the price cartel is contrary to the law due to its non-compliance with the relevant provisions of the APA (section 50). An infringement of the law can be established if the factual situation was not discovered to the necessary extent or the HCO's conclusion that there was a price cartel falls foul of the law, i.e., the balancing of the evidence was unreasonable. The relevant facts are not the same in the administrative procedure and the judicial review.

940. As noted by the Supreme Court in Case *Kf.I.35.827/2001*,[827] the authority and the court are obliged to discover the facts and take evidence in respect to the

---

822. *See* the session of 9 Apr. 1992 of the Supreme Court's Administrative College, quoted in Jenő Kaltenbach, *Közigazgatási mérlegelés és közigazgatási bíráskodás*, in *Emlékkönyv Dr. Kemenes Béla egyetemi tanár 65. születésnapjára* 187 (Károly Tóth ed., JATE 1993).
823. Section 50(1) APA.
824. 50(6) APA.
825. *See* 72(1)(eb) APA.
826. Section 206(1) CCP.
827. Case *BH2005.336*.

legally relevant facts; the relevant facts are delimited by the legal provisions governing the legal dispute. In the judicial review proceeding, the court can decide only on the legality or illegality of the attacked decision.[828] In Case *2.Kf. 27.565/2008/14*, the Budapest Court of Appeals considered the administrative decision to be lawful referring to the fact the authority balanced the available evidence in a reasonable manner.[829]

941. The burden of proof is to be grasped in the above context. As provided in section 164(1) CCP, the facts necessary for adjudicating the case are normally to be proven by the party, who is interested in that the court accepts them as true. Accordingly, in principle, the burden of proof rests on the plaintiff. However, the plaintiff need not prove that the facts underlying the decision did not occur; its burden covers those facts that underpin the illegality of the authority's factual statements (i.e., the fact pattern was not discovered properly, the balancing of the evidence was not reasonable). This approach is mirrored in section 336/A CCP,[830] providing that if the administrative proceeding was instituted ex officio or the administrative authority did not fulfil its duty to establish the fact pattern, it is obliged to prove the fact pattern underlying the decision is true, provided the plaintiff disputes it.[831] In other words, the burden of proof rests on the plaintiff, but this covers the question whether the authority discovered the facts[832] and whether its balancing of the evidence was reasonable. If the plaintiff is successful in this regard, the burden of proof shifts. Of course, the plaintiff may prove the illegality of the authority's factual statements by rebutting their truth, e.g., if it refutes the factual statements with three testimonies. However, the plaintiff is not required to go that far. This rule is logical, since the defendant in the administrative proceeding has the right to request the taking of evidence, and if this motion is rejected without a good reason, this may make the final decision illegal, provided this affects the merits of the case.[833] It is another case, if the authority is aware of the existence of additional means of evidence, the taking of these can be reasonably expected from it; for instance, the evidence suggests that eight persons were present at the cartel meeting but the HCO interrogates only one of them. In such a case, the HCO may violate the duty to discover the fact pattern.

942. The Supreme Court's judgment in Case *Kfv.III.37.690/2013/29 Railway Construction Companies* will probably lift the CC's margin of appreciation as regards the establishing of the facts. Although the allocation of the burden of proof remains intact (it rests on the plaintiff's shoulders), the standard of proof changes: it will be sufficient to demonstrate that there is a more reasonable assessment of the evidence. It is to be noted that as to facts the court's reviewing powers, as a matter of competence,

---

828. *See also* Case *Kfv.IV.39.399/2007* (Supreme Court), published under nr. *BH2009.91*.
829. Case *VEF2004.50*.
830. This provision entered into force on 1 Nov. 2005 and confirms the earlier judicial practice. *See* the explanatory memorandum of Act XVII of 2005 (remarks on s. 15). *Cf.* Case *2.Kf.27.578/2008/12* (Budapest Court of Appeal), published under No. *VEF2001.25*.
831. *See* Opinion No. 1/2007 of the Administrative College on the questions discussed on the consultation meeting (in Hungarian: '1/2007. KK vélemény a 2007. évi konzultációs értekezleten megvitatott kérdésekről'), answer to question 4, (3) *Bírósági Határozatok* (2008).
832. *See* Case *2.Kf.27.565/2008/14* (Budapest Court of Appeals), published under No. *VEF2004.50*.
833. *See* s. 72(1)(eb) APA.

Part III, Ch. 3, Challenging of the Administrative Decision

were unrestricted, so the new test is not expected to induce a material change in this regard.

II. The Abstract Interpretation (Construction) of the Law

943. In Hungarian administrative and civil procedural law, there is no specific provision on how the court may review the authority's abstract construction of the law. Since issues of competition law involve economic considerations, they may enable the authority to work out its own competition policy. Hungarian courts do have a full power to review this question de novo. The abstract interpretation of the law comes obviously under unrestricted judicial competence. It is to be noted, however, that Hungarian courts normally accept the HCO's abstract interpretation and policy-making, albeit this is not without exception. By way of example, as to excessive pricing the Supreme Court held that the legal test worked out by the HCO was flawed. There are two methods for defining the hypothetical competitive price. First, the analysis may proceed from the dominant undertaking's costs; second, the market price may be compared to a current or past market price on another market. The Court held: if excessive pricing can be ascertained on the basis of different methods of analysis, the HCO can take a position on the violation only if it examines the case on the basis of both methods and assesses the results of the two analyses together; the use of one of the methods does not exclude the other and does not exclude the possibility to establish the violation.[834]

944. The Supreme Court's judgment in Case *Kfv.III.37.690/2013/29 Railway Construction Companies* will not change the current judicial practice as to abstract interpretation, since the court's powers, as a matter of competence, have not been restricted anyway.

III. Application of the Law to a Concrete Case

945. The treatment of questions of law depends on the clarity of the language of the provision to be interpreted and applied. The authority has certainly no playing field as to clear-cut provisions; however, it does have such a give in case the language of the provision is not clear and its interpretation is uncertain. Hungarian administrative law recognizes the concept of 'discretionary acts';[835] i.e., if the legal

---

834. As to the legal test on excessive pricing *see* Case *Kf.II.39.048/2002/13* (Supreme Court). This case was connected to the HCO's decision in Case *Vj-152/2000*. In this regard, *see* Barna Berke, *Lehet-e tisztességtelenül megállapított, túlzottan magas ár egy versenypiaci ár?*, in *Studia Gy. Boytha Dedicata* 19–32 (Miklós Király & Péter Gyertyánfy ed., ELTE ÁJK Nemzetközi Magánjogi és Európai Gazdasági Jogi Tanszék 2004).
835. *See* Jenő Kaltenbach, *Közigazgatási mérlegelés és közigazgatási bíráskodás*, in *Emlékkönyv Dr. Kemenes Béla egyetemi tanár 65. születésnapjára* 181–188 (Károly Tóth ed., JATE 1993); János Martonyi, *A diszkrecionális mérlegelés kérdései* (József Attila Tudományegyetem, 1967); Miklós Molnár, *A mérlegeléses jogalkalmazás és a jogilag kötetlen döntéshozatal néhány kérdése az államigazgatásban*, in *Az ELTE Állam- és Jogtudományi Karának Aktái 1988. Vol. 30.* 91–100 (ELTE ÁJK, 1990).

provision's construction is not clear-cut, the court recognizes that the authority has a certain margin of appreciation and, accordingly, it will not second-guess but simply review the decisions as to points of law. Section 339/B CCP provides that a discretionary decision is lawful, if the administrative authority discovered the fact pattern properly, observed the procedural rules, the aspects of the balancing can be identified and the decision's reasoning reveals the reasonableness of the assessment of the evidence.

946. In Case *Büki Üdítő Kft. v. HCO*,[836] the Supreme Court held that in case of a discretionary decision the court has the power to inquire whether the authority took all potential aspects of balancing into account, explained why it accepted or rejected them; if the violation of the law cannot be established, the amount of the fine cannot be changed, the court has no power to second-guess the authority's decision.[837]

947. In Case *2.Kf.27.484/2008/7*, the Budapest Court established that the law conferred a wide margin of appreciation on the HCO as to the determination of the amount of the fine. In case more than one lawful decision could be made, the purpose of the balancing is to single out the most reasonable decision from all the potential lawful decisions. The discretionary power, however, cannot be unrestricted, irresponsible or based on unlimited discretion, but it has to remain within the framework delimited by the law.[838]

948. The Supreme Court's judgment in Case *Kfv.III.37.690/2013/29 Railway Constructors* will profoundly affect the way the fact pattern is subsumed under the abstractly defined legal norm. The Supreme Court's judgment expressly mentions section 339/B CCP as a provision that cannot be applied in EU competition law cases after *Menarini*. However, it is uncertain how this more activist judicial approach will be applied to the setting of fine: it is unsettled whether the principle that the CC's decision has to be treated merely as an 'indictment' related only to the question of illegality or it also covers the setting of the fine.

IV. Expert Questions

949. Expert questions are wedged in between questions of law and questions of facts; they are a mixture of legal and factual issues. These issues are questions that come under the expertise of court-appointed-experts, while they often influence the way the law is interpreted and applied. Furthermore, they may also be regarded as factual questions (at least to some extent), since experts enable the court to ascertain and evaluate facts.

---

836. Case *Kf.V.39.361/2001/4* (Supreme Court).
837. *See also* Case *2K. 30044/2008/18* (Budapest Court).
838. Case *2.Kf.27.565/2008/14* (Budapest Court of Appeal).

Part III, Ch. 3, Challenging of the Administrative Decision   950–953

950. According to the judicial practice, except the expert opinion is obscure, contains omissions or it is self-contradictory or contradicts with the opinion of another expert or the proved facts, or its accuracy admits of remarkable doubt,[839] the court cannot examine the expert question and cannot diverge from the conclusions of the expert opinion. Of course, it may appoint another expert, provided one of the parties requests this. Nonetheless, if the foregoing conditions are not met and no controlling expert is appointed, the expert opinion will be binding on the court.[840]

951. The status of expert questions had a pivotal role in Case *Vj-185/1994 Coffee Cartel*.[841] This case had been adjudicated prior to the entry into force of section 339/B of the Code on Civil Procedure;[842] however, it is to be noted that this provision was meant to simply codify the then-prevailing judicial practice.

952. The CC found that market players in the coffee market engaged in concerted practice, considering that the only reasonable explanation to their parallel behaviour was that they coordinated their market conduct. The court endorsed the legal test applied by the CC; that is, it is a concerted practice if the only reasonable explanation to the parallel behaviour is that the undertakings colluded. Afterwards, this legal test was to be applied to the fact patter, i.e., the question to be answered was whether there was indeed no other explanation to the parallel behaviour but the cartel. Since this question raised expert issues and required the economic assessment of market developments, the court appointed an expert and based its judgment on the expert's opinion.

953. The status and assessment of the expert opinion played a central role in the lawsuit. The first instance court appointed an economic expert, who considered that collusion was not the only reasonable explanation to the undertakings' parallel behaviour; the consequence of this economic assessment would have been that the enterprises' parallel behaviour cannot be regarded as concerted practice. However, both the first instance court and, afterwards, the appellate court affirmed the CC's decision, ignoring the expert opinion.[843] The Supreme Court quashed the judgment and remanded.[844] It held that the first and the second instance courts infringed the rules on proof and experts, and this had an impact on the merits of the case. The court of first instance did not explain in its reasoning why it disregarded the expert opinion's content and what evidence supported the legality of the CC's decision. The Supreme Court held that the expert's opinion may be disregarded only if this is supported by conclusive evidence. Failing this, section 182(3) CCP has to be applied. Accordingly, if the expert opinion is obscure, contains omissions or is self-contradictory or contradicts with the opinion of another expert or the proved facts, or its accuracy admits of remarkable doubt, the expert is obliged to provide the necessary information if the

---

839. Section 182(3) CCP.
840. *See* Case *Kfv.II.39.792/2002.* (Supreme Court), published under No. EBH2004.1082.
841. The case was based on the old Competition Act (Act LXXXVI of 1990).
842. Section 339/B CCP was inserted into the Code on Civil Procedure by Act XVII of 2005; it entered into force on 1 Nov. 2005.
843. Case *Kf.II.29.324/1999/14.* (Supreme Court).
844. Case *Kf.II.29.324/1999/14.* (Supreme Court).

court so requires; if one of the parties so requests, the court may appoint another expert; if the expert was appointed ex officio, the court may appoint another expert on its own motion. The Supreme Court ordered the court of first instance to call the expert to complete his expert opinion if necessary, and to appoint another expert if the conditions embedded in section 182(3) CCP are met. Furthermore, it also advanced that the judgment should contain the detailed reasons of the facts and circumstances that made the court not to accept the content of the expert opinion.

954. In the repeated procedure, since none of the parties requested the court to appoint another expert, the first instance court based its judgment on the expert opinion and accordingly quashed the HCO's decision. The court of second instance, without taking any additional evidence, including the appointment of another expert, reversed the first instance judgment. First, it considered the expert's opinion as dubious due to incompatibility issues. Second, it found that, contrary to the expert opinion, it was not proved that the parties engaged in parallel behaviour (and not in concerted practice). The plaintiffs challenged the judgment before the Supreme Court, which had to decide on it for the second time. The relevant legal question to be addressed was under what conditions the court may make a judgment that is contrary to the expert opinion, whether the authority's decision may be used as evidence. The Supreme Court held that the expert's opinion is quasi binding on the court, which may ignore it only under certain conditions: if the expert opinion's flaws and omissions could not be remedied and the well-founded, undoubted facts support that the court should disregard it. The Supreme Court's judgment suggests that if none of the parties requests this, the court may examine only whether the expert opinion contains contradictions, whether it is obscure, incoherent; these are questions a judge having no expertise in economics can hardly inquire. If the party to which the expert opinion is detrimental envisages raising expert (economic) arguments, it has to request the appointment of another expert. Since in *Coffee Cartel*, the HCO failed to submit such a motion, the court had to render a judgment on the basis of the single available expert opinion.

955. The Supreme Court also held that the CC's decision – as this is the subject-matter of the supervisory proceeding – is, in itself, no evidence. On the other hand, the facts and data revealed during the competition proceeding and the documents underlying the CC's decision do qualify as evidence. On the basis of this proposition, the Supreme Court held that the court of second instance erred in law when it decided on the acceptance of the expert opinion through contrasting the opinion with the administrative decision.

956. The Supreme Court's above judgment suggests that the court cannot 'legalize' the expert question, that is, it cannot make the economic assessment part of its interpretation and application of the law. This approach has been criticized in the scholarship, which advocates that due to the concept of discretionary acts and margin of appreciation, the question to be addressed to the expert is not whether the authority's assessment is reasonable and not whether it is the only acceptable assessment or whether the expert's assessment is in line with that of the CC. Since an economic question may have more than one plausible answers, the expert should not be asked to give a

Part III, Ch. 3, Challenging of the Administrative Decision

categorical answer on the economic question, because this would enable it to second-guess (instead of reviewing) the CC's decision.[845]

957. The above judgment is one of the rare cases in Europe that address specifically the role and status of expert evidence in competition cases. However, it is difficult to predict the precedential value of the above judgment. Although section 339/B CCP, which addresses the administrative authorities' margin of appreciation, was adopted subsequent to the judgment in *Caffee Cartel*, it was essentially meant to codify earlier judicial practice, instead of overruling it.

958. It appears that the Supreme Court treated expert questions rather as factual and not as an issue of subsumtion covered by the margin of appreciation doctrine. After the Supreme Court's judgment in Case *Kfv.III.37.690/2013/29 Railway Construction Companies*, this tendency is expected to accelerate. This would be very welcome in case the decision on economic issues would not be left to the court-appointed expert, but the court could make this part of the judicial legal assessment and balancing.

---

845. Csongor István Nagy, *Kartelljogi Kézikönyv. A közösségi és a magyar kartelljog kézikönyve* 692-693 (HVG-Orac 2006).

Selected Bibliography

BOOKS

András György Kovács. *Piacszabályozás és jogorvoslat – A piacszabályozói döntések bírói gyakorlata, különös tekintettel az elektronikus hírközlésre* (HVG-Orac 2012) (*Market regulation and legal remedy – the judicial practice of decisions of market regulation, with special emphasis on electronic communications*).

András Osztovits (ed.). *Az Európai Unióról és az Európai Unió működéséről szóló szerződések magyarázata* (Complex 2011).

András Tóth. *Az elektronikus hírközlés és média gazdasági szabályozásának alapjai és versenyjogi vonatkozásai* (HVG-Orac 2008) (*The economic foundations and competition law aspects of the regulation of the electronic communications and media*).

Boytha Györgyné (ed.). *Versenyjogi jogsértések esetén érvényesíthető magánjogi igények* (HVG-Orac 2009) (*Private claims enforceable in case of competition violations*).

Boytha Györgyné, et al. *Versenyjog* (HVG-Orac 2001) (*Competition law*).

Csongor István Nagy. *Kartelljogi Kézikönyv. A közösségi és a magyar kartelljog kézikönyve* (HVG-Orac 2006) (*Handbook of Restrictive Agreements. Handbook of Restrictive Agreements in Community and Hungarian Competition Law*).

Csongor István Nagy. *EU and US Competition Law: Divided in Unity?* (Ashgate Publishing 2013).

Imre Vörös. *Az európai versenyjogok kézikönyve* (Logod Bt. 1996) (*The handbook of European competition laws*).

Lénárd Darázs. *A kartellek semmissége* (Complex 2009) (*The automatic invalidity of restrictive agreements*).

Lénárd Darázs. *Vertikális kartellek* (Complex 2007) (*Vertical restraints*).

Péter Miskolczi-Bodnár. *A versenytörvény magyarázata.* (KJK-Kerszöv 2002) (*The commentary of the Competition Act*).

Tihamér Tóth. *Az Európai Unió versenyjoga* (Complex 2007) (*The competition law of the European Union*).

Virág Balogh, et al. *Magyar versenyjog* (HVG-Orac 2012) (*Hungarian competition law*).

Selected Bibliography

ARTICLES (IN HUNGARIAN)

Bálint Bassola. *A közösségi versenyjog eljárásjogi reformjának hatása a magyar versenyjogra*, in Jogi Tanulmányok 47 (Nagy Marianna ed., ELTE ÁJK 2005).
Chrysta Bán. *Az engedékenységi politika és a magánjogi igények kapcsolata*, in Versenyjogi jogsértések – magánjogi jogkövetkezmények 69 (Kisfaludi András ed., ELTE Eötvös Kiadó 2012).
Zoltán Bércesi & László Kecskés. *A bizalmas kommunikáció privilégiuma a versenyfelügyeleti eljárásokban. A legal privilege jelensége és érvényesülési keretei az európai és a hazai versenyjogban*, 5(4) Európai Jog 11 (2005).
Barna Berke. *Versenyjog, nemzetközi kapcsolatok, harmonizáció: kis magyar jogi imperializmus*. In: 52(9) Jogtudományi Közlöny 361 (1997).
Bodócsi, András. *Az árak megítélése a versenytörvény alapján*, 8(10) Versenyfelügyeleti Értesítő (1998).
Bodócsi András. *Az árak versenyhatósági ellenőrzésének kérdőjelei*, 5(2) Versenytükör 29 (2009).
Boytha Györgyné. *A közösségi versenyjogi gyakorlat tükröződése a magyar jogalkotásban és joggyakorlatban*, in Liber Amicorum Studia Gy. Boytha dedicata 49 (Miklós Király & Péter Gyertyánfy eds., ELTE ÁJK 2004).
László Burger. *A versenykorlátozó megállapodások jogi minősítésének kérdéséről*, in Jogi Tanulmányok 9 (Attila Harmathy Attila ed., ELTE ÁJK 2002).
Balázs Csépai & Dániel Krámer. *A közösségi versenyjogi reform hatása Magyarországon*, 54(11) Jogtudományi Közlöny 398 (2004).
Balázs Csépai, & István Szatmáry. *A magánjogi jogérvényesítés lehetőségei a versenyjogba ütköző magatartásokhoz kapcsolódóan*, in Versenyjog aktuális kérdései 36 (Tihamér Tóth ed., PPKE JÁK & GVH 2005).
Balázs Csépai & Ákos Újvári. *A versenyt korlátozó megállapodás közbeszerzési és koncessziós eljárásban való büntethetőségének kérdésköre. Reflexió a Btk. 296/B. par.-hoz*, 56(6) Jogtudományi Közlöny 221 (2006).
Lénárd Darázs. *Javaslat a versenytörvény hatályának komplex újraszabályozására*, in Polgári jogi és versenyjogi tanulmányok 47 (Attila Harmathy & Ottó Csakurda, MTA Állam- és Jogtudományi Intézet & ELTE ÁJK 1994).
Lénárd Darázs. *Javaslat a versenytörvény területi hatályának újraszabályozására*, 2(5) Gazdaság és Jog 14 (1994).
Lénárd Darázs. *A semmisség mint a versenyjogi jogsértések (kartellek és gazdasági erőfölénnyel való visszaélés) esetén alkalmazható polgári jogi jogkövetkezmény*, in Versenyjogi jogsértések – magánjogi jogkövetkezmények 119 (Kisfaludi András ed., ELTE Eötvös Kiadó 2012).
Tamás Éless, & Ágnes Németh. *Study on the conditions of claims for damages in case of infringement of EC competition rules. National report: Hungary* (Ashurst 2004) <http://ec.europa.eu/comm/competition/antitrust/others/actions_for_damages/national_reports/hungary_en.pdf>.
Gábor Fejes. *Attól, hogy kézenfekvő, még igaz: a közbeszerzés ajánlatkérője nincs felmentve versenyjogból*, 15(2) Gazdasági és Jog 9 (2007).
Gábor Fejes, Marosi Zoltán & Szabó Lia. *Miben áll az összefonódást tilalmazó GVH-határozat pogári jogi joghatása – dilemmák a versenyjog és a polgári jog határmezsgyéjén*, 61(11) Jogtudományi Közlöny 401 (2006).

Selected Bibliography

Ádám Fuglinszky. *A versenyjogi jogsértések esetén alkalmazható polgári jogi jogkövetkezmények*, in Versenyjogi jogsértések – magánjogi jogkövetkezmények 11 (Kisfaludi András ed., ELTE Eötvös Kiadó 2012).

Péter Misckolczi-Bodnár. *A kamarai szabályzat, mint vállalkozások társulásának döntése II.*, 2(4) Versenytükör 33 (2006).

Péter Misckolczi-Bodnár. *Vállalati döntés vagy állami aktus. A kamarai szabályzat, mint vállalkozások társulásának döntése I.*, 2(3) Versenytükör 35 (2006).

Péter Miskolczi-Bodnár. *Mentesülés mentesítés nélkül, avagy a versenyfelügyeleti eljárás palettájának fakulása*, in Kilényi Géza ünnepi kötet 313 (Barnabás Hajas & Balázs Schanda eds., PPKE JÁK & Szent István Társulat 2006).

István Molnár. *Versenykorlátozó kikötések a licenciaszerződésekben: a közösségi és hazai versenyjogi szabályozás kérdései*, 108(3) Iparjogvédelmi és Szerzői Jogi Szemle 3 (2003).

Csongor István Nagy, (2000). Felfaló árazás Magyarországon és az Európai Unióban. In: Versenyfelügyeleti Értesítő, n 8, pp. 394-414 (*Predatory pricing in Hungary and in the European Union*).

Csongor István Nagy, (2002). A felfaló ár megítélése a magyar versenyjogban. In: Collega. n 3, pp. 6-13 (*The adjudication of predatory prices in Hungarian competition law*).

Csongor István Nagy, (2002). Nélkülözhetetlen eszköz a közösségi versenyjogban. In: Új generáció a közigazgatásban. Tempus Közalapítvány – Miniszterelnöki Hivatal. pp. 199-218 (*Essential facilities in Community competition law*).

Csongor István Nagy, (2002). Túlzottan magas árak megítélése a magyar versenyjogban. Collega, n 4, pp. 38-47 (*Excessive pricing in Hungarian competition law*).

Csongor István Nagy, (2003). Nélkülözhetetlen eszközök és a távközlési infrastruktúra. In: Internetjogi tanulmányok. Ed: Kiss Daisy – Sántha Ágnes. Bibó István Szakkollégium Internetjogi Műhely, Budapest, pp. 231-245 (*Essential facilities and telecommunications infrastructure*).

Csongor István Nagy, (2006). Nélkülözhetetlen eszközök koncepciója az amerikai, a közösségi és a magyar versenyjogban. In: Európai Jogi Tanulmányok. ELTE ÁJK, Nemzetközi Magánjogi és Európai Gazdasági Jogi Tanszék. pp. 125-156. (*The concept of essential facilities in US, Community and Hungarian competition law*).

Csongor István Nagy, (2008). A leverage koncepciója az elektronikus hírközlési jogban: vissza a gyökerekhez. In: Infokommunikáció és Jog, n 3, pp. 113-121 (*The concept of leverage in electronic communications law: back to the roots*).

Csongor István Nagy, (2008). Egyetemes szolgáltatás és verseny. In: Infokommunikáció és Jog, n 11 (*Universal service and competition*).

Csongor István Nagy, (2008). Mégiscsak lehet viszonteladási árat kikötni? In: Gazdaság és Jog, n 5, pp. 8-12 (*After all: is it possible to fix the resale price?*).

Csongor István Nagy, (2009). A kartellkár egy speciális esete: a vétlen szerződő fél kártérítési igénye. In: Versenyjogi jogsértések esetén érvényesíthető magánjogi igények. HVG-Orac, Budapest, pp. 125-143 (*A special case of competition damages: the innocent contracting party's claim for damages*).

Csongor István Nagy, (2009). Jelentős piaci erő jogintézménye a villamosenergia-piaci szabályozásban: jogalkotói önellentmondás? In: Verseny és szabályozás.

Selected Bibliography

Ed.: Kiss Ferenc László – Valentiny Pál. MTA Közgazdaságtudományi Intézet. pp. 147-169 (*The concept of significant market power in electricity regulation: legislative self-contradiction*).

Csongor István Nagy, (2009). Kártérítési felelősség kartelljogsértések esetén: gondolatok a Tpvt. új szabályai kapcsán. In: Magyar Jog, n 9, pp. 513-520 (*Liability for damages due to cartel law violations: some thoughts on the new rule of the Competition Act*).

Csongor István Nagy, (2009). Vezető tisztségviselők személyes versenyjogi felelőssége: gondolatok az Alkotmánybíróság határozata kapcsán. In: Gazdaság és Jog, n 9, pp. 10-12 (*The personal competition law liability of executives: some thoughts on the decision of the Constitutional Court*).

Csongor István Nagy, (2010). A villamos energia egyetemes szolgáltatás az Európai Unióban és Magyarországon. In: A magyar villamosenergia-piac főbb aspektusai. Ed.: Fazekas Orsolya. Complex, Budapest, pp. 119-151 (*The electricity universal service in the European Union and in Hungary*).

Csongor István Nagy, (2010). Egységben a kartell? In: Ügyvédek Lapja n 5, pp. 30-35 (*United in Cartel?*).

Csongor István Nagy, (2010). Magánjogi igények érvényesítése a GVH határozatai alapján. In: Fogyasztóvédelmi Szemle IV. évf. 1. sz. pp. 43-48 (*Claims for damages on the basis of the decisions of the Hungarian Competition Office*).

Csongor István Nagy. *A versenykorlátozó megállapodásokkal kapcsolatos versenyjogi tilalom szerkezete*, 67(9) Jogtudományi Közlöny 321 (2012) (*The structure of the competition law prohibition on restrictive agreements*).

Csongor István Nagy. *A vertikális megállapodás mint a kartelltilalom küszöbfogalma: összehasonlító jogi elemzés és értékelés*, 7(1) Versenytükör 20 (2011) (*The vertical agreement as the treshold question of the prohibition on restrictive agreements: comparative analysis and evaluation*).

Csongor István Nagy. *A vertikális megállapodások új szabályai az EU-ban: régi és új örök harca dúl ...* , 19(1) Gazdaság és Jog (2011) (*The new rules of vertical restraints in the EU: the eternal fight of old and new ...*).

Csongor István Nagy. *A viszonteladási ár rögzítésének megítélése az amerikai, az EU és a magyar versenyjogban: kihasznált és kihagyott lehetőségek*, in Verseny és Szabályozás 2011 58 (Pál Valentiny, Ferenc László Kiss & Csongor István Nagy eds., MTA KRTK Közgazdaságtudományi Intézet 2012). (*The treatment of resale price fixing in US, EU and Hungarian competition law: exploited and missed opportunities*).

Csongor István Nagy. *Az egyetemes szolgáltatás metamorfózisai*, in Verseny és Szabályozás 2010 120 (Pál Valentiny, Ferenc László Kiss & Csongor István Nagy eds., MTA KRTK Közgazdaságtudományi Intézet 2011) (*The metamorphoses of universal service*).

Csongor István Nagy. *Az európai versenyjog magánjogi érvényesítése Magyarországon*, 11(3) Európai Jog 3 (2011) (*The private enforcement of European competition law in Hungary*).

Csongor István Nagy. *I. Fejezet: Versenypolitika*, in Az Európai Unió közös politikái (Kengyel Ákos ed., Akadémiai Kiadó 2010) (*Chapter I: Competition policy*).

Selected Bibliography

Csongor István Nagy. *Kötelezettségvállalások a GVH gyakorlatában*. In: Jubileumi kötet a modern magyar versenyjog 20 éves évfordulójára, 19(10) Gazdaság és Jog 3 (2011) (*Commitments in the practice of the Hungarian Competition Office*).

Csongor István Nagy. *Közgazdasági kérdések a mérlegelési jogkörben hozott közigazgatási határozatok felülvizsgálata során, különös tekintettel a versenyügyekre*, in Verseny és Szabályozás 2009 108 (Pál Valentiny, Ferenc László Kiss & Csongor István Nagy eds., MTA KRTK Közgazdaságtudományi Intézet 2010) (*Economics issues in the judicial review of discretionary administrative decisions*).

Csongor István Nagy. *Újabb kartelljogi roham az omerta falának áttörésére – gondolatok a feljelentői díj jogintézménye kapcsán*, 18(6) Gazdasági és Jog 3 (2010) (*A fresh competition law assault against the wall of omerta – thoughts on the informant's reward*).

Tamás Polauf. *A teljesítésre kötelezés mint a versenyjogi jogsértések esetén alkalmazható polgári jogi jogkövetkezmény*, in Versenyjogi jogsértések – magánjogi jogkövetkezmények 209 (Kisfaludi András ed., ELTE Eötvös Kiadó 2012).

József Sárai. *A magyar versenyszabályok változása a csatlakozás és a közösségi versenyjog eljárási reformja tükrében*, 8(4-5) Európai Tükör 92 (2003).

Pál Szilágyi. *A Legfelsőbb Bíróság ítélete a cementkartell ügyében*, 1(3) Jogesetek Magyarázata 63 (2010).

András Tóth. *Túlzó ár a Gazdasági Versenyhivatal gyakorlatában*, 16(6) Gazdaság és jog 3 (2008).

András Tóth. *Versenyjog alkalmazhatósága a szabályozott iparágakban*, 64(4) Jogtudományi Közlöny 183 (2009).

Tihamér Tóth. *A közösségi versenyjog alkalmazása a tagállami bíróságok előtt – egy reform, amelyre már a magyar bíróknak is figyelniük kell*, in PPKE JÁK Ünnepi Kötet Boytha Györgyné tiszteletére 115 (Bándi Gyula ed., PPKE JÁK 2002).

Tihamér Tóth. *A versenyfelügyeleti mai kérdései és a Gazdasági Versenyhivatal*, in Gazdasági kormányzás: változás és alkalmazkodás a magyar gazdaságirányítás intézményrendszerében 143 (Gusztáv Báger & Ákos Péter Bod eds., Aula Kiadó 2008).

Tihamér Tóth. *A vertikális versenykorlátozások aktuális kérdései, különös tekintettel a továbbeladási ár megkötésére*, in Az európai közösségi és a magyar versenyjog fejlődési irányai 9 (Vörös Imre ed., MTA Jogtudományi Intézet 2008).

Tihamér Tóth. *Az Alkotmánybíróság határozata a Gazdasági Versenyhivatal közleménykiadási jogáról*, 1(1) Jogesetek Magyarázata 12 (2010).

Tihamér Tóth. *Versenykorlátozó megállapodások a GVH 2009-es gyakorlatában*, 54(7-8) Külgazdaság 65 (2010).

József Zavodnyik, *A Gazdasági Versenyhivatalhoz benyújtott bejelentések megítélésének egyes kérdései a bírói gyakorlatban*, 12(9) Gazdaság és Jog 16 (2004).

József Zavodnyik, *A kartell versenyjogi megítélése a magyar és a közösségi joggyakorlat tükrében*, 12(6) Gazdaság és Jog 3 (2004).

Selected Bibliography

Articles (in English and German)

Árpád Hargita & Tihamér Tóth. *God forbid Bid-Riggers: Developments under the Hungarian Competition Act*, 28(2) World Competition 205 (2005).
Csongor István Nagy, (2010). *The judicial application of competition law in Hungary*, in Proceedings of the FIDE XXIV Congress Madrid 2010 Vol. 2 255 (Gil C. R. Iglesias & Luis O. Blanco eds., Universidad Complutense de Madrid 2010) <http://ssrn.com/abstract=1737808>.
Csongor István Nagy. *Commitments as surrogates of civil redress in competition law: the Hungarian perspective*, 33(11) European Competition Law Review 531 (2012).
Csongor István Nagy. *Das ungarische Verfassungsgericht zur persönlichen Haftung von Geschäftsführer und Vorstandsmitglied*, 57(1) Osteuropa-Recht 60 (2011) (*The Hungarian Constitutional Court on the personal liability of executives*).
Csongor István Nagy. *New Hungarian Rules on Damages in Competition Matters*, 32(2) European Competition Law Review 63 (2011).
Csongor István Nagy. *Predatory Pricing in Hungary and in Community Law*. in The perspectives of the legal approximation process in Central and Eastern Europe 147 (Bibó István Szakkollégium & Európai Jogakadémia 2001).
Csongor István Nagy. *Refusal to Deal and the Doctrine of Essential Facilities in US and EC Competition Law. A Comparative Perspective and a Proposal for an Analytical Framework*, 32(5) European Law Review 664 (2007).
Csongor István Nagy. *Schadensersatzklagen im Falle kartellrechtlicher Rechtsverletzungen in Ungarn: neue Schadensersatzvorschriften des ungarischen Kartellgesetzes*, 60(9) Wirtschaft und Wettbewerb 902 (2010) (*Claims for damages in case of violations of the law on restrictive agreements in Hungary: the Hungarian Competition Act's new rules on damages*).
Csongor István Nagy. *The Constitutional Court Condemned Hungarian Statute Imposing 'Occupational Ban' on Executives of Cartelist Companies*. 30(8) European Competition Law Review 371 (2009).
Pál Szilágyi & Katalin Cseres. *The Hungarian Car Insurance Cartel Saga*, in Landmark Cases in Competition Law: Around the World in Fourteen Stories 145 (Barry Rodger ed., Kluwer Law International 2013).
Pál Szilágyi. *Bidding Markets and Competition Law in the European Union and the United Kingdom. Part II*, 29(2) European Competition Law Review 89 (2008).
Pál Szilágyi. *Bidding Markets and Competition Law in the European Union and the United Kingdom. Part I*, 29(1) European Competition Law Review 16 (2008).
Pál Szilágyi. *Hungarian Competition Law & Policy: The Watermelon Omen.* 10(2) Competition Policy International 2 (2012).
Pál Szilágyi. *Versenyeztetési eljárások hatása az érintett piac meghatározására és a versenyfeltételekre a közösségi jogban versenypolitikai szemszögből*. 64(5) Jogtudományi Közlöny 220 (2009).
Tihamér Tóth. *Competition Law in Hungary: Harmonisation Towards EU Membership*, 19(6) European Competition Law Review 358 (1998).
Tihamér Tóth. *Enforcement of EC Competition Rules Since 1 May 2004 by the Hungarian Competition Office*. in Antitrust Reform in Europe: a year in practice 77 (Philip Lowe & Michael Reynolds eds., International Bar Association 2005).

Selected Bibliography

Tihamér Tóth. *EU Enlargement and Modernisation of Competition Law: Some National Experiences.* in Modernisation and Enlargement: two Major Challenges of EC Competition Law (Damien Geradin ed., Intersentia 2004).

Tihamér Tóth. *Hungary*, Competition Cases from the European Union 629 (Ioannis Kokkoris ed., 2d ed, Sweet & Maxwell Ltd. 2010).

Tihamér Tóth. *Hungary*, Competition Cases from the European Union: The Ultimate Guide to Leading Cases of the EU and all 27 Member States 629 (Ioannis Kokkoris ed., Sweet & Maxwell Ltd. 2008).

Selected Bibliography

Index

The numbers here refer to paragraph numbers.

Absolute territorial exclusivity, 194, 198, 547, 559, 569, 570
Abuse of dominant position, 18, 22, 26, 31, 46, 74, 120, 237–241, 315, 441, 463, 473, 514, 734, 735, 755, 833
Access to file, 782–795
Active sales, 559, 561
Agreements of minor importance, 29, 67, 71, 72, 126, 183, 197, 198, 200, 208–222, 522, 547, 549, 550, 558, 570, 571, 577
Anti-competitive effect, 72, 110, 113, 114, 184–206, 214, 530, 670–685
Anti-competitive object, 72, 110–113, 181, 184–206, 525
Association of undertakings, 69, 72, 128, 153, 178–181, 190, 207, 323, 338, 341, 490

Black-listed agreements, 539, 574
Block exemption, 22, 32–34, 73, 126, 182-183, 200, 224, 225, 233–236, 304, 430, 535–537, 539, 540, 543, 544, 550, 552, 559, 569, 574, 575, 578, 579, 811
Bundling, 241, 639–645

Concerted practice, 47, 49, 69, 70, 72, 153–181, 206, 207, 351, 352, 468, 486, 490, 527, 696, 952–954

Dawn raids, 296–299, 352, 353, 718, 721, 746, 753, 755–758, 761, 763–766
De minimis, see agreements of minor importance
Discrimination, 107, 199, 241, 604–610, 663
Dominance, see dominant position
Dominant position, 18, 22, 26–28, 31, 46, 74–77, 100, 105, 116, 117, 120, 125, 136, 145–152, 237–241, 299, 315, 370, 406, 441, 452, 463, 467, 473, 514, 597, 602, 612, 639, 640, 647, 649, 659, 669, 671, 686–688, 707, 720, 734, 735, 755, 761, 765, 773, 778, 833, 906–908

Economic unit, 92, 118, 120, 123, 126, 127, 129–131, 147, 338, 830, 836
Effects-analysis 113-115, 126, 188, 196
Excessive pricing, 241, 441, 583, 584, 588, 589, 943
Exclusivity, 350, 560, 563, 667–685

Hardcore agreements, 453, 515, 525, 547, 720
Horizontal agreements, 193, 206, 213, 350, 351, 404, 515–546

Individual exemption, 22, 33, 47, 100, 112, 195, 198, 224, 226–234, 312, 473, 515, 552, 554, 556, 557, 569, 570
Informant's award, 718–733
Inter-brand restrictions, 653
Interrogation of witnesses, 746, 753
Intra-brand restrictions, 653
Invalidity, 83, 435, 862
Investigating powers, 296–302, 776

Judicial review, 23, 32, 396, 505, 510, 709, 716, 724, 775, 929, 934–958

Legal privilege, 301, 747, 754, 767–772
Leniency, 38, 317, 337, 345–381, 455–457, 459, 468, 469, 492–495, 497, 512, 514, 719, 729, 730

Margin squeeze, 628, 662
Market share, 106, 126, 136, 151, 168, 197, 198, 209–215, 247, 336, 516, 517, 523, 537, 540, 543, 547, 548, 550–552,

263

Index

558, 559, 568–572, 576–578, 671, 821, 856, 871, 874, 877–883, 921
Market-sharing, 193, 210, 215, 218–222, 451, 452, 517, 518, 520, 522
Merger analysis, 687, 906–914

Notification duty, 85, 89, 103, 243–245, 247, 274, 276, 313, 325, 821, 841–843, 847–850, 861

Passive sales, 194, 198, 559, 570
Predatory pricing, 28, 238, 241, 613–638, 666
Price-fixing, 193, 195, 197, 210, 215, 216, 222, 452, 516, 527, 546, 550, 554, 720, 738
Price squeeze, 658–666
Private enforcement, 389, 427, 440, 452, 455, 739

Relevant market, 38, 75, 76, 99–101, 135–145, 149, 161, 172, 188, 190, 201, 210, 212, 214, 225, 241, 247, 309, 333, 425, 542, 543, 550, 559, 572, 578, 605, 635, 647, 675, 690, 691, 694, 802, 821, 871, 875, 877–881, 898, 910, 912, 913, 915
Resale price fixing, see resale price maintenance
Resale price maintenance, 18, 28, 195–197, 232, 550–557
Rule of reason, see effects-analysis

Self-incrimination, 302, 750
Significant impediment to effective competition (SIEC) test, 116, 687, 907
Simplified merger procedure, 247, 821, 871
Substantial lessening of competition (SLC) test, 101, 687, 907

Tying, 241, 629, 639–645

Undertaking, 46, 69, 118, 302, 519, 584, 686, 703, 818, 930

Vertical agreements, 22, 34, 194, 211–213, 235, 350, 547–582, 684
Vertical restraints, see vertical agreements